AF676238

Animal Guides

Marie-Louise von Franz, Honorary Patron

Studies in Jungian Psychology by Jungian Analysts

Daryl Sharp, General Editor

ANIMAL GUIDES

In Life, Myth and Dreams

An Analyst's Notebook

Neil Russack

Foreword by Joseph L. Henderson

INNER CITY BOOKS

For Suki, and for
Joseph and Benjamin

National Library of Canada Cataloguing in Publication Data

Russack, Neil
Animal guides in life, myth and dreams: an analyst's notebook

(Studies in Jungian psychology by Jungian analysts; no. 97)

Includes bibliographical references and index.

ISBN 0-919123-98-8

1. Animals—Symbolic aspects.
2. Psychoanalytic interpretation.
3. Jungian psychology.
I. Title. II. Series.

BF173.R87 2002 150.19'54 C2001-901445-7

INNER CITY BOOKS
Box 1271, Station Q, Toronto, ON M4T 2P4, Canada
Telephone (416) 927-0355 / Fax (416) 924-1814
Web site: www.innercitybooks.net / E-mail: admin@innercitybooks.net

Honorary Patron: Marie-Louise von Franz.
Publisher and General Editor: Daryl Sharp.
Senior Editor: Victoria B. Cowan.

INNER CITY BOOKS was founded in 1980 to promote the understanding and practical application of the work of C.G. Jung.

Cover: "Herons," woodcut by Vicki Cowan.

Printed and bound in Canada by University of Toronto Press Incorporated

CONTENTS

See final pages for descriptions of other Inner City Books

Foreword

Ever since Paleolithic people learned to draw animal forms on the walls of caves, we humans have shown a mixed reaction to the animal world. On the one hand we have worshipped animals as if they were gods, and on the other treated them as personal possessions to be loved and cared for.

In the early 1950s, I had the good fortune to visit the great cave at Lascaux in France when it was still open to the public. In that vast space there were drawings of large bovine creatures in their deified splendor. The guide pointed to some horses on another wall, saying, "Ladies and gentlemen, look at those adorable horses!" Later I learned that this guide had been one of the two boys who discovered the cave, hence this personal, loving feeling.

The power of this response is brought into play even as the totem animals in tribal rites were killed and eaten on ceremonial occasions. When the Ainu of northern Japan killed a bear, they blessed its animal soul and sent it on its way, telling it to come back again, reborn as an Ainu.

Dr. Russack has given us a beautiful narrative of his experience of animals, adding his psychological commentary to this ancient tradition. In harmony with Jung's theory of the collective unconscious, he places his animals each in an archetypal setting represented by the traditional four elements: air, earth, water and fire. The means by which he describes these elements is made possible by another archetype, which is the initiatory act of going into the unconscious. The most immediately accessible way to do this is through the dream. Since much of my own early work lay in using dreams to reveal important aspects of initiation, I have been especially appreciative of this approach which in Dr. Russack's exposition gives my intuitive approach a more realistic focus. Above all he honors the animals in their own life, so that we get the feeling of what they might mean not only to him and his patients, but also as natural science for us all.

I had a foretaste of this method years ago when I was training to become a Jungian analyst. I dreamed I was standing near the sea accompanied by an older man, a doctor friend. He pointed to the water and said I should consider a vocation of sea-farming. What I understood, at the time of having this dream, was that the sea represented the unconscious and what I would fish for would be the memory of dreams and their interpretation.

This dream came back to me as I read Dr. Russack's account of the waterbird as a fisher by nature, but also as a symbol which, we are told, is to be understood as initiation by water. But the bird as symbol is much more. We learn that the Greek name of the crane, or stork, is likened to Demeter herself, founder of the eighth-century Kabirian Mysteries, more archaic than the Eleusinian Mysteries: a mythology of the divine mother and her daughter, expressing the destiny of woman and her initiatory role as the giver of birth and rebirth.

Many other denizens of this symbolic water come to light in Dr. Russack's elucidation of the contents of the dreaming mind and their emergence into consciousness. They are shown to embody a transcendent function of the psyche, beautifully represented by Aphrodite riding on the back of a goose in flight (page 85). Such symbols of transcendence are especially well anchored in the author's account of his practical work as a therapist.

Joseph L. Henderson

Preface

This book begins in water and flying. It begins with a waterbird. One afternoon, in the woods of Montana, I left a Blackfoot Indian sweat lodge because I had begun to experience a tightening in my chest and thought I might have a heart attack. Exiled by my pain, I stood outside for some time, listening to the continuous chanting inside and watching the skin of the lodge turn white and begin shimmering. For two days, curled on a makeshift bed in a tent, I endured the pain. By the third morning I gave up all hope of freeing myself of both the pain and its underlying fear: "fear in the pit of your stomach," the medicine man called it. In that moment of giving up, the image of a bird appeared to me.

It was an egret, pure white, and wrapped around my heart. Gradually, very carefully, the elegant bird began to unwind its long legs and open its great folded wings. Unfurled, it flew out of my heart into the beyond. My pain left and I felt free. Much later I realized that the white bird had become this book.

The waterbird flies free across the waters, away from the known to the world beyond. As a dreamer, reader and therapist I witness this flight again and again. In a colleague's dream a flock of geese suddenly becomes airborne, inspiring him to chance an artistic career. In a patient's drawing, a duck fetches a woman who is trapped on dry land and carries her on its back into the waters. In the weeks that follow, the patient discovers that she is able to love for the first time. In a Japanese fairy tale, a man rescues a crane. In gratitude, this non-human female transforms herself into a woman and marries him.

The waterbird is a weaver, moving between the elements of water, air and land, stitching together the different worlds. Just as the waterbird can shift between realms and link them, this book will take you, the reader, in and out of many different realms. Along the way, you will hear various kinds of voices: the intimate accounts of those who come to see me as a psychiatrist, the stories of friends, and my own personal story, which is inevitably touched by what people bring to me. Threaded throughout are some of the great myths that belong to all of us.

We will meet other animals along with the waterbird. Each one has a unique voice, a voice you cannot find in a guidebook or a compilation of symbols. How the beast appears, what it brings, what emotion it evokes, what healing link it fashions: this is the story.

This is not a "how to" book: It is a book to stir the imagination. Animals link us to the mythic realm. They are messengers of the gods, and I hope that this book itself will become a kind of messenger, like the waterbird, attuning us to older and deeper ways of life. As you read, I hope that you will remember animals you have encountered—wild creatures, pets, dream animals—and that you will be touched as I have been. I hope you will be renewed through reconnecting to the animal life we humans left behind long ago.

This book is a map tracing journeys in which people are guided by animals into a richer humanity. Animals break down barriers and bring a healing presence into our lives. The waterbird, weaver of worlds, is the original and guiding image.

The story begins with my own early life, introducing the themes of alienation, the suffering that comes from being cut off from animal life, and the quest for love. Then a variety of healing paths are described, involving the initiations by animals into their elemental realms: air, water, earth and fire. In the final chapter, animals restore us to the human world.

The narrative has been guided by C.G. Jung's diagnosis of the modern condition as a state of fundamental estrangement:

> As scientific understanding has grown, so our world has become dehumanized. Man feels himself isolated in the cosmos, because he is no longer involved in nature, and has lost his emotional "unconscious identity" with natural phenomena. These have slowly lost their symbolic implications. Thunder is no longer the voice of an angry god, nor is lightning his avenging missile. No river contains a spirit, no tree is the life principle of a man, no snake the embodiment of wisdom, no mountain cave the home of a great demon. No voices now speak to man from stones, plants, and animals, nor does he speak to them believing they can hear. His contact with nature has gone, and with it has gone the profound emotional energy that this symbolic connection supplied.[1]

By encouraging the soul's interest in animals, we can embrace what animals have: resilience, pleasure and a link to the elemental forms that sustain and renew us all.

---

[1] C.G. Jung, ed., *Man and His Symbols,* p. 95.

1
Isolation and Alienation

Early Years with Animals, Family, Nature

Mr. Glickstein and his pet shop

I was eight or nine when I bought my first canary at Mr. Glickstein's pet shop. The shop was on East Federal Street, the poorer, seedier half of the main business street in Youngstown, Ohio. Was Mr. Glickstein really missing half of his penis, from the War? Surely my mother didn't tell me that. She did confide in me that she thought my father should have an affair, in order to take care of his sexual needs. Was I supposed to tell him? My mother and I wondered together how Mr. Glickstein peed and what his penis looked like. Intrigued by the missing half of Mr. Glickstein's penis, perhaps my mother was wistfully reminded that a penis was missing from her life too. Like Isis attending to dismembered Osiris, my mother had ideas for finding and restoring these missing penises, Mr. Glickstein's and the one meant for her. But she was no help to me. She wasn't aware that little boys had penises they needed to use, hoses that reached out into a life that a boy could follow. Whenever my mother was overtaken by a particular kind of restlessness, she would drag me down to Mr. Glickstein's pet shop. There in the store was everything missing from our house: animal smells, birds squawking, dark soft bins of seeds . . . it reeked organic.

In our house everything was labeled. Tasteless and odorless, objects were exhibited as if on display. Knickknacks and pieces of inexpensive china were neatly arranged in a faux-antique hutch as if they were sacred objects. They sat sentient over the worshippers at formal dinners. There were no mysteries, no wandering nymphs or flute-playing Pan to lure you into secret hideaways. No birthdays joyously celebrated: instead, functional shirts were cautiously presented, carefully unwrapped. No animal would come crawling out to give you a lick. When my father peed in the toilet, he ran water from the tap to cover up the real sounds of his body. Furniture encased in plastic was uncovered only on special occasions. Sterility was the order of the day. Nighttime did not exist; nothing unknown was acknowledged.

Mr. Glickstein was a large burly man with a cigar. He seemed gruff and natural, more like a man was supposed to look than my father who was always too eager to please. He filled in for my father and relieved me of being husband to my mother. Since Mr. Glickstein would tease and flirt with my mother, I could save my penis for myself.

One after another, I bought three canaries from Mr. Glickstein, each rapidly succumbing to colds. It wouldn't work. I knew it. I couldn't keep the birds alive. It was too drafty in our converted porch that had been tacked onto the kitchen and was now used for informal meals. With my little yellow friend gone and no warbling song to inspire my imagination, I was back to mother's milk. Each day I was made to sit at the table until I finished drinking my milk. Ritually each day when my mother left, our intelligent and insightful black maid Margaret, who I secretly believed was my real mother, would pour the milk down the sink. I had already taken in more than I could stand as my mother's confidant.

No wonder I would want a singing bird to keep me company during this ordeal. But they were all drafted back to the spirit world. It must have been too painful for them to sit with this dispirited youth. They were all named "Terry," and to this day when I meet my next door neighbor named Terry I can't help but think of my dead canaries. My father would bring a vaporizer from the drugstore and cover the cage until each Terry succumbed. I wasn't sure if Mr. Glickstein's cut-off penis had something to do with their deaths, or was it the vital member missing from my parent's relationship? Why couldn't these canaries breathe?

Woolworth's Five-and-Dime

Up the street in the basement of Woolworth's was a big tank teeming with little turtles, each the size of a quarter. I don't remember if the goldfish were in a different tank. There was a steamy, almost putrid smell, unlike anything going on in our artificial home. Girls with painted nails and fancy hairdos were ready for their next adventure. Perched on tiptoes to fish out the turtles, they would laugh, moving with the same quick spontaneity as the turtles. These young girls were on the make—looking, like the turtles, to see where life would take them. Imagine a little boy with eyes wide staring up at this tank. Could I capture some of this life? Would these turtles, displaced to my tank at home, infect me with the same excitement as these girls? Would the murky organic smell along with the memory of the perfumed girls carry me along in a cloud of vapors and protect me from the poison of my house? These little turtles looked like me; though they were tiny and frantic, they had my hands and feet.

The tank at Woolworth's was right at the bottom of the stairs so people climbing in and out of the basement would pass right by the turtles. Cheap clothes in vivid pastel colors attracted working girls hunting for bargains and matronly mothers shopping for their kids and themselves. It was a warm atmosphere; people were close, touching the fabric and each other, laughing, gesturing, holding the fabric up against their bodies, talking with the clerks. They were not self-conscious and careful, not like the stranger I seemed to be to my mother. Rather they zipped around like the turtles. I wanted to be a turtle, one that an expressive sexy girl would scoop up to take home with her. I wanted to capture the life in that basement. Instead, it evaporated when I ascended the steps. Everyone else seemed to have this vitality without asking. Why didn't I?

Teeth

Dr. Louis Goldman was actually my first psychotherapist, though officially he was my dentist. Now I realize that for me he was an early model of a man who kept his instinct alive in the midst of his professional life. He gave me a glimpse of another way. My mother stopped going to him when he pulled a toothpick out of his pocket ordering her to "Bite down on this" to test her new filling. "He is unhygienic," she said and moved uptown to the newer, more upscale dentists. Dr. Goldman was located in Central Towers on the square, an older building that was part of the original downtown. His office was up so high that my stomach flew to my neck every time I rode the elevator. I would go each week, one stretch for seventeen weeks in a row, to have new fillings replace my old cavities: I can still taste the silver. He did not use Novocain, instead he would stuff my mouth with cotton to soak up the saliva, and with a huge old fashioned drill he would work my mouth over.

Somewhere in the middle he would stop work, perhaps as the fillings were drying, and talk to me. "Elementary schools should have mandatory psychotherapy, then a little boy or girl could talk to someone about their personal problems." These long discourses on education and social justice were presented while he looked out the window with his back to me. He loved to talk and his voice was so reassuring that perhaps I listened more to the feeling than to the actual words. Of course, when he was expostulating, I couldn't respond because my mouth was full of cotton. Big black women in the waiting room, having waited an hour or more, would bang on the glass door, "Dr. Goldman, *what* are you doing in there?" "Can't you see I'm working on this boy?" and he would go on philosophizing as if dentistry, mouths, teeth were of little consequence.

Attached to his small office was a back closet containing a work table with many dentures in various stages of completion. Snapping the uppers and lowers together, he would demonstrate: "You see, it doesn't quite close" and point to where the problem was, as if we were undertaking this project together. A Bunsen burner was continuously lit, though there was no window for ventilation. No apparent order was discernible; tools and dentures in molds lay every-which-way, intermingled with cans of solder and heaps of assorted work materials. At heart, he was a mechanic and loved working with his hands. Everything else was secondary. This was the creative chaos missing from my family.

It wasn't just that the order in our house was compulsory but that it had become an ordering of nothing, to make it seem as if life were happening. The fact was that we lived and worked in the drugstore, seven days a week. The house was for show. No one really lived there.

Dr. Goldman would eat lunch across the street from Glickstein's pet shop at a grill on East Federal where ordinary people ate, a lower class version of the "Brass Rail" further up the street. It seemed mysterious and exciting. He told me to have lunch with him there one day, but I didn't, I don't remember why not. Probably because I was afraid. He was a Jewish intellectual, a real one, his brother a Communist. He would take all my mother's opinions and replace them with real thought. My mother's idea was that people should not make a lot of money, but she envied those who did. "I like to get paid," he said. "I don't want to work for nothing." Yet, in fact, he catered to a poor clientele and didn't make a great deal of money. I learned later that when he turned seventy, a grateful patient left him a million dollars.

What I remember most about him was his voice, alive and confident. He loved to think and talk about anything. He fixed my rotten teeth but more importantly he filled my head with new ideas and emotional hope. I left his office happy and faced the angry looks of his ever-waiting patients. When years later, I called my friend Leonard Specter, the local Youngstown historian, to inquire about Louis Goldman, Leonard said he had never heard of him and added that he was not aware of any Jews living there whom he did not know. This raised my esteem of Dr. Goldman all the more. He was obviously not part of the usual social fabric—which was why, of course, my mother would have nothing to do with him. "Bite down on this"—that's how you knew if he fixed your tooth. That's how you knew if your life was real. My mother wanted him to put braces on my protruding front teeth, but he wouldn't because he said my bite was good as it was. What did it matter how I looked? Instinct replaced appearance. Actively biting my way through life was better than passively being observed.

The box turtle

The other turtles we encountered besides the ones we bought in the five and dime were the box turtles. Seeing the solitary turtle strike out on its own across the road was somehow reassuring, perhaps because it was too hot to do anything—even think. To see this slow independent shell with legs move with a plan and direction gave me hope. They were wonderful to pick up and hold. They had real weight. It was a solid piece of real life I could hold in my hand with its legs slowly moving and beautiful mosaic patterns on its belly.

The magical thing was its searching head peeking out from a long red-and-yellow lined neck, which could swell and elongate, stretching far beyond its shell. Our fascination with such extensions preceded the knowledge that our own penises were capable of such feats—yet somehow we felt that the colorful stripes expressed our own hot passion. Their sturdy legs were slow, yet demonstrated that such heavily burdened life can indeed move. The house I lived in was so big that once in, I couldn't easily get out. Cut off from the outside world, our house suffocated and enveloped. Seeing the turtle uninhibited from movement despite its big house gave me hope. It was possible. You simply had to take the whole thing with you.

My brother was always trying to catch birds in the backyard. He would set up a trap with a collapsing stick once the bird entered. Sometimes the bird would break a wing trying to escape. It was horrible to watch—a blue jay flashing brilliant blue each time it smashed against the tiny cage. But I never said anything, nor did my parents. My brother did achieve flight one day when he escaped my Aunt Miriam by climbing down the drainpipe from the second floor. What a surprise for us to see him right before us in the kitchen window. When we screamed he jumped and ran to my father in the drugstore.

Having an older brother was a mixed bag. From a distance I could watch him struggle with new challenges, but he also had entitlements. He got half the parking money I collected from spectators parking their cars in our yard to see the football game. The stadium was located right across the street from where we lived. Once when I tried to keep all the money myself (since my brother didn't help) my father got so angry at me that he picked me up and threw me across the room. Though I landed on the couch, the vehemence of the gesture shocked me. We parked the cars with more care than my father parked me.

The games were always Friday and Saturday nights. We charged twenty-five cents per car for high school games and fifty cents for the college games. "Park your carcass right in here," we would yell, trying to direct cars with our flashlights into our driveway, competing with our neighbors. We parked the cars in the backyard, the front lawn, the driveway. The cars became the animal night life that messed up the compulsive order of the house. These Fords, Chevies, Plymouths, crashed through the compartmentalization and sterility of my mother's world, a world she tried to keep in place as tidily as her hairdo. All the while, her carefully manicured hands wrung each other, in a desperate longing for feeling. In contrast, these cars went in and out of the driveways, off the lawns into life. They carried students and football fans who could express their emotions, who weren't afraid of making a dent in the world, as evidenced by tire tracks in the lawn, by condoms and empty bottles of booze freely discarded on streets and sidewalks.

After parking the cars, we would sneak into the game under the fence. There was excitement, bright lights, the crowd, the announcer blasting downs and yards to go, and bands at half-time. You could hear it blocks away, and my father, just one block away, got the overflow crowd in the drugstore asking for milkshakes, hot chocolate, cigarettes. Sometimes when we were bored we would steal reflectors off cars. They came in different colors and shapes—yellow and red, round and flat or pointed like a strawberry. These colors, feelings really, I hid away in cigar boxes in the secret of the closet, someday to reflect the colors in the rainbow. You don't see reflectors on cars nowadays. They were attached to the screws holding the license plates and we would just leave the license plate on the ground or the hood of the car if we felt particularly civic minded.

Circling the store on football nights and other unpredictable times were the popcorn people: a short chunky white woman and a tall black man who lived together down the street. Sometimes they would be accompanied by her younger brother who was in and out of the mental hospital. They would push their glass popcorn case on wheels. It was all warm and the fiery ring that heated and exploded the popcorn seemed transcendent. At night the lit carriage moved slowly and mysteriously down the street as if by itself. I can see it now under a street lamp or parked outside the gate of the football stadium. The owners were a silent trio. They never talked to anybody. You would just see them circumambulating the neighborhood as if they knew something no one else knew, with their black and white faces lit up by the gas ring. As I remember them, they seem unkempt in clothes that didn't quite fit. They belonged to another realm that was present but indecipherable. Still, their presence made the world a little warmer. I remember standing at night close to the glass, fascinated by the popcorn striking against the sides of the glass. Although I must have hungered for the warm buttery lightness, I never thought of buying any. Sometimes now, as if in apparition, I see the two wheeling their magic lit carriage and I feel nostalgic for an effervescent magic I could never quite attain.

Red McKensey lived next door. He was the son of a policeman and sometimes when he got really angry, he would get his father's police revolver and wave it at us. I would hide behind a bush thinking I was safe, but he never fired. Norma Chill lived down the street and once she volunteered to show me her thing if I showed her my thing. We urinated together by the side of her house. My best friend was Jimmy Ring who lived on the other side. His father was a bus driver and one day I stole a carton of cigarettes from the drugstore, all different kinds, Chesterfields, Lucky Strikes, Camels, Parliaments, Philip Morris, Raleigh's and we smoked them all down in the hollow under the bridge. I think I turned yellow and then green and became deathly sick. In high school I regretted this experience because after that I was never able to smoke like my friends.

These working class surroundings felt alive, and when we moved into our new house I never really fit into the neighborhood. That's when the trouble began, big time. That move isolated us and made me feel self-conscious. I could no longer relate to my old friends, and we didn't socialize much with the upwardly mobile middle class. I knew that I was in deep trouble when one spring day I caught a baby rabbit in the gasoline powered rotary lawn mower. He was pretty badly chewed up but living, and I was alone at the time. Deep down I felt panicked, horrified in fact, but I put on a smiling persona, fantasizing to myself as to how I should end his life. Should I grind him up in the kitchen garbage disposal? Here I was, mowing the grass—a chore I hated but dutifully performed in a new backyard. Did my parents work there because they enjoyed gardening or only to keep up appearances? I always caught the glint in my mother's eye when she said she was going out to weed. With her gloves on, holding and pointing a pair of snippers, she exuded a nervous energy, private, charged.

On this spring day, when I should have been with friends, I was halfway between a lifeless garden and a sanitized kitchen holding a bleeding rabbit in my hands. To this day I remember that moment as the most desperate in my life.

My most un-animal experience

When I was eight or nine I began piano lessons on a small cardboard piano, nothing more than a shortened keyboard made out of flat cardboard. The black and white keys were clearly demarcated but nothing moved. In looking back I can't believe this actually happened to me. My mother, the essence of caution, did not want to invest in a piano until I showed "real interest." She didn't seem to grasp that real interest could not exist if there was nothing real to engage with: no sound, no polished wood, no ivory keys. Needless to say, I never displayed any excitement. I remember pressing the numbered cardboard keys until

I memorized the sequence of fingered notations, playing by the numbers. Then I would play the same tune on my teacher's real piano, which to my ears didn't sound much different! What I remember most were the big fat fingers of the German piano teacher's hands. I always wondered how he could fit them on the keys, striking one note at a time instead of two or three. I was so fascinated by the deftness of his fat fingers that I couldn't pay attention to his voice.

What my parents seemed to lack was the sense of a person's real nature. Their idea was that if you studied hard enough, you could accomplish anything. Aptitude and talent did not exist. It was the opposite of Gerald Durrell's description of his family in his autobiographical book, *My Family and Other Animals.* As a child he spent time on the Greek island of Corfu. His older brother Lawrence, author of *Four Quartets,* would notice all manner of animals hanging out of Gerald's pockets when coming into the house and would complain to his mother, who would respond, "Can't you see the boy will become a zoologist?"

Of course it was left for me to have such premonitions about my own vocation. When I was twelve, I told my mother she was depressed and needed to see a psychiatrist. She seemed intrigued by the idea, but because money was so overvalued and because my father was so practical and unpsychologically minded, she never really considered it. Later, when I became a psychiatrist, I pointed out something about her behavior and she put her fingers in her ears: "I cannot hear one word you are saying." So much for being receptive to her son's calling.

The drugstore

Our drugstore, Benita Drug Co., the archetypal neighborhood drugstore, located in the north side of Youngstown, Ohio, on the corner of Benita Avenue and Elm Street, where the trolley ran, served a wide range of people: from the poor who lived close to factories by railroad tracks, to the steel mill owners who would drive up in their Rolls Royces. The main draw was the soda fountain, jammed three deep after high school let out. Students poured into the store grabbing counter stools and demanding ice cream cones, sodas, milkshakes, and on hot days, limeade. This was a to-die-for concoction prepared from fresh limes squeezed, with ice and sugar, into a missile-shaped metallic canister and beat up in the blender, condensing the ice and cooling the hand. It sold for ten cents and was the best buy then or ever. Hot fudge sundaes made of two scoops of rich vanilla ice cream topped with too-thick-to-pour hot fudge and nuts selling for twenty-five cents was the real thing. Three people, including me, worked the soda fountain during the rush. Students yelled, laughed, pushed; books piled high fell off the counter. Chewing gum hastily removed from mouths joined generations of predecessors under the counter top. No one could get from one side of the store to the other; mild chaos reigned, noise loud and wonderful, the complete opposite of our house where I would become lonely and depressed, walking through emptiness from one room to the other. Money often dropped onto the counter and bunced to the floor. The high school crowd ate sitting and standing. They touched, flirted, made dates, arranged parties, gossiped, complained about teachers, then slowly filtered out by twos and threes. Magazines at the front of the store were read, stolen, replaced, occasionally sold.

You could say I grew up in the drugstore. I learned more than most boys my age about people and their lives, but I was still an observer. What was left out was the animal inside who hungered to experiment and explore his own relationship to friends and the world. During the student rush hour I talked to and took care of my friends, but I was on the wrong side of the counter. I wasn't part of it. Instead of going out with girls my own age, I would pat the asses of the women employees as they bent over the ice cream coolers, until the women complained. Instead of buying a present for my mother on her birthday, I tried to appropriate a mechanical singing apparatus that contained perfume from the women's gift section of the store, only to be told by my father that I couldn't do that. I was never paid for working so I had no spending money. No one ever thought I might have needs of my own separate from the family. And I never asked.

The drugstore, wonderful in many ways, was also a trap. It kept all the libido inside me. I had a dream once that my secret girlfriend was there with me inside the store. It was lovely to be together, but we couldn't get out. It was a ghetto. No one else saw it that way. My mother, too, worked in the store. Although she would get up to wait on customers, I remember her sitting at the counter month after month doing the statements. It was a laborious task, unending, sad. We all had become slaves to something that was sapping our lives. What I was missing was the animal on which I could ride out into my own existence.

However, the life in the store gave me an understanding of people that I drew on later to become a psychiatrist. My father was the vital hub of the store. Like many pharmacists of the day, he was well liked. "Hey Sid, how ya doin'?" the locals would call out. Above the din of telephones and pin-ball machines, he listened to their medical problems and then prescribed, sold and sometimes applied the necessary medication. He took care of all the ailments people didn't want to pay their doctor for or were too embarrassed to share.

While my father took care of the somatic side of medicine, I took care of the customer's psyche. Curious to know why people's lives turned out the way they did, I had a way of letting people tell me their life stories and their dreams. Sailors and soldiers on furlough during World War Two would tell of their experiences. Dr. Spec, our local mental case, would come into the store on a hot and humid summer day wearing a heavy beige overcoat and smoking a fat cigar. He had been an ears, eyes, nose and throat doctor (otolaryngologist), who lost all his money in the Depression and went off the deep end. Spying me first behind the cigar counter he would haul out his latest renditions of U.S. government treasury notes done in great detail. In the center of the bill, instead of a picture of George Washington, would be a picture of my father. My name would be listed as United States Treasurer and Dr. Spec's name as secretary. Then after buying his El Producto cigar he would search out my father in the back room. No one treated him like a lunatic, we were all quite polite. As a nine year old, I knew it couldn't be true, but I was hopeful. It would be nice to be rich. Who wouldn't want their father to be president? Besides, I liked his gruff manner and voice and all that attention. And I actually got paid. He would leave the treasury notes with me. There was a larger world out there, one that included other planetary systems with strange currencies.

Another cigar smoker with the same husky body type as Dr. Spec was Joe, an old black man with white hair and gleaming eyes. He would tell me stories on his way out to the garage, his big sure hands easily arranging and hauling empty boxes. He was so much himself, so at ease, so natural in his bodily movements that just watching him made me feel happy. I loved being near him, smelling the tobacco on his warm body. I would watch him move the chewing tobacco or his cigar around in his mouth showing the red inside of his cheek and lips while he carefully felt the smooth cardboard surface of the box with his outstretched fingers until his hand reached the corner. Then he would glide down the next plane as if these empty boxes contained all the valuable information life had to offer. He made me feel that had access to a store of wisdom, a wisdom he would impart to me. When he told me stories, I wanted to stay forever. The whites of his eyes would flash, he would smile his great big smile and laugh, lighting up my soul.

I don't remember anyone else talking to him or calling his name, he seemed to be there just for me. His presence gave me something. It was the way he talked, the way he rolled his eyes and moved his head and hands. It was a physical thing. I don't remember the words. I think it had to do with the kindness he showed me and his great kindness toward the world. I don't remember when he left, but as I got older he was not there anymore. By the time he was gone, I had already lost whatever magic there was in my childhood. It's all memory now; no one is alive who might have known him except maybe Leonard Specter, another local who hung around the store a lot. Joe had a dignity, a certain kind of knowing, that allowed him to be in his life, in the movement of the boxes, doing the simple things that were required of him in a way that made him seem like a god or an animal. No one I knew had this kind of manna. In comparison, everyone else seemed like a stick figure, pretending.

As well as cleaning our store, Joe also cleaned Sackville's fancy grocery store next door. Sackville's was a busy, family-owned business that delivered food to all the wealthy people on the north side of town. When I entered the grocery from the back to borrow Elizabeth Sackville's bus pass to downtown, I was always greeted by the two butchers hauling great sides of meat out of the refrigerator, cutting it up with huge cleavers and then carefully slicing it with marvelous long carving knives. I liked the activity, the talk and the smell of fresh sawdust on the floor, piles of it. You could almost slide on it.

Underlying the two-story corner brick building that comprised my father's drugstore and Sackville's on the first floor and a doctor's office upstairs was a huge cool windowless basement. From what I pieced together, on Saturday nights in the 30s, the basement was used for partying, poker playing, carousing and drinking. On the walls now hidden behind stored cases of canned food for Sackville's and barrels of Coca-Cola syrup and sacks of sugar belonging to my father were murals of nude women, big breasted, big hipped, in deep shades of orange and green. They were all wonderfully evocative and erotic. The entire cellar was dimly lit by three light bulbs strung along a wire. These were turned on by a funny looking circular switch you could never find in the dark. It was like going into a cave, scary, dark, alone, with no sound. All the life that was buried in me was here in this cellar in the dark. It was for me alone.

At Christmas vacation, I would spend days in a little room off this cellar adding up the store's receipts. I was isolated from my friends, cut off from the outside world, fearful of using the odd-smelling old toilet next door that was inside a closet that didn't close and had no light. Concerned about my tabulations, I would ask my father, "How will I know if I've made a mistake?" "It doesn't matter," he would respond, as if he paid taxes according to some secret inner code in his head. What meaningless numbers was I adding? What was I doing? I was adding up to nothing.

The Napa Years and After

Immersion in nature

My mother clapped her hands over her ears. Now in the office where I listen for hours to my patient's stories, there hangs a *thanka* of Avalokitesvara, the god who hears the cries of the world. How did I arrive from the sealed orifice of my childhood home to the office where I now sit, all ears? Not by professional training alone. As much as the books, the lectures, the papers, the consultations, and the analysis, my contact with nature was essential to my formation as healer of souls. In fact, my psychiatric residency began and ended with a pig.

When I moved to California from Ohio to begin my psychiatric residency at Napa State Hospital in 1961, I longed to live in the country. As soon as I arrived, I was introduced to animals. On my very first day I noticed a posted announcement: "Pig stolen from farm, anyone with information contact administrative office." Not mentioned was the fact that the pig had been served the evening before at the retirement dinner for Theo K. Miller, superintendent since the 1930s. The announcement was a cover-up. Alas, I had arrived one day too late.

But the pig did not abandon me. After completing the three years of my residency I accepted an offer to serve as psychiatrist in charge of M-6, a boys' adolescent ward. That's where my pig came for me. One day the "psych. techs" insisted I buy a ticket from the ward football pool. Embarrassed when I won the hundred dollars, I invited the whole ward, 50 kids and 25 staff members, to a pig roast at my Sonoma mountain retreat. After overcoming administrative red tape, mostly insurance anxiety, and armed with a pig bought from the cook's butcher, half the male staff and I set out at dusk the evening before to dig the pit. By early morning, under moon and stars and to the accompaniment of strong bourbon, I tasted my first "cracklin's"—cooked fatty animal skin.

The technicians were from Texas, and that night we traveled far over the Texas prairie with reminiscences of many animal roastings. By morning the caravan of buses and cars arrived with the remaining staff and patients. It was like Renoir's movie *Day in the Country*. The usual woodenness in the bodies of the schizophrenic patients seemed relaxed; on this day they were flexible as the trees. Our "schizo-paths" (Dr. McGrath's term, he being in charge of the children's unit) were kids who were sociopathic when they functioned well, but became psychotic when they regressed. On this day they seemed almost normal, acting as if they were children of the staff. There were no incidents, no tattling about the staff's drinking. By the end of the day there was a quietness as if something sacred had happened; it was a day long remembered by all.

I also realized I was breaking an ancient semitic taboo. It had been a totemic meal. Accompanied by my non-Jewish wife, I must have known I was leaving my own family. As a Jew, I had grown up understanding that the flesh of the pig was considered "unclean" because of the possibility of disease. Later, from my study of animal symbolism, I learned that there is more to the story. The patriarchal religion of Abraham, Isaac and Jacob suppressed the older matriarchal tradition of the Great Goddess who might tempt their people to resume pagan worship.[2] From the early Neolithic period the pig was considered to be the sacred animal of the earth goddess. As Marja Gimbutas, the Lithuanian archeologist, tells us, it was "a rapidly growing animal and highly prolific," and thus was compared to the abundance of the harvest. She reveals how, from the third millennium, people carried ceremonial vases in celebration of sowing and reaping. These offerings were made while dancing with pig masks.

> Similar festivities . . . . took place in Classical and Hellenistic Greece at which time suckling pigs were sacrificed to Demeter and her daughter Persephone. . . . During the fall harvest holiday of Thesmophoria, women would bring the remains of suckling pigs that had been buried and rotting in the earth and place them on altars (mixing these) with seed to be sown in the fields, thus helping to evoke an abundant harvest of crops.[3]

Four years before this Napa pig feast, when I had finished my internship, I had a most propitious encounter. I had loaded up my car and set out from Napa north toward St. Helena. Stopping to buy a loaf of bread baked by the Seventh-Day Adventists in Anguin, I was approached by a woman. As if reading my mind, or perhaps seeing my loaded car, she inquired if I needed a place to live. Following her back to Zinfandel Lane, just north of Rutherford, I arrived at an idyllic red cottage set right up against the last row of a vineyard. I had grown up in a steel town in the Midwest where the river ran yellow from iron ore deposits since the Civil War and the smoke from the mills coated our houses and gardens, so my sense of smell was not delicate. But here the luxuriant deep fragrance, musty and sensual, would draw me on evening walks among the vines. Weekends I helped a neighbor load the small sweet plums, dark purple with whitish dust and intoxicating perfume, for hauling to the St. Helena co-op for drying, and later on in the fall I helped my landlady collect fallen walnuts.

Handling the fruit on these early autumn days I felt as if time had stopped. I remember reading outdoors in a chair on the grass, as though houses and the

---

[2] See Rivka Shärf Kluger, *Satan and the Old Testament,* esp. pp. 49, 145.

[3] *The Civilization of the Goddess,* p. 229.

material things they contained were no longer necessary. Mother Nature was ripening the fruit of the valley, as well as transforming my habitual anxiety into a new responsiveness. Nature was reflecting something back to me, and for the first time I experienced my own being in a wholesome way. It reminded me of this poem by James Wright, called "Beginning":

> The moon drops one or two feathers into the field.
> The dark wheat listens.
> Be still.
> Now.
> There they are, the moon's young, trying
> Their wings.
> Between trees, a slender woman lifts up the lovely shadow
> Of her face, and now she steps into the air, now she is gone
> Wholly, into the air.
> I stand alone by an elder tree, I do not dare breathe
> Or move.
> I listen.
> The wheat leans back toward its own darkness.
> And I lean toward mine.[4]

My landlady was not completely in the service of Mother Nature, however. When she espied my girlfriend with long red hair swinging on the porch, she evicted me for being immoral. Hastily I contacted my cousins, who had heard of a place for rent on Mount St. Helena, overlooking the Napa Valley. It was a large piece of land far above the valley floor, with a main house above and two small houses on either side below. It was unoccupied, and for $65 a month I could have one of the little houses. Sitting in the bathtub, I could look out over the whole valley. Yet the house was very remote, and one day, after playing hooky from work and watching the solitary hawks circling above, I realized the danger of being too isolated. There was no telephone, and I remember that after eating breakfast in Calistoga, a sleepy little town during the week (on weekends people came for the mudbaths), I would pass only two or three cars on the Silverado Trail all the way into Napa.

During my first year one of my fellow psychiatric residents had befriended a long-time employee at Louis Martini Winery, and on occasional afternoons we would all knock off early and drink there with the old man. This was when I was living in St. Helena in the early 1960s before the valley's wineries got all gus-

---

[4] *Collected Poems.* p. 127.

sied up. The tasting room, cool and smelling wonderful, was right there alongside the big barrels. Sipping the different wines opened up a new world for me. I discovered not only my nose but also my palate. You could buy a bottle of Cabernet Sauvignon for $2.80 and a good red table wine for 99 cents.

In 1965 I moved to Lokoya Lodge, near Mayacamus Winery, located on the west ridge of the Napa Valley under Mt. Veeder. The original lodge had long since burned down, but a long beautiful swimming pool remained with cottages surrounding it in the redwoods. In the morning I would awaken high above the fog in the valley and swim. My inner life was exploding and I began painting and working in clay. I repetitively painted pictures of wicker chairs in reds and browns twirling in space. I covered my walls with them. (Perhaps these animated chairs represented an attempt to find my own place to sit, like a king on his throne.) I also took my clay figures to be fired in the kiln in the art building of the hospital. The firing was a disaster—my pieces exploded, burying the work of the patients who later shook their fists at me in outrage. To calm myself I would take my sleeping bag up to the winery and sleep between the terraced rows of vines. One weekend my friends and I picked the luscious Chardonnay grape. Mayacamus was noted for its Chardonnay wine, and I remember squeezing bunches of grapes into my mouth, the juice running down my face. I never tasted anything, before or since, so luxuriant, so rich in flavor and sweetness. Perhaps it was like having sex for the first time when you are in love.

Around the same time I met a Sioux Indian woman who had six children and lived at the bottom of Lokoya Road where it intersects Redwood Road. Carrying too many responsibilities and living too close to psychic reality, she had been in and out of the state hospital as a patient many times. It was from her that I learned to trust myself. "Will I make it, Fay?" I would ask, meaning, "Will I become the person I'm meant to be?" One night after eating mushrooms I thought I would die, and she held my head all during those early morning hours before dawn. "The spirits are walking—do you hear them?" she would ask. From her I learned about people from the inside. She read people the Indian way. She was a large woman, about six feet tall, yet when she walked over twigs and pine needles to visit me there was no sound. When we parted she gave me a glass box with this note inside:

> Man—this small glass cage is for the meaningful things you are collecting. No need to lift the lid and peek—no danger of runaways. Very practical when one realizes the fantastic number of meaningful things lost in one day.
>
> *(Signed with her Indian mark)*

No land was so imbued with spirit, so powerful and frightening as those hills and ridges under the eye of Mt. Veeder. When I walked in the evening twilight, the Manzanita skin would glow as if from an internal light—where? Even though there were a few people inhabiting this land, it was decidedly remote and felt uninhabitable, being high up, hilly and arid with scrub brush and rocky soil. Some amusing things happened to me in this setting. One week I asked a neighbor to call in sick for me because I wanted to paint. I hadn't realized the extent to which Dr. McGrath—though he was of another generation with superior education, including mastery of Latin—considered me a kindred spirit and son. Worried about my illness in the wilderness, he sent a search party from the hospital. Fortunately they never found me. My cabin was too remote.

One beneficent autumn day we all took a picnic lunch and Chardonnay wine to an abandoned persimmon orchard. The leaves from the trees were gone, but the luminescent globes of orange fruit hung like Japanese lanterns from the trees, all warm and sweet, and we sucked them up with the wine.

Around then I met the woman who would become my wife, and moved west to the east ridge of Petaluma, to Sonoma Mountain about 1500 feet above the valley floor. Open sprawling meadows punctuated with live oak and an old olive grove made the land seem warm and friendly. The ranch was originally owned by friends of my wife's family, the Moreaus. I think the rent for the whole place, house plus studio, was $150 a month. There was no other house within a mile except for Robert McChesney and his wife Mary Fuller McChesney who lived up the road a piece, having traded a painting for a piece of Moreaus' land.

The McChesneys were artists, he among the famous group that attended the San Francisco Art Institute following World War Two. This group included Clyfford Still. One evening they came over for me to do a tarot reading on the question "Is Clyfford Still a Manichaean?" Never having heard of Clyfford Still, I assumed he was a friend of theirs and that they wanted to know if he was "still" a Manichaean! McChesney helped me see the aesthetic in nature, in our walks in woods and meadows along the mysterious "sinks." He would stop in contemplation to study the light as it reflected off the moss of the California oak, or he would stoop down to examine a single flower. He chided me for not touching the grasses, the flowers, the bark, the earth. Sometimes he would laugh; a quiet joy had entered his heart and he would show me how the grasses and trees were all brought together in a single moment. We looked at things from such a different perspective that I hardly recognized where I lived by the time we returned.

My wife's house was made of redwood logs built by Moreau, McChesney and my wife's family, including her grandfather. It was basically one large room which faced out through a wall of windows to a downward-sloping meadow. The floor of the house was level with the ground so there was no stepping up from the earth to enter. The effect on the occupant was like that in many California houses; the inhabitant feels no separation between inside and outside. Life is open and waiting, anything can happen. These Californians were intuitive, quick as lightning, free to change, accomplishing tasks spontaneously, so unlike my Midwestern relatives with all that planning and preparing. I knew the first moment I entered that space that I would never leave.

My mother-in-law, a woman close to the land, is psychic, and continues to this day to slip me advice as the Indian woman did. She encouraged me to find a place of my own in nature by the ocean; it was as if she had a vision of me there. And in later years, when I was in a muddle, I would pour out the problem, including my dream, and I would get a response completely other than how I was thinking. She wasn't afraid to challenge me. After my analysis was completed, she was my ace in the hole.

After Napa

When I look back at it now, I see that over the course of my professional life, cycles of intense vitality have alternated with periods of relative dryness and isolation. And always, in the periods of dryness, it is contact with nature that has been the source of revitalization.

After my wife and I moved to San Francisco, I began my career in psychiatry. Coincident with developing my outer professional life, I felt a need to better understand certain powerful experiences and visions. In one of these, which I had while living on Mt. Veeder, I was visited by the image of a warm woman figure, Death. My colleagues and friends thought it was enough to have had these visions, but the awakening analyst in me was not satisfied to have met this figure of Death without knowing more about her. From a recent dream, I painted an Indian woman stirring a large pot over a fire while I looked on. Proudly showing this depiction to the Jungian analyst I consulted, he expressed concern that it might be me she would cook. He meant that I was too taken up with unconscious exploration and I needed to tend to my life. My beatific inner world had the potential of capturing me in the way that Circe had entranced Ulysses. There were other practical things requiring my attention, and gradually I entered the world more fully as psychiatrist, analytic student, husband, father, homeowner, collector of Oriental art, devotee of Thomas Mann. I enjoyed these early professional years, and it seemed that I made a good adaptation.

Eventually, however, over many years of successful work, I began to see how cut off from nature I had become. Simultaneously something quite unexpected began emerging in my own analysis. Through the transference I began to see that I was not the person I thought I was. I could not emulate my analyst because he fit the Jungian model as an intellectual thinking type and try as I might, that just wasn't my nature. So I began the painful process of consciously discovering what the "metal" or substance was that composed my own deepest self.

What I discovered I didn't much like: earthy, with too much feeling and sensitivity, not suited for the world. I understood now what Miss Craver, my high school algebra teacher, told my parents when my younger sister entered her class: "Here's the child you have been waiting for. She has a brain. Send her to private school." And I understood an earlier experience when, in the fourth grade in Youngstown, Ohio, I was kept back a semester in Miss Deem's class because I was emotionally upset and not doing well. To the teacher's credit she placed me in a seat at the back of the classroom closest to the closet containing all the art materials. There were rows of large jars of poster paint; yellow, red, blue, green. Day after day, instead of participating in regular class assignments, I painted on large sheets of butcher paper. Eventually I was moved ahead to join my regular class, reunited with old friends.

Slowly it dawned on me that I couldn't compete with my colleagues in teaching or writing. I just didn't measure up, and when I decided to withdraw from such scholarly pursuits, much to my horror my analyst concurred. He commented coldly, "I'll accept that." I surmised that he had no feeling for me, that this was an empathic failure on his part and that my suggestion that I withdraw came as a relief to him. I would not be an embarrassment to a highly sophisticated professional community. His consolation was, "You work well with people." I felt ashamed and humiliated, but what I was not aware of at the time was that I had to go deeper. My analyst must have known that I was capable of finding my own way. I could suffer "the analytic transference" as they say in the vernacular, in order to have a life for myself, not dependent on collective approval or the adoration of my mentors. Then I remembered the words of a woman friend who advised me to "let life put you where it wants, rather than you deciding. Then you will live in the moment without regret." In my youth I had missed opportunities by turning down dates with girls whom I felt were socially inferior.

Besides my analyst, there were other people in authority who were tough-minded toward me, my high school algebra teacher, for one. When I stuttered in her class one day, she said, "Neil Russack, you stop that right now. I won't have any of that in my classroom." And by God I did stop—though only in her class. Sometimes I miss someone ordering me around as if they really know what I should be doing. People now appear supportive of anything I do. Is such support a form of care? When I was little and stubborn as can be, my German grandmother came to care for us, replacing my hospitalized mother, and when I refused to come downstairs, she hollered up: "Neil Russack, you come down here right this minute," and I did. Her forthrightness made me realize she loved me.

My analyst's three-word response, "I'll accept that," implying that I was not ready to teach, sent me into a professional identity crisis. I didn't know that I wasn't standing on my own feet. In my earlier student years I did not have the emotional strength and focus necessary to pursue a career close to my heart. Now, the professional path of writing and teaching seemed closed to me. I suffered terribly from this confrontation. I began to write as I had begun to paint in the fourth grade when I was stopped from going forward with my classmates. I wrote what I called my "Potato Paper," in which I identified with a potato, underground, alone, but with eyes that can see, eyes out of which new sprouts grow, eyes from which underground inner visions could develop.

And at the same time, remembering those years in Napa, where I knew I could be myself and where I had enjoyed that burst of creative energy, I literally retreated into nature, down into the depths again—away from civilization—like Merlin retreating to the forest. This shift in my psyche crystallized on one autumn day. I was hiking in Pt. Reyes as I often did, yet I knew something fateful was about to happen. I knew this in my bones, deeper than anything I had ever known. It was during the week, with not a soul in sight. I hiked the trail from the end of Pierce Point Road to Tomales Point—the northern five mile tip of the Pt. Reyes peninsula. It is a spectacular high trail that moves down a long spine overlooking the vast Pacific on one side and the long narrow Tomales Bay, created by the San Andreas fault, on the other side. It ends at a point where the fault line, now bay, creates a break in the coast.

From this vantage point, looking across the inlet to the town of Tomales, I pulled out my bread, cheese, and a lovely red bell pepper I had picked from a truck farm near my mother-in-law's in Sonoma county. Astonished, I watched my red pepper roll off the paper bag down the drop-off to become an offering to the sea below. An immediate emotional sense of loss overcame me. I realized that my feeling life had been contained by the warmth of my wife's family and would now be replaced by something of my inmost self.

On the way back I saw more hawks than I had ever seen before and I was struck by the beautifully soft and rich looking mottled beige and brown color of these powerful birds. Being alone need not be so austere or removed. Solitude could nourish and bring wonderment. A rare spirit flame caught me. The hawks and rocks of Robinson Jeffers' California now claimed me too.

Thus I began living alone in Inverness on and off for many years; taking long walks by the seashore with my dog, reading by the fire or under a tree, sleeping outside by hooting owls; all this became a way of life for me. Strangely enough, I never felt alone. I was always having intense conversations with myself, going over analytic hours, thinking about things I had read, revisiting my past as well as observing the beauty and wonder of my surroundings. I was fascinated by the shore birds. Occasionally my older son would visit me. One day on the beach he discovered Velella, or By-The-Wind-Sailors, little floating marine animals characterized by a sail, a gas-filled float in soft blue color. Thousands covered the seashore and he wrote a lovely paper about them for zoology class. He learned to enjoy eating barbecued oysters by moonlight and starlight.

"What do you do out there all that time?" asked a worldly woman friend. I couldn't really say. I had never thought of it as "doing," but rather as a way of being. It was always a shock to return to San Francisco, though it was only an hour away. For a long time I moved back and forth between both worlds.

Two significant events marked the end of my ten- or twelve-year stay in Inverness. My dog died, and I had begun collecting animal and nature dreams from my patients. From that material I started giving seminars. Also, with the urging of my wife, I took on some additional work. Suddenly my life in the world caught fire. I had drawn energy from the red fox lying in the sun, the waterbird taking off into the sky. Now this energy flowed into my work with patients' dreams. My patients' experience of the healing power of animals became congruent with my personal inner nature quest. The two worlds came together: my outer professional life and the more secret world of animal imagination. Sometimes it took my breath away to hear a patient's animal dream. My professional life had moved inside the ancient caves where painted animals vibrated with a mysterious life. Seeing a mountain lion at Pt. Reyes was one thing, but feeling the large cats walking with their paws on the earth inside the psyche's cave was Inverness times ten. I returned to the office, but with the listening ears of a knowing animal. I had learned to fly with the waterbirds, moving from one realm to another.

2
Animal Healing

Animal Soul

Humans and animals are capable of a deep and healing intimacy with one another. Joseph Henderson, among the first to disseminate Jung's ideas in America, told me the following story about Jung that relates animal to soul.

> Jung used to tell a story about a little circus elephant he knew about because the circus had its off-season winter quarters in Rapperswill, the town nearest his country house at Bollingen on the Lake of Zurich. He used to talk to the animal trainer about his relation to the animals. One winter a little elephant became sick. The trainer, following the veterinarian's advice, medicated him, but after many trials the animal continued to be sick and he despaired of saving him.
>
> In desperation he tried talking to the elephant, much as if it could understand human language. Asking questions seemed to interest the elephant. What these questions were Jung did not know, but presumably they were accompanied by the trainer's feeling for the animal's inner identity, one might say its soul. Slowly, watchfully, the trainer began to sense a change, and in a short time the little elephant was well again. What made the story so memorable was in Jung's telling it as if he were in the shoes of the trainer, and he talked as if he were speaking to a sick patient whose sickness was healed in a similar way by reaching the patient's inmost self, through feeling.

When animals, like this elephant, are thrust into the human environment, they sometimes suffer the same soul-loss that is so common among humans. More often, however, as is evident in the following pages, it is the animal who brings vitality to the human.

Animal Energy

Just as the trainer coaxed the failing elephant back to life, so my own little dog kept me linked to life when my vitality was fading. When I took him with me to the country, we would take a long walk during the day, then spend the evening by the fire. Sometimes we walked at the dead of night in the dark woods, and the white tip of his tail would lead me home in the starlight. He was the one who, by helping me find my way, showed me who I was. This all happened at a time when there was something dead in my life. Without knowing it, the dog changed me through the touch of his intimate companionship. My energy returned. My time of retreat ended. I became interested again in the things that people do, and I went back to my work refreshed.

Then something unexpected happened. Just at the point when I returned to life, my dog died. He couldn't cross the threshold with me. I buried him there on the country property. As I was crossing back over into the human world, he had to return to his world. Was he a god? Was he part of myself? To simply tell people that my dog died didn't communicate how important he was to me. Now that he was dead, I would be on my own. I had tried communicating with my colleagues now and again what my life in retreat was about, but they always seemed to measure me according to worldly values and with reference to the risk to my professional life. When a friend asked, "What do you do out there all that time?" I couldn't reply. I had nothing to show for it, and yet everything flowed from that solitude and immersion in nature—and my dog was with me through every moment. Sometimes I felt he alone understood.

The transition from animals to people was easy. The animals who accompanied me in my solitude followed me back into my interactions with others, appearing in dreams and stories that people reported to me. Animals broke into their lives, frightening them and creating havoc. Sometimes, the animals brought them blessings. A patient told me with alarm that her two-and-a-half-year-old daughter woke up from a dream holding her head in pain. "A baby monster bit my head, he bit my knee, and then my other knee. A crocodile bit my knee, he got my foot, he got my toe." She woke up looking for the crocodile in her bed, under the covers.

Once, I encountered on a trail in Pt. Reyes a man ashen with fear. Trembling, he stammered out a warning to me to turn back. Just moments before, after rounding a bend, he had come upon a mountain lion lying on a grassy area not fifteen feet away. He froze. The lion had looked him over, then after a long two or three minutes had slowly risen to its feet and ambled off into the bush.

Later I ran into a woman on the same trail who had a different response to crossing paths with a mountain lion. "I was excited," she said and a big smile spread across her face.

When a dangerous animal truly touches us, we feel both terror and exhilaration—it breaks through our ordinary way of being, rousing us from our routine existence. In this way, animals shock us open; they kick us out of ego consciousness. Suddenly, through facing death by a dangerous animal, we experience the big life, bigger than our problems, bigger than our worries about work, spouse, money. The animals evoke an instinctual response. They are the life that bites us.

Animals that befriend us can also protect us from these bites. They can cuddle us in cozy warmth as they did for a lively five-year-old girl, the daughter of one of my patients. She was having difficulty adjusting to kindergarten: frightened by nightmares, she was discovered walking in her sleep. She told her mother that when she was frightened in the middle of the night she would bring her mother her lamb who sings, "Mary had a little lamb," or her horse that glows in the dark. Her mother was then to wake up, come into her room and put a special protective lotion on her.

Animals can soothe our stress and release our energy. When a woman in graduate school finished a long term paper at the end of a school year she was ecstatic She dreamed:

> Our whole family and our neighbors were at a swimming pool like the one at Sea Ranch. The water was blue and clear. It was doggie swim time and the water was churning with exuberant dogs and kids and anyone else brave enough to dodge the feet of paddling pups, the dogs jumping into the water and the rough waves generated by all the activity. Joseph, my son, was a 10 year old having a wonderful time in the water. There was one big black dog with short hair and lumpy wrinkled skin like those Chinese dogs who was cavorting in the water. This dog just had puppies and her teats were swollen with milk.

The dream dropped her back into an older, deeper, more feminine mode from which she could respond without thinking. It was summertime, with its freedom from responsibilities. Letting go in water dissolved this woman's work mode, releasing her from the discipline of analysis and allowing her to return to the relative ease of being with children and dogs. The excitement and exuberance of all this young life rekindled her joy. The mother dog's affection for its pups, the renewal of fertility, were as far away from academic hurdles as she could go.

People have always enjoyed an animal's closeness, its physicality. I often wake in the morning to find the cat sleeping right in the curve of my wife's neck, and I like to lie down alongside my dog next to the hearth by the fire. Many people find that they can open themselves to animals in a way that is different from their relationship to even the most loved family members.

Sigmund Freud explains the psychological reasons

> why one can love an animal like Topsy or Jofi with such extraordinary intensity . . . affection without ambivalence, the simplicity of a life free from the almost unbearable conflicts of civilization, the beauty of an existence complete in itself, and yet,

> despite all diversions in the organic development, that feeling of an intimate affinity, of an undisputed solidarity.[5]

"Basic stuff" is how one woman referred to her dog, who stayed by her side as she shed a relationship and moved to another home. Lovers can come and go, but dogs remain. We call or whistle to them and put our noses up to theirs, exchanging breath. My male border collie greets women by putting his nose into their crotches. Moss the Nose, he's called. There's a moment of embarrassment and recoil; yet my friends continue to pet Moss while holding him at a discreet distance. They seem to accept the intrusion. The dog smells who they are and the women respond: "Yes, this is how animals are, and isn't that what life is about, being included?"

Animals also respond to the flow in our lives, marking who has come home, who has left, what the fighting or excitement is about. They gravitate to the dark places in us. At times, I imagine my wife thinking, "There he is in another of those moods again," and the children stay away until "Daddy feels better," but not the dog. Animals resonate with our emotions, no matter how irrational. They help us bring them to the surface by responding to our feeling life. They give solace and comfort. Perhaps I have a cyst behind my ear, and when I forget myself and start to scratch it, there is my dog, licking it, caring for it.

It is not right to describe animals as our inferiors, for they bring us gifts, even if we only half notice them. They are gates through which we shift our consciousness. Coming upon a deer in the woods, a waterbird on shore, I feel its living presence. My body becomes alert, I stand poised. If I am quiet inside, the animal doesn't move. We can just be, the animal and me, in our living stillness. Then I feel whole again, no matter what difficulties have befallen me in the work-a-day world. Touched in this deeper way, I neither want to leave nor want the animal to leave. When the animal outstays me, I leave with sadness. My old life draws me back across the boundary; that's how we're different, the animal and me.

Henry Beston expressed his respect for animals in a novel written in the early 1920s, during the year he spent in a small cottage on Cape Cod:

> We need another and a wiser and perhaps a more mystical concept of animals. Remote from universal nature, and living by complicated artifice, man in civilization surveys the creature through the glass of his knowledge and sees thereby a feather magnified and the whole image in distortion. We patronize them for their

---

[5] Quoted by Eleanora M. Woloy in *The Symbol of the Dog in the Human Psyche,* p. 15.

> incompleteness, for their tragic fate of having taken form so far below ourselves. And therein we err, and greatly err. For the animals shall not be measured by man. In a world older and more complete than ours they move finished and complete, gifted with extensions of the sense we have lost or never attained, living by voices we shall never hear. They are not brethren, they are not underlings; they are other nations, caught with ourselves in the net of life and time, fellow prisoners of the splendour and travail of earth.[6]

Because the animal world is different from ours, the wounds which impair us in our human world actually open us to the realm of animals. In this way, people who are half mad can be guides to the animal world. One day I was walking in Pt. Reyes with a tall, gangly young woman. She sometimes fell into episodes of manic depression, and through this terrible condition became wide open to life. That day we came upon a flock of black-shouldered kites. These birds have mysteriously beautiful faces and are not often encountered in such numbers. They perched on fence posts and hovered above us. It was an ecstatic moment. I looked into the faces of the birds and felt I was entering another world. I thought, "These birds do not belong in our realm." The girl and I, and the dog too, it seemed, all entered the birds' world. My chest filled with light and warmth. Immersed in a different reality, the birds, the girl, I and my dog were one. I saw through the birds' eyes and face; I flew into the sustaining air.

Since then, I have searched for that place by the road. It's close to where I live, but I have not been able to find it again. I thought it was so natural that I could return whenever I wished. The place, the girl, the dog are all gone, but I cannot look into the face of a kite without remembering.

Now, looking back at the experience, I realize that its aesthetic beauty is what captured my imagination. It had a quality of light and stillness like a Vermeer painting. Remembering this, I want to retell the story, to get the light right: We spotted the birds from the road. To get there we had to navigate the shrubs that grew thicker than we expected. We were excited, and in our hurry we ran, stumbling and laughing. The dog raced ahead, but returned to herd us along when our feet became entangled in the underlying roots. Then suddenly we were there: the light behind us outlined the birds, and we couldn't take our eyes off them. Everything stopped. We stopped. In the immensity of the present moment, everything around us grew still except for the birds that were perched and hovering, slowly ascending and descending like the people in Blake's painting, *Jacob's Ladder.* We dissolved into the moment. We were in the air, ascending and de-

---

[6] *The Outermost House,* pp. 19f.

scending with the birds. We were like the man and woman in Wallace Stevens's poem, "Thirteen Ways of Looking at a Blackbird":

> A man and a woman
> are one.
> A man and woman and a blackbird
> are one.[7]

How long we remained there, I couldn't say. Then we left, quietly bearing the knowledge that something had happened to us. We didn't talk after that.

Over the years, animals have settled the doubts in me. If I have an identity, it is rooted in such experiences as with the birds. A voice in me used to say I was wasting those years, but my animal self has shown me otherwise. After this period in Inverness ended, I had completed something and was ready to reenter life. I was no longer searching. I had found something for myself, for me alone. What is it? I feel I am in my body in the moment and can respond to my emotions as they are. Comfortable being the person that I am, I feel a fundamental belonging on earth—quite apart from whatever my achievements might be.

My closeness with Moss evokes another lost dog, Skipper, my childhood pet, my first and most powerful link to the animal world. With my dog always at my side, I felt I belonged. He represented my place in the family. When I was five-and-a-half-years old, my sister was born. My parents had waited a long time for a girl and felt protective of her. They gave away Skipper, a male standard schnauzer who would take on anything and everything. They were worried about what an aggressive dog might do to a baby girl. It was a terrible loss for me and I held it against her—that unwelcome little princess. Somehow the loss of Skipper was healed in my later life by Moss, the dog who led me home in the starlight. Though I am still angry when I think of losing Skipper, he left me with the sense of an animal life and his loss was a kind of hole where light could later pour in.

When I told a colleague about my starlit dog, she told me a dream she had had about her dogs:

> Inside a small stone Romanesque church I am walking arm in arm with my mother coming up a side aisle or cross aisle. We are to be married. In front of me are four dogs sitting in pews in a balcony as they lean with their elbows over the ledge of a stone banister. They are watching us. These short-haired dogs, perhaps hound dogs, are sitting just like humans might and if I didn't know they were dogs I

---

[7] *The Palm at the End of the Mind: Selected Poems and a Play*, p. 20.

> would think they were people. With my mother on the left side of me we turn left with our backs to the dogs toward a light sunny altar place but in fact there is no altar. The dogs leap down out of the balcony and completely devour me, and then vomit me up into a pile of vomit on the floor. As I rise from the vomit, I am turned away from my mother and am facing the front of the church. I then realize what's happened to me. I am resurrected with an incredible feeling of independence.

This woman's mother occupied an important social and political position in this country and expected her children to take up similar positions eventually, so no special interest was given to their individual differences. In the dream my friend continues to look for an intimate link with her mother through a marriage ceremony in this small lovely church. Instead of an altar, there is a place filled with light. Instead of people to witness the marriage, there are dogs. This suggests to me that the occasion required an instinctual response. A social role alone is not enough to sustain us. We need an individual life. The dogs ate up her social position and turned her away from her mother and onto her own path. Rising from the disgusting vomit, so organic and animal-like, so offensive to her diplomatic training, she becomes free.

Dreams very similar to this—archetypal dreams—have been reported from time immemorial. As in the shamanic tradition, she is devoured, dismembered and arises new born. She is given a sense of renewal and independence from the dream which will anchor her life work. She herself is an analyst, a vocation which in its own deep way is consistent with the ancient healing tradition of shamans, supported by the animals.

The dog doesn't always have to rescue people; sometimes people on their own have the good sense to be dog-like. On my evening walk I often notice the resemblance between dogs and their owners. A well-trimmed poodle has in tow a fastidiously dressed man; a beautiful young German shepherd bounding ahead, superior and aloof, encourages a tall young aristocratic Italian woman; a Belgian Bouvier accompanies a burly, successful gent. One morning I passed an old man whose dog had inadvertently wrapped his leash around a tree while peeing. I overheard the old man say to his dog in response, "Sometimes I wonder about your mental make-up, Sirrah." Dogs often reveal a hidden side of their owners.

An animal image can capture the essence of a person's character. It can represent a part that doesn't change. We think, "He is a lion," or "He is a horse's ass." A friend of mine, newly employed as an administrator at a small college, had begun to worry about his relationship with the college's financial officer, who was encouraging him to delay reporting certain expenses to the Trustees until they knew him better. Over a period of time, the financial officer, a gracious, fatherly man, persuaded my friend to continue this questionable practice, convincing him that he knew the system and had only his interest at heart. The night following one of their discussions, my friend dreamed that he was sitting face to face with an elegant, beautiful older woman. Out of the corner of his eye, he noticed some movement under her skirt, but felt it would be rude to stare at the legs of such a lady. Steadfastly, he kept his eyes focused on her head and torso as she continued to talk and charm him with her presence, but finally he could no longer restrain himself. He looked down in the direction of her feet just in time to see a weasel run out from under her dress.

When my friend awoke, he realized that the financial officer and his advice, despite their elegant seductiveness, were, underneath, sly and weasely to the point of being psychopathic.

The evolution of nature has created some odd animals, animals that we humans wouldn't think could function well. A giraffe with its large lower body sprouting a long tapering neck and small head can nevertheless run like the wind. A porcupine with its impenetrable needles can still mate. Seeing these incongruous and seemingly contradictory elements combined can be reassuring to us. A colleague of mine knew he had completed his analysis when he saw that the energy of his mind was not compromised by the anxiety of his spirit. This insight was occasioned by a dream that presented to him the image of the head of a beautiful strong horse, very like one of those on the Parthenon frieze displayed in the British Museum. Like the horse, this man is high strung and sensitive, yet powerful and swift in his professional life. He had always imagined that to be entirely effective in the world he would have to get over his sensitivity. Reflecting on the horse as a healthy image of himself, however, he realized that it was his nature to be on edge and alert and that this need not impede him on his journey through life.

Animal Guardian

Often it is through loss or absence that we realize what holds meaning for us. This is true both in waking life and in dreams. People who are cut off from their emotions might dream they have lost the ability to move or that they are an animal trapped in a cage. Their energy, dammed up inside, can't get out into life and their dreams wake them up to their deeper values. The poet Rilke was already breaking away from certain constricting notions as to what constituted value in art when he met the sculptor Rodin.

> As a yaung poet, Rilke was for a while secretary to the sculptor Auguste Rodin. "What made you the artist that you are?" he inquired. Rodin advised, "Go to the zoo and study the animals."[8]

Rodin sent him to the zoo to discover a kind of primal vital energy that is unencumbered by the hierarchical tendencies of the rational mind. Rilke expresses the power of this primal vitality, and the sadness of being cut off from it, in "The Panther":

> His vision, from the constantly passing bars,
> has grown so weary that it cannot hold
> anything else. It seems to him there are
> a thousand bars; and behind the bars, no world.
>
> As he paces in cramped circles, over and over,
> the movement of his powerful soft strides
> is like a ritual dance around a center
> in which a mighty will stands paralyzed.
>
> Only at times, the curtain of the pupils
> lifts, quietly—. An image enters in,
> rushes down through the tensed, arrested muscles,
> plunges into the heart and is gone.[9]

Can our emotional fire be made conscious, or are we like the caged animal, experiencing our life only as a flash of possibility? Rilke's poem has become a metaphor for my work with patients, as I measure sickness in their restriction, healing in their freedom.

Healthy people, like my friend eaten by dream dogs, allow themselves to fall into crisis, permit old structures to break apart, opening the way for new life. Crisis can involve the death of a family member, loss of love or a career, or illness. At such times, in dreams, a freed animal will often appear to guide and comfort us. After breaking off a long relationship with a man, a friend of mine dreamt she was accompanied by a huge bear:

> He is so big that if he covered me, I would be hidden. I can feel the pads of his feetÑtwice the size of my palms—soft but big. We are walking hand in hand, his paw warmly enclosing mine. Somehow he puts his arms around me and hugs me.
>
> People are looking at us as if we are strange but I know I'm on the right path. (I've had it with people so I don't care what they think.) I'm proud of him—not

---

[8] Wolfgang Leppmann, *Rilke: A Life,* p. 214.
[9] *The Selected Poetry of Rainer Maria Rilke,* p. 25.

> embarrassed of him. He talks very softly and interestedly and nobody can understand him but me. The bear belongs to me. We claimed each other.

She said further about the bear:

> He gave me peace and trust, an expansion of safety because I can conjure him up again. I can feel his whole body and spine. I feel whole when I feel that dream. Afterward I came to the realization that there is no one who can really take care of me. Initially I experienced a period of loneliness, sad but exciting. Now I'm okay. There is a peace when I think about this dream.

When we're in crisis, we need comfort and reassurance from our animal nature. Later, when the crisis subsides, it is time to enter into a new life. This is a different kind of moment. For this transition we need energy, confidence and playfulness. For this moment, too, an animal can serve as guide. I had a friend who hadn't been connected to the world. She had kept herself in a kind of closet as a gentle, artistic woman lacking self-confidence. One night she dreamt of tigers and lions coming right into her bedroom, embodying her new life. Indeed, her friends began to find her alive and dangerous. This was her dream:

> I am in a beautiful old house. Large rooms furnished with art, exquisite antiques of different styles and periods, oriental rugs. Flowers in vases, magazines and books on shelves on tables. Although neat and well-cared for, the rooms feel comfortable and lived in. This could be my house. A teen-age tiger comes leaping across the furniture, over the table, playfully, not harming anything. I'm amazed and amused. I hear a roar. The front door opens and a huge lioness walks toward me. She comes right up beside me and looks directly into my eyes. We know and love each other and are coming together after being apart for a long time. I run my fingers through her thick fur. The love between us is deep and old. I feel warm and happy.

The dream opened up in a big beautiful house filled with art and complexity. A teen-age tiger came bounding in, supplying the woman with the adventurous energy needed to get out in the world. Enjoying its playfulness, she was then able to encounter a mature lioness—the regal female empowered with full authority. The direct eye contact between this animal and the woman forever sealed this loving reconnection. There is a strong tactile quality, a powerful physicality, in these animal encounters, both real and imaginary: a woman meets a mountain lion in Pt. Reyes, a little girl searches for crocodiles under the covers of her bed. The big cats, independent and powerful, filled the artist-dreamer with awe and reverence, the lion representing sun and heat, the tiger representing the dark and the mysterious. She seemed noticeably relaxed and more easily accessible. The inner power of these cats reminds me of William Blake's poem:

Tyger! Tyger! Burning bright
In the forests of the night,
What immortal hand or eye
Could frame thy fearful symmetry?

In what distant deeps or skies
Burnt the fire of thine eyes?
On what wings dare he aspire?
What the hand, dare seize the fire?[10]

In dreaming of a wild animal, we sometimes seize the fire. True to its nature, the animal lives in the moment. It teaches us to trust our instincts without calculation. It helps us return to a more immediate, powerfully embodied way of acting in the world. We begin to listen to our emotions, trusting a true response. We wake up in the morning and suddenly know in our bones what we have to do. And, curiously, we are not afraid. We know what is right and we do it. We don't have to prove anything or justify our response; we are like the animal, valued for its own sake. It no longer matters how we dress or whether we find the correct words for our intentions.

The reality that comes from sharing in the power of the animal and the dream world makes our life feel natural. We become like an animal, experiencing reality directly, without premeditation. "Spontaneous response, great precision," exclaims the Chinese master painter as he captures in a few brushstrokes the spirit of the monkey holding his orange.[11]

When I dreamt of a large owl flying silently at night, its great wings outspread and its eyes seeing everything, I am awed. This bird is both stealthy and effective, sneaky and predatory. The owl is the analyst's bird who sees in the night, whose intuitive radar finds what will feed the process. Through such a dream, something happened in my psyche that was even deeper than my work with patients. Indeed, from that owl dream arose the impulse that led to the writing of this book, and then the book itself became a bird.

In his *Visions Seminars,* Jung speaks of the instinctual response. A patient of his painted her vision of a human face turning into an animal face. Jung said that she was emotionally stung from looking into

> the melancholy eye of [a dark hairy-faced] animal. You see what really happened was that they traveled back, not only to ancient Greece but farther; the animals led

---

[10] "The Tyger," in *The Portable Blake,* p. 109.

[11] See Yuan and Chuan, *The Mustard Seed Garden Manual of Painting*, p. 20.

> her inevitably back to the animal age. That is, you remember, the purpose of the Dionysian mysteries, to bring people back to the animal; not to what we know as the animal, not that they should identify with it as we understand it, but to the animal within. . . . She looks here into the very soul of the animal and that is the experience she should have, otherwise she is disconnected from nature.[12]

Often, however, dreaming of a healing image alone is not enough. The image needs to be swallowed, absorbed. Then it can come out into life. It needs to become active in our lives. When we use this new energy, we experience more directly every interaction: eating, sleeping, working, making love. Then this integrated response becomes a sacred action. Vital animal energy becomes a healing ingredient, not just a static image. Too often, we dream a healing symbol and think simply understanding it will bring the cure. Then we are on to the next thing and promptly forget about the image, until to our surprise it appears again in another dream, reminding us that we have not fully absorbed it. In the words of Aniela Jaffé, it is vital that people "integrate into their lives the symbol's psychic content—instinct. . . . The foundation of human nature is instinct."[13]

Of course, instinct is not in itself always positive. As a civilized society we constanty struggle with our aggressive instincts, often with harmful results. And nothing is more disastrous than when such instincts are mobilized on a grand scale in the form of mob violence, war, genocide. Jaffé makes this distinction between healthy and unhealthy instincts:

> Suppressed and wounded instincts are the dangers threatening civilized man; uninhibited drives are the dangers threatening primitive man. In both cases the "animal" is alienated from its true nature; and for both, the acceptance of the animal soul is the condition for wholeness and a fully lived life. Primitive man must tame the animal in himself and make it his helpful companion: civilized man must heal the animal in himself and make it his friend.[14]

In talking about the healing power of instinct, then, we are not referring to a simple acting-out of sexual and aggressive impulses. We are talking, rather, about heeding the deep promptings of the psyche. Something within calls us to actualize our natural talents, to pursue our deepest longings, to bring into being the deepest essence of our being.

It is one thing to speak of healing the animal within, but how do we actually do it?

---

[12] *The Visions Seminars,* vol. 1, pp. 62f.

[13] "Symbolism in the Visual Arts," in Jung, ed., *Man and His Symbols,* p. 239.

[14] Ibid.

A friend once asked, "How can anyone ever know what sex is like from a description? You have to have the experience yourself." It is the same in relation to our animal nature. First, we must experience the animal—in dream, in reality, in artistic creation. Experience leads to integration. The friend mentioned earlier who dreamed of a bear, dreamed again of a bear dancing around her. She moved from just observing, to being taken up with the action of the bear, infused with its energy. She did not simply see a bear dancing, she *became* the bear dancing.

In a similar vein, the poet Carl Sandburg knows how to integrate animal images so that he experiences them as a part of himself. He has taken them in alive, as we see from these three stanzas of his poem, "Wilderness":

> There is a fox in me . . . a silver-gray fox . . . I sniff and
> guess . . . I pick things out of the wind and air . . . I
> nose in the dark night and take sleepers and eat them and
> hide the feathers . . . I circle and loop and double-cross.
>
> There is a baboon in me . . . clambering clawed . . . dog-
> faced . . . yawping a galoot's hunger . . . hairy under
> the armpits . . . here are the hawk-eyed hankering men
> . . . here are the blonde and blue-eyed women . . . here
> they hide curled asleep waiting . . . ready to snarl and
> kill . . . ready to sing and give milk . . . waiting—I keep
> the baboon because the wilderness says so.
>
> There is an eagle in me and a mockingbird . . . and the eagle
> flies among the Rocky Mountains of my dreams and fights
> among the Sierra crags of what I want . . . and the
> mockingbird warbles in the early forenoon before the dew
> is gone, warbles in the underbrush of my Chattanoogas of
> hope, gushes over the blue Ozark foothills of my wishes. . . .
> And I got the eagle and the mockingbird from the
> wilderness.[15]

As we experience an animal's presence, we enter its skin in the same way that early humans, donning animal masks, became the animal. Even now, in still intact hunting-gathering cultures, the practice is not simply to identify with the totem animal in the way a modern person might assume, but to *become* the animal incarnate. When the shaman turns himself into an animal, he takes on a new identity and "becomes an animal-spirit, and 'speaks,' sings or flies like the ani-

[15] *Harvest Poems,* pp. 47f.

mals and birds."[16] The shaman is the animal spirit that "incorporates or represents the ancestor of the tribe and the clan, and therefore the primal god himself. He represents, and is, the 'totem' animal."[17]

Mircea Eliade, the great scholar of ancient religions, describes the shaman's identification with the animal:

> We know that the shaman plays a definite part in ensuring an abundance of game and good luck of the hunters. . . . but we must not forget that the relations between the shaman (and, indeed, "primitive man" in general) and animals are spiritual in nature and of a mystical intensity that a modern, desacralized mentality finds it difficult to imagine. For primitive man, donning the skin of an animal was becoming that animal, feeling himself transformed into an animal. . . . We have reason to believe that this magical transformation resulted in a "going out of the self" that very often found expression in an ecstatic experience.[18]

The dream animal can display our wounds. Often, its image represents a way of being that we have not been able to express because of earlier trauma. The animal seems to say, "You are wounded and cannot behave like me, but if you can begin to relate to me and let yourself express me, then I will heal you and bring you back to life." In the case of the dancing bear woman, the bear inspired confidence and trust. When we don't pay attention to our animal nature, the animal within turns against us and we may dream of an animal biting us or chasing us. Jaffé tells of the dangers which occur when instinct is cut off:

> The familiar dream in which the dreamer is pursued by an animal nearly always indicates that an instinct has been split off from consciousness and ought to be (or is trying to be) readmitted and integrated into life. The more dangerous the behavior of the animal in the dream, the more unconscious is the primitive and instinctual soul of the dreamer, and the more imperative is its integration into his life if some irreparable evil is to be forestalled.[19]

Integrating these split-off instincts becomes an ethical responsibility. Normally, instincts are integrated through the socialization process. Sports, for example, become the container for some young people to work out aggressive instincts, in keeping with the principles of good sportsmanship. Psychotherapy is a modern method of helping people to understand their defense mechanisms and open up, allowing a deep form of vitality to find its creative channel.

---

[16] Mircea Eliade, *Shamanism*, p. 93.
[17] Jaffé, "Symbolism in the Visual Arts," in Jung, ed., *Man and His Symbols*, p. 236.
[18] *Shamanism*. p. 459.
[19] Jaffé, "Symbolism in the Visual Arts," in Jung, ed., *Man and His Symbols*. p. 239.

Animal Body

When I first came onto the grounds of Napa State Hospital, a mental hospital, I was struck by the way the psychotic patients moved. Their limbs seemed wooden and their gait stiff, as if no one inhabited their bodies. A psychotic person's body is not a unit coordinated or focused toward some directed intention. This was a most unsettling sight, and there is nothing compared to it in the animal world, except perhaps a sick animal, a rabid dog or a cat with distemper.

Normally the animal's instinct, which is the root of its behavior, determines a clear bodily intention. When I arrived at the hospital each morning, I stepped into an unnatural world where bodies enacted an eerie trance in slow motion. At the other extreme was a severely autistic child who neither spoke nor looked me in the eye but whose body was so agile that he could practically walk sideways on an inner tube or even a wall. This is because autistic children, bombarded by stimuli, withdraw from life. Their bodies don't take on the same gravity as normal children, but remain uncannily agile, as if inhabiting a spirit realm. Jung talks about the split between body and psyche:

> The body is the original animal condition; we are all animals in the body, and so we should have animal psychology in order to be able to live in it. Yes, if we had no body then we could live with contracts and marvelous laws which everybody could observe and a marvelous morality which everybody could easily fulfill. But since we have a body it is indispensable that we exist also as an animal, and each time we invent a new increase of consciousness we have to put a new link in the chain that binds us to the animal, till finally it will become so long that complications will surely ensue. For when the chain between man and animal has grown so long that we lose sight of the animal, anything can happen in between, the chain will snarl up somewhere.[20]

My work at the state hospital was my first real experience with people whose communication was primarily nonverbal. I learned that the body and psyche belong together, that the body is the visible container that expresses our discomfiture and dis-ease. The rigid person moves rigidly. The fearful person moves tentatively. Women with eating disorders take the culture's view of a perfect body to an extreme, starving themselves or bingeing and purging, unable to simply let go into the process of life.

My interest in the relationship between psyche and body was not limited to a hospital setting but continued into private practice. When I completed my four

---

[20] *Nietzsche's* Zarathrusta, vol. 2, pp. 967f.

years at Napa State Hospital, I married and moved to San Francisco where I worked in hospitals and clinics while slowly building up a private practice. One of the clinics where I worked was the Center for Special Problems, so named because the patients treated there suffered from characterological disorders, ingrained behavioral patterns that often expressed antisocial behavior, specifically sexual dysfunction, criminal violations, alcohol and drug addiction. Because of the poor "cure" rate of these problems, and because more interaction with social agencies including police was required, a clinic with a particular focus and intervention was established.

One of the patients I was assigned to was a heroin addict, required by a court order to come for mandatory treatment in lieu of going to jail. He was intelligent and came from a wealthy family. Being good looking, immaculately dressed and highly verbal, he was able to take people in, so much so that one day he walked into a grocery store without knowing anyone, and walked out with a check in his pocket for several thousand dollars, given to him by the store manager.

Despite his many talents, this man was cut off from his emotions and had absolutely no connection to his body. Miraculously, he came regularly to his weekly appointment. He said he liked me because I was more interested in him as a person than in just trying to help him discontinue taking drugs. When I left the clinic, he transferred to my private practice.

All seemed to go well until one day when he was riding on the San Francisco trolley car. The only other people on the trolley, he told me, were an old lady at the back of the bus and the driver. He was looking out the window and saw reflected in the glass the image of a man. He couldn't understand who this was because there was no other man on the trolley. He looked and looked and it finally dawned on him that the image was his own. It terrified him. He had never consciously seen himself before. He had no internalized body image. His conception of himself did not include a body, which is probably why he was able to do such destructive things to it. He shaved in the mirror every morning, but never really looked at himself. He had no objective sense of himself. He had gone through many painful experiences, but the day he told me the trolley story was the first time he was visibly shaken.

I never saw him again. He must have felt incapable of accepting anything so physical as his own body, unable to be an object in his own right. If he had recognized his body, he would have had to reckon with his tangible self. He might have had to care for himself and make something of his life. It seems he couldn't make the passage into having a body. He couldn't connect to that living presence that exists in all living things, made manifest in the animal body. Because he couldn't accept the animal, he couldn't quite become human.

What is it like to be alienated and then healed? Not long ago, I was fortunate to meet Pansy Hawk Wing, a Lakota medicine woman, who was healed from alcoholism in the traditional Indian manner, in a sweat lodge by an animal visitation. She explained:

> When I was having difficulty, I was told Coyote would come and turn me in my path. He is cunning and so I came to a fork in the road—to the left was my old ways, but to the right was the road to health, to spirit, body, nature. There was sun, dew on the grass, an early morning chill, reflection of sun on dew creating a rainbow effect.

She related to the spirits in animals, plants, water, rocks, and mountains. Through her visions in the sweat lodge and on vision quests, she experienced the animals with the intense intimacy that we might know in dreams. When a buffalo came, she said,

> You feel his presence, you smell him, feel his warmth, his coat, feel everything—when he shifts hoofs, you hear that. You experience him huge behind you, all around you. Your own body opens up, your senses respond, it is tactile, smell, you feel it. It is nonverbal.
>
> When Elk comes, he has a different smell, his coat is coarse. You feel the warmth through his nostrils. Sometimes he will stroke my hair, sometimes pat my head, relaxing me, meaning that I am too hard on myself. Or he might tap me next to my heart meaning that I have some work to do with my feeling. Or he might give me a handful of herbs which I can smell. Animals teach humor saying, "You're worrying too much," implying you're O.K. as you are.
>
> If Eagle comes, it has to do with trust. I have to trust to fly with him.

I was interested to know how she related differently to animals than to people when they appear to her. She said that when human ancestors appear she may ask a question. "Grandfather" *(Wakan-tanka,* who represents great mystery), "I am your granddaughter. I know nothing." Then he may respond. With ancestors, verbal teachings are given; with animals, the contact is through physical presence. As I was talking with her I had the sense that when she was in the presence of an animal, her body responded directly to its body. Directly experiencing an animal's presence deeply touches the psyche and expresses itself in the body. Instead of talking about trust, the initiate experiences trust by flying with eagle. Actually experiencing trust in the psyche and the body helps one to reexperience this trust in daily life, in relationships or in reaching out in a more trusting way.

"You have to let your body move," Pansy said, "get into the sound, sing or yell. People today are not tuning in to what their body is saying. They need to experience their body. When you're in your body, you lose track of time"—meaning you are focused inside, aware of your own experience, not with what is going on in the world; it is sacred time. Then you are connected to the emotions in your body.

"The body carries emotion," says Ruth Amman, Swiss analyst and former architect who teaches the therapeutic use of the sand tray. She told me that when she first looks at a patient's completed sand tray, she observes the body or emerging form the patient has shaped from the sand itself underneath the more visible picture created by figures. "When people put their hands in sand, they awaken emotionally. Sometimes dreams are too far removed." She added that animal images help people connect to body and emotions. Animals that most often appear in the sand tray are snakes, turtles and the black panther for women. The panther symbolizes the dark, fierce feminine passion that is always independent, subject to no man. Turtles with their shells often stand for life that is contained and protected. We will meet the snake a little later on.

When we are at ease with our instinctual life, we are more like animals. As Ursula LeGuin says, "An animal is beautiful, it acts with certainty; it acts 'rightly,' appropriately."[21] Animals are always true to themselves. They can never be anything else. In this sense they are religious. They always act out of their deepest self. A dog always behaves like a dog, never like a cat or mouse, and there is no such thing as a vegetarian lion. The animal, at one with its body, spontaneously responds to its needs: mating, eating, running. By observing its body, we learn what the animal is up to.

The poet Robert Hass explicates Rilke's portrayal of animals as "at home in the world in a way that human beings are not."[22] Rilke's animals open out to the world, to a timeless eternity before consciousness; they are at one with it, whereas we humans are taught to come back to ourselves as objects always comparing ourselves to others, to some image of how we should be. This is why Rilke's poem about the caged panther is so poignant; the panther's longing for freedom is experienced only in the body.[23] And what does it say about us? Perhaps, that we too have lost something huge and can only imagine what that original experience must be like through the eyes of the animal.

---

[21] "The Language of the Night," in *Harper Perennial,* 1993, p. 61.
[22] "Introduction," *The Selected Poetry of Rainer Maria Rilke,* p. xxiv.
[23] "Duino Elegies" (the Eighth Elegy), ibid., p. 193.

Animal Guide

The term animal guide is used here in a different sense than animal guardian spirit. Animal guardian spirit, previously described, originated in the hunting-gathering culture before totemism, and represented the spirit of the animal that came to a person individually for one's whole life, not to be shared with anyone. The term animal guide refers to an animal that may guide a person through a transitional phase in life, whether it be puberty, marriage or death.

Animals are smart about their instincts. They know what must develop for the next phase of their life. Perhaps for this reason, the life passages of human beings are often heralded by the dream of an animal, especially a female animal for a girl coming into womanhood. It makes her aware that an energy deep inside is awakening. She is excited, curious, and she wonders: "My life is changing, where is it headed? What do I have to learn? Suppose I don't like sex. Suppose no one will take an interest in me. Mommy, how will I know?"

A thirteen-year-old girl found a bird that had flown into a plate glass window and stunned itself. She mothered the little creature until it was well and flew away. That same night she dreamed she went down to the beach and found a mother and baby dolphin. The baby dolphin had beached itself, and the young girl helped it back into the water. In response she received a blessing from the mother dolphin who asked her if she wanted to take a ride on her back. Some nights later, the girl's mother, having heard her daughter's dream, dreamed that a whale came and invited her to sit on it and take a ride with the whale pod.

When the young girl takes care of the bird, she receives a blessing in her dream. She is on the threshold of life. It's quite possible to get lost or stranded at such a time, but she makes the passage beautifully. The small action of caring for an injured bird, a compassionate concern for a life beyond her own, has led to a psychological shift: the young dolphin returns to the elements, the girl enters the next phase of her life, young womanhood. When one person dreams, it can affect another. The whales come to the young girl's mother, affirming her mothering of her child. They honor the mother by including her in a life larger than the one she imagines.

Animals reunite us with our instinctual life in various ways. How do they do that? They can herald future transformation, as the bird and dolphin did for the young girl. They can awaken us emotionally, renewing our confidence and trust as they did for Pansy. Being themselves, they inspire spontaneity, reminding us to enjoy our body. The animal's instincts define its life. Its natural sense of limit helps us to feel content with our life the way it is. We see too often that humans are not satisfied with the life they have.

Walt Whitman, in "Song of Myself," understands that the animal cannot desire anything that is not in its nature. It simply obeys its instincts.

> I think I could turn and live with animals, they are so placid
> and self contained;
> I stand and look at them long and long.
> They do not sweat and whine about their condition;
> They do not lie awake in the dark and weep for their sins;
> They do not make me sick discussing their duty to God;
> Not one is dissatisfied—not one is demented with the mania of
> owning things;
> Not one kneels to another, nor to his kind that lived thousands of
> years ago;
> Not one is respectable or industrious over the whole earth.[24]

Animals are our prototypes, our natural models. They move through life with grace and dignity. Their absolute acceptance of their own nature evokes a kind of wisdom that instills within us the desire to live our unique life. These values animals hold for us give yet another degree of urgency to the disappearance of so many species. With each species that disappears, our models for comparison diminish. I once heard the poet Gary Snyder ask in a lecture: "Will there still be inner images of animals in our psyche after they have become extinct?"

What we've lost is an awareness of our own internal connection to animals, the way we give birth to them within our souls, the way they give birth to us. If we listened to what the animals tell us, we would develop a more trusting relation to the process of life's unfolding, a more spontaneous and playful attitude and a more intuitive feel for choices and decisions. We would come away with renewed energy to meet whatever challenge life has brought.

The creatures in their elements, on forest path or seashore, visit and heal our psyches, companion our griefs, guide our transitions. Radiating an instinctual courage in their simplicity, they show us paths out of our problems and the way back to our deepest nature.

---

[24] *Complete Poetry and Selected Prose,* p. 47.

3
Through the Gate of the Snake

The instincts are a far better protection than all the intellectual wisdom in the world.
—C.G. Jung, *The Visions Seminars.*

Throughout history, and around the world, the snake is given a healing initiatory role. In Genesis, the serpent initiator in the tree of knowledge entices Eve to eat the apple of consciousness. If only as a child I had heard Moses' words, "Make thee a fiery serpent, and set it upon a pole: and it shall come to pass that every-one . . . when he looketh upon it, shall live."[25] When the snake is elevated and wrapped around the vertical axis of a tree, its hidden knowledge becomes healing. It is known to us as the caduceus, the symbol for medicine. This symbol originated in classical Greece, from Aesclepius, the wounded-healer, who is pictured with a serpent entwined around his staff.

In Greek antiquity, if you were sick, you would come to the temple of Asclepius at Epidaurus to be cured. You would lie in the temple baths to purify the soul, then move to the sanctuary to sleep, to incubate the vision and dream the sacred dream. The sickness created by the gods must be cured by the gods. Asclepius, the wounded healer, would bring his snake, and as snake he would enter your soul. You would let him bite you, then you would be rid of sickness and pain and could be restored to your ancestors.[26] No longer isolated, you would be reborn just like the snake that sheds its skin. Carl Kerényi, a classical philologist and authority in comparative religions, describes the function of the Aesclepian temple in Epidauros:

> The purpose of a visit to the sanctuary of Epidauros was to meet this divine power halfway. This was no visit to a doctor who simply administers medicine; it was an encounter with the naked and immediate event of healing itself.[27] . . . Characteristically, this cure is sought in sleep and dreams. In sleep the patient withdraws from his fellow men and even from his physician, and surrenders to a process at work within him.[28]

---

[25] Numbers. 21:8 (King James Version).

[26] *Asklepios: Archetypal Image of the Physician's Existence,* pp. 18f.

[27] Ibid., pp. 34f.

[28] Ibid., p. 35.

In India snakes are nagas, "demons of divine earthy energy," according to Indian scholar Heinrich Zimmer.[29] They are symbols of fertility and vegetation. They are the spirit "keepers of the life energy that is stored in the earthy waters of springs, wells, and ponds."[30] Zimmer tells the story of Muchalinda, the Serpent King:

> Now Muchalinda, a prodigious cobra, dwelt in a hole amongst the roots. He perceived, as soon as the Buddha had passed into the state of bliss, that a great storm cloud had begun to gather, out of season. Thereupon he issued quietly from the black abode and with the coils of his body enveloped seven times the blessed body of the Enlightened One; with the expanse of his giant snake-hood he sheltered as an umbrella the blessed head. Seven days it rained, the wind blew cold, the Buddha remained in meditation. But on the seventh, the unseasonable storm dispersed; Muchalinda unloosed his coils, transformed himself into a gentle youth, and with joined hands to his forehead bowed worship of the savior of the world.[31]

The snake has a connection to spiritual wisdom of life. It shelters that wisdom and helps it. Yet the snake is also a creature we fear.

An Australian man I know grew up with three different kinds of poisonous snakes in his yard. "As a child I stepped on a snake," he once told me. "I was proud and thrilled. While the snakes were poisonous and we were terrified of them, we were also fascinated by them and under the spell of their beauty." His words testify to the balance of fear and attraction that snakes carry.

Where I grew up, there were no snakes. If there had been, they would have been antithetical to the atmosphere of my mother's house. Our house was a sealed container unto itself—no drafts, no dirt, no bugs. A snake would have been the ultimate transgressor. However, snakes can get in through an orifice or crack. My mother might put her hands over her ears, but she couldn't really protect snake from slithering in.

Why do we have such a fear of snakes? There are many reasons. The snake is so remote from human consciousness that it is very hard to relate to it. One can establish rapport with almost all animals, but the snake remains so aloof that trust cannot be established. A friend told me: "I think people who are very feeling-oriented often have difficulty relating to snakes; it's so hard to look into their eyes." When hibernating, the cold-blooded snake is stiff and appears inanimate. Even warmed, the limbless snake can appear like an inanimate object

---

[29] *The Art of Indian Asia*, p. 161.

[30] Zimmer, *Myths and Symbols in Indian Art and Civilization*, p. 63.

[31] Ibid., p. 67.

that can suddenly spring to life—as though a shoe or a log were suddenly to move—striking terror in the human soul.

Barbara Hannah, an analyst close to Jung, who studied the symbolism of animals, says about the snake; "Warm-blooded animals have an idea of man; they are either friendly, or they avoid him and his habitations because they dislike or are afraid of him. But snakes are absolutely headless,"[32] meaning they have no brain power. A snake's small head slides imperceptibly into a long undifferentiated body, all spinal cord, that ends in a tail. This extended sympathetic nervous system with its tiny brain accounts for its lack of intelligence. The snake orients itself by using different senses than we do; not seeing or hearing well, it uses its tongue as a sensing organ. They are fearless, even of their worst enemies, and as pets they can never be trusted. Some are venomous; some can dislocate their jaws and swallow prey larger than themselves, characteristics which make the snake seem strange and threatening to our way of living.

The snake is uncannily invisible, appearing unexpectedly. This strange animal, which belongs to unknown earthly realms, materializes out of nowhere. Arriving at the oddest times, it reminds us of uninvited intuitions come to reveal things furthest from our mind. My mother was afraid of her intuitions. She was scared to death they might be true. If she let them in, then she would have to take responsibility for them. By not accepting nature's whispers, my mother gave them even greater power, finally becoming immobilized by fear.

As my mother's son, I was also prey to this fear. I suffered from lack of action. I could not do what the Australian man was able to do: step on snakes and feel proud. As a young man, I dreamed I was venturing out into life on the back of a horse. Wrapped around the horse's body and legs was a long snake. The snake paralyzed the horse. It took me years to understand why this image was so disturbing—the snake had a hold on my heroic life-bound horse.

When I had started my practice and needed to learn how to take care of the financial end of things, I asked a financial consultant to come to my house. He knew I was a psychiatrist. When he entered my study, his body jerked with terror as he pointed to a large glass jar with marbles and gasped, "Can that snake crawl out of the jar?" He had mistaken the reflected circulating light from the marbles as something alive. He was a man totally cut off from his body, and the terror of being with a psychiatrist, who is comfortable with irrational thoughts and emotions getting loose, was projected onto the image of a snake arising

---

[32] *The Symbolism of Animals,* lecture 2, p. 5.

from the jar. Like my mother who had a snake phobia, he managed this fear by staying in rational control. He would only let in what was familiar. Relieved that he didn't have to actually face a snake, he then presented to me in cool snake-like fashion a number of schemes to avoid paying taxes. It was himself he saw reflected in that jar, but he didn't know it. He had become the snake.

I, too, was not in touch with the snake within me which might have helped me go after what I really wanted. However, I was not afraid of snakes; I just didn't pay enough attention to them. If I had, I would have avoided the painful process of seeing all those tax shelters go bust. Letting in a little snake energy might have freed me to express something of my own unique nature without worrying so much about what other people thought. Jung, whose beady little snake eyes would sometimes unnerve people, said that the hero has "the cold eyes of the snake, expressing the fact that the extraordinary individual is . . . [known] for a certain strangeness and inhumanity which impresses people like the inhumanity of a snake."[33]

A woman had sacrificed her own course of study in college for one prescribed by her tyrannical father. She had a fear of snakes. She dreamed that when she reached into her refrigerator for asparagus, she found that two asparagus heads had turned into snake heads. The other two asparagus with stalks had transformed into snakes with long bodies and long tails. As she grasped the two tailed snakes by their midsections, they began whipping around her in the kitchen, trying to bite her. She awakened trembling.

She told me that she came from a family that was cold, selfish and withholding and that she herself was cold. This cold woman from a cold family reaches into a cold refrigerator only to find cold snakes. In the past, she expected her lover to supply the warmth in the relationship, which he was not always able to do. As she became healthier, she could ask, "So, why can't I supply the feeling? It's not fair for me to expect that from him."

Awakening to her emotions, she discovered the excitement and fascination of the snake in a way that recalls the Australian man. The image of snakes in the refrigerator startled her into awareness, aliveness. Emily Dickinson captures this startle in the grass.

> A narrow fellow in the Grass
> Occasionally rides—
> You may have met him—did you not?
> His notice sudden is—

---

[33] Ibid., lecture 2. p. 7.

The Grass divides as with a Comb—
A spotted shaft is seen—
And then it closes at your feet
And opens further on—

He likes a Boggy Acre
A floor too cool for Corn—
Yet when a Boy, and Barefoot—
I more than once, at Noon—

Have passed, I thought, a whiplash
Upbraiding in the sun—
When stopping to secure it
It wrinkled, and was gone—

Several of Nature's People
I know, and they know me—
I feel for them a transport
of cordiality—

But never met this Fellow,
Attended, or alone,
Without a tighter breathing,
And Zero at the Bone—[34]

Meeting this fellow is one of the great goals of the inner journey, but the encounter is not without its dangers, as Dickinson concludes. Something startles us and takes us by surprise. We shudder and recoil from the cold texture of snake skin on human skin. We are frightened, but this can also be good. In Western mythology, the snake is dangerous. When the python of the Delphic oracle revealed the deep plan of fate, the lives of individuals and nations were changed forever. In the Bible, the snake is the dark and cunning animal that initiated Adam and Eve into the painful human world of mortality and transgression. That is the power of the snake. Initiation can go either way. Any transformation can be dangerous, bringing both power and danger. This danger gives us our lives. The analyst Joseph Henderson wrote a book about snakes. He says:

> The wisdom of the serpent, which is suggested by its watchful lidless eyes, lies essentially in mankind's having projected into this lowly creature his own secret wish to obtain from the earth a knowledge he cannot find in waking daylight consciousness alone. This is the knowledge of death and rebirth . . . [symbolized by]

---

[34] "A Narrow Fellow in the Grass," *The Complete Poems of Emily Dickinson,* pp. 459f.

> its yearly period of hibernation ...[during which] the snake sheds its skin and reappears as if renewed.[35]

This transcendent function of the psyche that can bring contents of the unconscious to the light of day is symbolized by the snake. These dreams and intuitions that come unannounced to bring wisdom or foretell danger were what my mother was so afraid of. I had to hunt for snakes alone.

An early image of a snake impressed itself upon me. Rabbi Gordon, from our neighborhood temple, served as a chaplain in the U.S. Army during World War Two and was stationed in India. As a young boy, I saw a newspaper photograph in which he was standing with a python he had killed lying at his feet. At that time in my life I was isolated from boyish adventures since I worked all the time in my father's drug store. It was striking for me to see a Jew, our Rabbi, involved in the great struggle of the time. When I first saw the photo, I did not think much about the snake, but many years later it returned in one of the most powerful dreams I ever had.

The dream occurred at a time when I was serving on the committee of an analysts' training institute. It had been an honor to be invited onto this committee, but soon after I joined I realized that the conditions weren't right. Although I liked the task of supervising training, intractable quarrels drained my energy. For three years we struggled, but as there seemed no way to resolve the conflict I was left too fatigued and distracted to take up other tasks nearer to my soul. The night before I presented a seminar on animal symbolism I was tired and worried. And I dreamed:

> I am in the square or center of a small village in India and the first thing I see ("Wouldn't you know?" I say to myself in the dream) is a large python perched on top of a tall pole, visible to all around. I am afraid—it sends chills down my spine. Suddenly it awakens and with lightening speed travels down to the ground. Small brown Indians scatter in every direction. The next thing I see is an Indian man standing nearby who has swallowed a live snake whole. Only its tail is visible, hanging down to the man's chest and wriggling frantically. Was this the python? I think so.

In the wake of this dream, I awoke invigorated, able to shed the dry skin of duty. At the time of the dream, I had not made a formal study of the psychic significance of snakes, but intuitively I knew already that *the snake is life*. The serpent awakens underneath your feet. It coils from below. It is cold and its

---

[35] Henderson and Maud Oaks, *The Wisdom of the Serpent*, pp. 36f.

scaly skin is strange to the touch. Coiling, it moves irrationally. It is indiscriminate and powerful. It will eat anything. It bites you. It destroys the toxic part of the ego, the inertia that stems from correct social attitudes. When bitten, like Adam and Eve, you are awakened never to sleep again. You are tortured into action. The snake sheds its skin, dies and is reborn. It invokes a serpent "wisdom which comes from nature herself."[36] Abraham the patriarch is afraid of it.[37]

In Indian kundalini yoga, the snake travels up and down the spinal cord, activating the different chakras. In my dream the snake went down the pole and brought me with it. My view of life was a little too elevated, and I was a little too aware of what I "ought" to do. The snake taught me to lie closer to the ground of my own being.

My dream image is an incongruity. Usually we think of a snake as devouring people. ("Python Swallows Man" is the imaginary headline), but in this instance a man has ingested a snake. It is dangerous and exciting to take in snake energy. The kundalini is awakened, the snake man is on the move, devouring everything in his path. There is no stopping him. He is eating life. He cannot get enough. He no longer sleeps. The man is awakened. The world cracks open.

When we meet the snake, it stops us dead. It's a shock. But shock is not always a bad thing. It cleans out the cobwebs and allows new understanding to follow. In China, the dragon is the mythological form of the snake, initially hidden in the earth, but which begins to stir as man awakens to his spiritual nature. Inspired, man then mounts the arousing dragon which carries him toward heaven in six steps. The dragon is a symbol of the creative yang power of heaven that energizes and gives form to all thoughts; its image is experienced in an electrically charged thunderstorm.[38]

The snake's power enters our life more quietly, subtly, through the medium of our dreams. The snake gives us the power to connect with our deepest instincts, with our animal life, and in this way comes to our aid. When we meet the snake, the shock of that meeting poses a question for us. And the question always has something to do with whether we can be true to that deep level of feeling and instinct and the sustenance that comes from that.

This is the problem a patient of mine was struggling with. She grew up in a severely patriarchal household where individual behavior had to conform to the strict conventions of a fundamentalist Christian religion. In a dream she experi-

---

[36] Hannah, *The Symbolism of Animals*, lecture 5, p. 6.

[37] Kluger, *Satan and the Old Testament*, pp. 41, 145.

[38] *The I Ching or Book of Changes*. Hexagram 1, p. 7.

enced this instinctual snake power by actually witnessing a man turning into a snake. As her dream reveals, there is a tremendous energy that can break out in the most domestic garden:

> I am at a party with a man friend of mine. We are talking in the garden. As we walk toward the rose garden standing behind the arbor, we see a man, army general, being changed into a snake. He is very large. The person who changes him into a snake seems to be a wizard or some other magical person who looks around to see if he is being watched. After doing the "magic" he disappears.
>
> While the general is in the process of changing from man to snake, I take hold of him. As I am holding him in my hands I look into his eyes. He knows me. I cannot tell what the expression means. He is changing very quickly but his head changes last. I think he wishes that I had not seen the transformation because he knows I will have to live with the knowledge and will want to understand what it means. He knows that no one will believe me and that I will be in danger if I tell anyone about this event. He seems to feel sorry for what I am going to have to go through because of what I am witnessing.
>
> In the dream I am not afraid of the snake man; I am confused about the meaning of the transformation. I wonder if it is "against the rules" and needs to be exposed to someone. I wonder if civilization is now in danger because it is possible to change men into snakes. I know there is some purpose in the transformation that makes the snake man capable of something men are not usually capable of doing. I know he made the choice. I know he has increased power in his transformed form.
>
> I tell the man I am with that we should tell someone before the general is completely changed. The man says that no one will believe me. I argue with him because I know I am telling the truth and the truth should be believed. I know what I know and that knowledge should be accepted. He explains (as to a child) that no one will accept what I know.

One day when this woman was a girl of fifteen, she had missed her bus after school. A clean-cut, pleasant looking man drove by and asked her if she would like a ride home. Instantly she knew something was wrong about this man and she knew better than to accept rides from strangers, but he had a nice appearance and seemed friendly so she accepted.

Initially he headed in the right direction, but then turned toward the country and into the woods. She was becoming more and more frightened. He stopped in a secluded spot, locked the car doors and ordered her to take off her clothes. She tried to get out of the car, but he pinned her down. She struggled to free herself and—just as it seemed he would overpower her—she gave a violent kick to the door handle which miraculously opened. She leaped out of the car and ran up a hill. He followed her for a long way, but she ran with every ounce of energy she had and escaped. She was too ashamed to tell anyone, but she knew he was the rapist-murderer of several teen-age girls. He killed one more girl after this incident with her and then was caught.

This is a story of how our relationship to the snake energy can go wrong. She didn't trust her instincts but rather followed a false rationality, one she learned from her parents, that was all bound up with being proper, good, pleasant. If you disregard your own snake energy and your relationship to it, you become vulnerable to someone else's instinct—the evil snake energy that can get into your life. Both the victim and the criminal take in snake energy in the wrong way. The victim has no relationship to the snake, and the criminal identifies with it. He has lost human values and so he becomes a snake. The serial killer didn't eat the snake, the snake ate him.

The dream shows that while the initial potential rape experience was terrifying, she is now working with snake energy on her own terms. She embraces a snake-man as she looks into his eyes and forms a relationship with him. The dream leaves her with the question: how do I relate to this snake energy? Because she embraces the question, she is growing. As the man changes into a snake, his potency increases, indicating that something positive is occurring. But she is still faced with her question. Should she report this to the authorities, as she didn't do with the earlier real-life encounter? She is like many women who have been wounded by sexual molestation: she doesn't know whether to trust men or not. Her instincts have been damaged, so the snake in her dream awakens her need to believe in herself. Then she will be able to find her own life.

There seems to be a resonance between the human and the snake. The contact point of this resonance is the autonomic nervous system, the snake being all spinal cord. So, when we are in snake brain mode, our body responds autonomically, involuntarily. Literally speaking, nobody changes into a snake except in a dream. The dream shows a man changing into snake. But this is a dream that implies an inner change.

How does a person change when they move from everyday human consciousness to experience life as a snake? What state of consciousness does transformation into a reptile represent? Being the animal furthest from consciousness, the serpent represents the instinctual world. When we meet the snake, our whole being goes on alert, we awaken.

In Africa, snake is revered. I once heard an African song in which a young woman encounters snake-man. The song portrays the reverse transformation in which a snake turns into a man. This African song of a snake that turns into a man and the dream of a Western woman in which a man is transformed into a snake, move in opposite directions. The African snake-man becomes human and the Western woman connects to her instincts.

My niece and her new Senegalese husband came for a visit last summer. He is a Griot, meaning an oral historian for the king, singing the age-old stories to the accompaniment of African instruments. He had never seen a Western harp. He asked my wife to play and as she did he began to improvise, accompanying her on the other harp, while singing a beautiful, haunting song. It was an extraordinary collision of worlds: in our San Francisco living room, a young African man improvised on this most elaborate of European instruments.

The song was like nothing I had ever heard before, and it sent chills down my spine. The melody seemed to emanate from the earth itself, transporting our living room back to a village in Africa. The song was very long, and it was past midnight when he told us that the song describes a love affair between a woman and a snake. Because he was leaving in the morning, I knew it was now or never to try to record the words of the song for my animal studies, and so I asked him if he would stay up to tell me. For the next two hours, he sang a part of the song, then translated it into English. If I asked a question, he would first sing the verse again, to capture the feeling and the experience, and then he would tell me the words. We continued until early in the morning, alternating between melody and words, until I felt the kitchen table turn to African wood. Here is a synopsis of the story, entitled "Joulowo":

> A young woman goes out to gather wood in a dark forest. There a snake sees her and is filled with desire for her. In order to meet her, he transforms himself into a man. He courts her and she, not knowing that he is a snake, marries him and goes to live with him in the forest. There, to her horror, she discovers that she has married a snake. Frightened, she runs back toward her village and on the road she meets Joulowo, a traveling man, to whom she appeals in song, "Joulowo, Joulowo, you tell my mother and father that the man they married me to is not a man, but a big, big snake." Joulowo, like the villagers, is perplexed when confronted with this strange story. Her parents consult medicine men who examine her husband and detect snake skin. After much consultation, snake agrees to let the medicine men permanently seal him as a man. The couple, joyfully reunited together with the entire village, relocate to snake's forest.

This is a love story comparable to our Western story of "Beauty and the Beast." Beauty and Mamouna, the African girl, through loving Beast and Snake, transform them into prince and man. In both stories girls leave their virtuous life with their families to include erotic feeling which matures them into women. In "Beauty and the Beast," Beauty as a young girl leaves her father for Beast in order to satisfy a claim that Beast has on her father's life. After overcoming her initial fear, Beauty realizes her love for Beast when he becomes threatened with illness, thus releasing him from an evil curse and transforming him back into a handsome prince.[39] The African story is a little different because the young woman never really accepts Snake as Snake, but loves him only after he is transformed into a man. The importance of the snake component is acknowledged, however, by the villagers when they move their home into snake country.

In the African story, Mamouna goes looking in the forest for wood to fire her emotions. She enters a dark magic woods, a moist forest, outside her village, beyond the perimeter of relationship. It is scary and exciting. She searches for the forest of that wet and wild lower place, away from her heart, between her legs, into the mysterious, into the creative.

The snake has fallen in love with a girl. To woo her, he becomes a man. He changes his scaly snake skin for human skin, snake eyes for human eyes, snake oil for feeling. He is a snake with a human soul. He is lured out of the dank dark forest into the open, into a village, into the place where human feelings exist, where people care about each other. He is, however, still snake-vigorous and powerful. His long body tenderly coils around the woman. He slithers, he charms, but with care.

We have Joulowo, the traveling man, magician and teller of stories, who weaves things together. He weaves together things that don't ordinarily belong together. He lubricates. He brings forest to village. He unites nature's juices with human love.

This is an African story, not European. In Africa, snake is venerated, not killed. He is wooed and tamed, allowing his sacred knowledge to heal. He has the ability to change shape. Snake transforms into man and then back into snake. We saw this change from human form to animal form earlier in this chapter in the woman's dream in which a man's body turned into a snake. This fluid metamorphic process of transformation, of human changing to animal and back again, is what keeps us alive.

Some of us may find the transformation frightening. My mother refused to change herself into a snake. She refused to identify with snake. She rigidly rejected engaging in this process and so lost the capacity to change. Changing

---

[39] Henderson, "Ancient Myths and Modern Man," in Jung, ed., *Man and His Symbols*. p. 137.

from one form to another allows us to relate to different aspects of ourselves. We move from human brain to animal brain, up and down the phylogenetic scale. We let our ancestors speak to us in our dreams. We encounter them when we soar like birds, crawl sinuously into forbidden places, snap back angrily when irritated. We change overnight from passionate sexual animals to rational sentient beings.

I experienced this change with a woman colleague at a weekend professional conference. Following an evening banquet, she and I danced together all night. She was sexy and very much a woman. We let our bodies coil around one another all over the dance floor. The next morning she was transformed into suit with glasses and notebook. Although we sat together, it was all business and thinking. The Navajos have a name for her: Changing Woman.

The serpent as a death-dealing and life-sustaining symbol touches on the changing quality of woman as she moves through her moon phases, through the death and rebirth of her fertile times. A woman's body is more changeable than man's. Her womb sheds its lining every month, her belly grows huge in pregnancy. Is this why from ancient times, she was seen as more open to divine penetration, in both its benevolent and malevolent aspects? And is it this openness that makes her consort of the snake, that changeable creature who sheds his skin, who can move so quickly between worlds, from deep underground to the highest branch of a tree?

In one woman's experience, an early encounter with a snake taught her something about the relation between life and death. Her story exemplifies some of the snake's ancient role as the linker of realms. When she was five years old, she went with her parents to a summer cabin in Maine. Playing by herself near the river one morning, she befriended a little green frog. Suddenly, a big black snake slithered up the bank and swallowed the frog. Terrified, the little girl screamed for her mother. The landlady, who lived in the cabin next door, heard the commotion and came running with an ax. The child watched in horror as the woman severed the head of the snake. The next morning, when the little girl went back down to the spot by the river where both animals had met their death, she was surprised to see a little black frog jumping about. She says

> To me this black frog was none other than the little green frog, turned black by the body of the snake. From this moment on, I have had some kind of faith that there is something about us that does not die. Years later, I realized that the little green frog could not possibly have survived—yet the faith which this incident inspired remains.

In the young child's consciousness, the diabolical black snake of death eats the green frog of life and then is cut to pieces. Miraculously, the next day, the dismembered snake disgorges its prey, transformed. The black frog now contains both death and life. The adult woman knows this black frog is not the same frog, and she has retained an intense horror of snakes. Yet contained within this very horror is a sense of the snake's profound initiatory power.

The snake resides in all of us. The old brain and long snake-like spinal cord with its ancient animal is there. It comes out in different ways. The spouses of Alzheimer's patients find that the loss of the fore-brain turns their loved one into a vacant-eyed reptile. If the girl who went off with the murderer had been a bit snake-like herself, she would have recognized him. If the woman who dreamed of refrigerated asparagus-snakes had a livelier snake life, she would have been able to enjoy an intimate and more mutual relationship with her lover. A homeopathic injection of cold blood can sometimes provide just the right balance.

Many years ago when I took up Tai Chi, I experienced the sinewy movements of the snake that flowed upward into the aspiring position called "White crane spreads its wings." Only then did I hear about the legendary origin of Tai Chi, which began as an eternal struggle between the snake and the bird.

We know also that in evolutionary development reptiles and birds are closely related. Now as we spiral up toward the birds from deep under water, we will fly with the white crane and other birds of the water, waterbirds.

4
Initiation by Water

Octopus and Spiral

We now enter the water-world, the free and liquid place where change occurs, the waterworks of transformation. When we are in need of renewal, we must submit our learned selves to nature's way, called in the *Tao Te Ching*, "The Watercourse Way."[40] The old forms, the old masks, must dissolve before the new molds can set up. We must seek a new solution, beginning with the scary part of our journey, the deep descent that precedes the soaring.

Sometimes when we descend into places of great disintegration and suffering, we meet the animals who belong to these realms. We drop into deep water where it is dark and disorienting, and nothing is familiar. Isolated and afraid, we lose our motivation, forget our intention, and become vulnerable. There, in the depths, we encounter mythological creatures. We see animals that we have read about in books or that appear only in dreams: fierce creatures with tentacles that wrap themselves around ships and pull them under, then squeeze the life out of their victims. Such an image is seen on this Minoan terra cotta funerary pot, which shows the octopus with glaring eyes and sucker arms:

Figure 1
Pre-Hellenic. Crete, Post-Palace period, ca. 1500 B.C.
(Heraklion: Mus.,, Archaeological; No. A870. Lentoid flask)

[40] See Alan Watts and Al Chung-Liang, *Tao: The Water Course Way.*

Because the huge octopi live in the depths of the ocean, not much is actually known of them, but they have given rise to terrifying stories of mythological intensity. Most are of modest proportion, however, and live in shallow waters, in holes or crevices along the bottom of the sea. The common octopus is best known for its large head and eight contractile arms, each lined with rows of strong, fleshy suckers. Its mouth has a pair of horny beaks and the file-like *radula* for drilling and scraping its shellfish meals.[41]

Considered very intelligent, the octopus is endowed with excellent sight, great flexibility of movement and an extraordinary ability to learn from its experience. When alarmed, it shoots backward via a jet of water. Lacking a shell, it is extremely vulnerable; when endangered, it ejects an inky substance as a screen and camouflages itself by quickly changing color. This underwater creature with large staring eyes, a rasping beak, and long tentacles, might well frighten anyone alone in deep water. Psychologically, it symbolizes the devouring aspect of the unconscious—the fear that overtakes the hero on his night sea journey. As recently as 1947, when Thor Heyerdahl crossed the Pacific in his Kon-Tiki, each man carried a machete to bed with him, for fear that the giant arm of an octopus might reach onto the raft and drag him down into the depths of the night sea.

Heracles succeeded in conquering his fear. Figure 2 portrays him in a lion skin, holding a club and bow, crossing the water in the golden vessel of Helios.

Figure 2
(Terra cotta , detail; Rome: Mus. Vaticano; ca. 480 B.C.)

---

[41] *Encyclopaedia Britannica, Micropaedia,* vol. 7, p. 478.

Some thirty years ago, in a lecture at the Jung Institute in San Francisco, Dr. H.K. Fierz discussed the remarkable case of a woman he treated on the psychiatric unit at Bellevue Hospital in Kreuzlingen, Switzerland.[42] The patient was in her mid-fifties and had been living on the back ward of a mental hospital in England for many years. An initial photograph showed a toothless, bald-headed woman with unfocused eyes. She had not spoken a word for decades and purportedly smeared feces on the walls of her room. Dr. Fierz was dubious about taking her on but the family was so determined that he acquiesced.

Early in the treatment, he encouraged her to smear clay on the walls, and after some weeks a form gradually emerged. It was an aquatic animal, an octopus. Gradually, other images emerged—including a mandala—and within a year the patient began speaking. Some time later she was discharged. A second photograph showed her as a rather unremarkable-looking woman with a wig, dentures and glasses.

At Dr. Fierz's lecture, he was questioned about the healing role of the octopus, which had represented a critical turning point in this remarkable recovery. The other analysts were inclined to see the octopus as symbolizing the negative, devouring mother complex, given its use of tentacles and suckers in overpowering its prey. Dr. Fierz explained that this animal had been healing for this patient because it was a life form emerging out of the depths of the unconscious.

Why the octopus and not some other form? Perhaps the answer is to be found in further exploration of the ancient symbol of the octopus, which is abundantly present in Mediterranean pottery of the Pre-Hellenic period. Although some images present an engulfing threat, others present a delightfully lively and engaging spirit. On a painted terra cotta sarcophagus from Crete, an octopus with two great eyes stares out at us from a figure-eight body, its ten undulating tentacles each ending in a spiral design (Figure 3).

For the Greeks, the spiral was a healing symbol, whether explicitly linked to the octopus with its undulating tentacles or in a more abstract form "related to the wheel, the swastika and the equal-armed cross, [expressing] the primeval urge to creative power,"[43] evident in the spiraloid movements of the tentacles. This generative aspect of the spiral evolved as a fertility symbol associated with the Great Mother goddesses of the agricultural era, which I will discuss later in this chapter.

---

[42] See Fierz, *Jungian Psychiatry,* pp. 139ff.

[43] Federico De Luca Comandini, *The Octopus: Metamorphoses of an Imaginal Animal,* pp. 94f.

Figure 3
(Pre-Hellenic. Crete, Post-Palace period, ca. 1400-1350 B.C.; Heraklion Museum)

Italian analyst Federico De Luca Comandini describes such a creature as bearing "an expression of profound subjectivity."[44] The emphasis on the head and eyes suggests the physicality of a human being, the embodiment of a consciousness that, while highly reflective, is nonetheless open to a deep sense of nature. Referring to the octopus's high intelligence and wide repertoire of defensive strategies, Comandini ascribes to this image of the octopus the human characteristics of "intuition, the ability to foresee things and get out of tight squeezes, versatility, and subtlety—a knack for adapting to the changeable fleeting aspects of reality."[45] He adds:

> The tentacles don't merely suffocate or suck one in; they are rather living bonds which intelligently set up and define relations among things. They express a way of understanding which does not proceed by way of separation but through contact. They are the flowing lines of the spirit of Eros.[46]

In their song, "Octopus's Garden," the Beatles present us with an octopus who behaves very much like Comandini's octopus. In this joyful song, the octopus seems to be extending an invitation to girls and boys to hang out in his garden. Curiously, this octopus knows about the people he is inviting even before meeting them:

---

[44] Ibid., p. 93.
[45] Ibid.
[46] Ibid., p. 95.

> I'd like to be under the sea
> In an octopus's garden in the shade
> He'd let us in, knows where we've been
> In his octopus's garden in the shade...
>
> Oh what a joy for every girl and boy
> Knowing they're happy and they're safe...
> I'd like to be under the sea
> In an octopus's garden with you . . .[47]

The Beatles' imaginative octopus may not be so different from Comandini's living octopus who is gifted with a rare intuition. He quotes a zoologist for whom "the unusual aura that surrounds the animal" is a sign of its strangely unique intelligence. This would correspond to our notion of the unconscious psyche, which, by bringing dreams and new insights, is often experienced as an "alien intelligence."

This process of transformation, which both expands and absorbs, bringing the new into the familiar, is itself a kind of spiral. Perhaps this is why Comandini regards the octopus as a symbol of "profound subjectivity." In linking the spiral of the octopus to its symbolic meaning of creativity in the human, he further points to an image of a humanoid head of an octopus he has seen, an extraordinary being whose head "bore an expression of profound subjectivity":

> The emphasis on head and eyes suggestively stirs the physicality of human being. Indeed, they arouse reflective ideas in a consciousness open to a deep sense of nature: the image of the octopus as a living physical presence could not but bring closer to the human being the archetypal significance of the spiral.[48]

Did Dr. Fierz's patient somehow know, at the deepest level of her being, that the image of the octopus would help her escape her desperate condition, to give birth to her own subjectivity and find her way back into human speed and interconnection? In any case, it is clear that in the octopus we find an animal whose psychic significance is vastly richer and more complex than the simple reflective horror that many of us might feel upon actually encountering one.

Long ago I published an account of how the symbol of the spiral brought a patient of mine to life.[49] He was depressed because several people close to him

---

47 Richard Starkey (a.k.a. Ringo Starr) on *Abbey Road* (Parlophone/EMI Records).

48 *The Octopus,* p. 92.

49 "Amplification of the Spiral," in *Journal of Analytical Psychology,* vol. 29, no. 2 (1984), pp. 125ff.

had died. Amog them was his academic advisor whose death paralyzed him in the process of trying to complete his dissertation. The man, a sensitive middle-aged teacher, sought treatment for his anxiety and lethargy, which interfered with his ability to work. Because his mother was schizophrenic, he had always been cut off from his emotional life. Like Dr. Fierz's patient, this man had to descend to a primordial level to awaken new life.

There is a virtue in going down to the primitive level, to the early forms of life, allowing the gradual development of an anima, or soul figure, of a most primitive nature. A mollusk containing the image of the spiral began to infiltrate and awaken this man's life. His initial dream, depicting a dead octopus in a tree, showed how skewered and out of balance his life had become. In order to get well, he had to go far back in the phylogenetic scale to find less well-developed but healthy animals. Here is the dream:

> I was walking down an old street. To my left there was a garden wall. I could see over the wall what I at first took to be an elephant's head stuck in the crotch of a tree. It was a non-bearing fig tree. I went round to the corner where the wall joined the house and climbed over it. There was a clay finial which was broken in my climbing. I walked across the garden which was mostly paving stones, like a patio, to the tree. I could see when I got close that it was an octopus in the tree, and that the two arms closest to me had been stuffed, taxidermized, and that's why I had mistaken it for a head. The two dead arms were close together and separated from the other arms and I had mistaken them for a trunk. I reached up and touched the treated arms. They had a hard leathery texture and I could see stitching in them. I turned to see if anyone in the house had discovered me in the garden.

I asked, "What is a dead, partly stuffed octopus doing in a tree?" He did not know and even appeared apologetic. I said the octopi I knew about were only found in water. The patient identified with the octopus's vulnerability from being exposed and unprotected. He said this was how he had felt most of his life.

Then a miraculous thing happened. In the weeks that followed he dreamed of scores of living snails crawling on the underside of the leaves of a small tree. As they journeyed, they left behind silver trails. These little snails with their spiral motif had been awakened in his psyche.

I was excited to see where these animal tracks would lead. I was also excited to learn about the life of the mollusk—where it lives, what it eats, where it is in the food chain. I wanted to know all about these marine animals, and so I fondly dug out my old college zoology book. Just the smell of leafing through it, bespattered with laboratory juices, filled me with the wondrous curiosity I had enjoyed as a student. And later as an analyst, when I began to understand the archetype behind the images, I began to see how a newly created living form, a symbol, can take hold deep in the psyche, and what this meant for the patient.

The patient, too, grew excited seeing these living snails moving about, and he dreamed of other members of the mollusk family; chitons, and this time, living octopi. Then the spiral appeared in food to be eaten. A pastry snail supplying nourishment and giving him a sense of well-being eased his doubts and fears; afterward it coiled out neatly in spiral-shaped excrement. The symbol had gone completely through the digestive tract and come out the other end, indicating that the process of healing was being integrated. The patient himself became intrigued with the spiral image. I didn't say a word about it. I just listened as he followed the image with thoughtful interest. From there the spiral extended into all aspects of his life, including a spiral-shaped casing of the gear shift of his car. The sequence culminated in a new image of his house: a beehive in a spiral shape, indicating that now he could live in a more natural way.

The psychological process was not always positive, however. Along the way, he had a frightening dream, again of a mollusk, but this one with teeth:

> I went down the steep back stairs into the garden. It was overgrown and full of animals. They were not ordinary animals, but strange. As I herded them, I saw a round, egg-shaped chitinous object and picked it up. There was a small hole in the top. I put a pencil into the hole and serrated edges moved out and gripped the pencil so that I could lift it with the pencil, the grip was so strong. Then I could see that there were tiny holes all over it and slimy pseudopodia oozed out through the holes. It was a monstrous and dangerous thing.

He was frightened by the dream. The description of this strange animal fits that of one of the mollusks described in my zoology book: "mouth with a radula bearing transverse rows of minute chitinous teeth to rasp food."[50] This animal is a symbol of the *vagina dentata,* the devouring aspect of the feminine that underlay his fear and anxiety. However, this regressive dream image did not stop the slow forward spiral movement of the snail.

As I continued my study of the spiral, I learned that women from East Africa and Oceania wore cowrie shells around their pelvic girdles, connecting the symbol of the spiral to reproduction.[51] The depth of this cultural expression is symbolized in sculptures and other art forms of the great goddesses of the Neolithic Period, Hathor and Astarte or Ishtar, who were adorned with spiral configurations (Figure 4). According to Henri Frankfort, a scholar of Egypt, Mesopotamia

[50] Tracy I. Storer, *General* Zoology, p. 416.
[51] E.G. Smith, *The Evolution of the Dragon,* p. 140, fig. 20.

Figure 4
The Goddess Ninhursag ("Lady of Birth").
(Mesopotamia, ca. 2117-1763; terra cotta, height 4 in. Baghdad, Iraq Museum)

and the Ancient Near East, the motif of the spiraloid form "is the sacred symbol of the Lady of Birth who is identified in Mesopotamia as Ninhursag, or Nintu, from the earliest of times."[52] He has argued that this spiraloid form is actually a linear rendering of the bicornate uterus of a wild heifer and is therefore a reasonable symbol for birth. He further observes that one Mesopotamian list of divinities refers to Ninhursag as "the Uterus" and that her association with cattle is of the greatest antiquity.[53] Psychologically, then, the symbol of the spiral is related to the generative function of the Great Mother and to the death and rebirth mythology of the planting culture.

---

[52] "A Note on the Lady of Birth," pp. 198ff.
[53] Ibid.

I juxtaposed this healthy archetypal imagery against the destructiveness of the patient's schizophrenic mother. By using him to fill her needs, she had undermined his independence. Gradually, through his dream-work, his depression lifted and his anxiety disappeared. He seemed freer and looked forward to his new teaching commitments.

The original spiral is associated with the primordial movement in one's unconscious toward creating new life. Jung sees this spiral motif in dreams in which the developmental process revolves around a center.

> The way to the goal seems chaotic and interminable at first, and only gradually do the signs increase that it is leading anywhere. The way is not straight but appears to go round in circles. More accurate knowledge has proved it to go in spirals: the dream-motifs always return after certain intervals to definite forms, whose characteristic it is to define a centre. And as a matter of fact the whole process revolves about a central point or some arrangement around a centre, which may in certain circumstances appear even in the initial dreams.[54]

In dreams, the spiral process mirrors the balanced plant growth up and around a center. Plant growth, unlike human growth, sometimes unfolds according to a precise mathematical formulation. Leonardo Fibonacci, a mathematician of the Middle Ages, discovered that in some plants each leaf or flower petal germinates at a fixed distance from the preceding one, following "a sequence of numbers, each of which, after the second, is the sum of the two preceding numbers; i.e. 1, 1, 2, 3, 5, 8, 13 . . ."[55]

The spiral is a universal form that underlies the structure of both our psyche and the biological world. It is seen in the pattern of galaxies and in Neolithic ziggurats that aspired toward the heavens. It appears in the pine cone and extends, as we have seen, to the cephalopods, noticed also by poets. Like many a physician-poet, Oliver Wendell Holmes drew his inspiration from the physical world. He saw the soul illustrated in the bodies of his patients as well as in sea creatures. In one poem he compares the growth of the nautilus to the growth of the soul, with each new chamber representing a new level of development. Like Comandini, he ascribes to a cephalopod human characteristics of the soul.

> Build thee more stately mansions, O my soul,
>   As the swift seasons roll!
>   Leave thy low-vaulted past!

---

[54] *Psychology and Alchemy,* CW 12, par. 34. [CW refers throughout to *The Collected Works of C.G. Jung]*

[55] *The New Encyclopaedia Britannica. Micropaedia,* vol. 4, p. 120.

Let each new temple, nobler than the last,
Shut thee from heaven with a dome more vast,
  Till thou at length art free,
Leaving thine outgrown shell by life's unresting sea![56]

Animals grow and humans grow. The chambered nautilus, Dr. Fierz's patient and my patient all were able to outgrow their shells. Initiated by the spiral, life begins anew. From primitive forms of life, more developed creatures evolve.

Released from the earth, we now take new wing with a creature that is at home in both water and air, the waterbird.

Waterbird

Early one morning my dog and I had the beach to ourselves. We had walked quite a ways, dodging the waves, letting our feet sink deep into wet sand, stretching our muscles, releasing our bodies. Feeling restored I stopped to consider whether to go on or turn back when loudly spoken words were addressed to me, "There are too many people on this beach." "But I am the only person present," I thought. "Am I too many people?" I laughed and laughed. Then suddenly I was not there. My psyche was present but I no longer had a body. My seeing eye was drawn to the shore birds all in motion. They ran, stopped, turned, sat, fed and flew. Mesmerized by their eyes I joined them, seeing from above the rhythmical pattern of the waves moving toward shore. Living between sea and sky seemed so natural; life was going on as it always had been, and now I was part of it. I belonged with the birds. Their shrill cries pierced my soul, yet they weren't calling to me. I no longer had to take things personally. Seen through these winged creature's eyes, I had become something objective—on the same order of being as a rock, a wave, a log washed up on shore.

The experience ended when I began to feel self-conscious. I wondered if I were in danger of becoming more removed and isolated than ever. I began to feel humiliation and shame, but a deeper wave of healing passed through my body, releasing me.

My dog Moss, belonging both to the wild world and the human world, was there with me, my link between these two realities. On the way back he would lick my ear or just collapse as dogs do after vigorous exercise, and then I too would let go. My world had become porous. I was as free as the birds.

Like many people, I have sometimes had transcendent experiences: the sweat lodge and the waterbird, walking on the beach with the egrets, and with my dog

[56] " The Chambered Nautilus," in *America in Literature,* vol. 1, p. 1479.

at Pt. Reyes. These initiations are available to us. They do not represent a final goal or a once-and-for-all transformation, but afterward we feel more fullness and participation. We seem to be more at home in life and we feel its energy running through us, like a herd of elk running across a prairie or whales sounding off shore. We are part of life and life is in us.

After this visitation with the shore birds and the visit from the egret near the sweat lodge, there were other visits. The waterbird took up residence in my office, linking my professional and personal life. One morning a patient brought in a picture she had drawn of herself as a young girl. Nude, and with an expression both demure and alluring, she was sitting on the back of a large white duck. It was like Leda and the swan, and as she spoke about the picture, she expressed a degree of trust in the duck that she had never felt for anyone or anything before. In the wake of this experience, she began a love affair. Through her I experienced the initiatory power of the waterbird, on whose back she had discovered a new reality of feeling.

Meanwhile I began to discover historical evidence linking the bird to the feminine world. Lithuanian archaeologist Marja Gimbutas found representations of waterbirds—geese, cranes, swans and ducks—in Paleolithic art in bone carvings and cave drawings. She also found a hybridization of waterbird with womanly form in a Neolithic terra cotta sculpture (Figure 5). Gimbutas writes, "This is an identification of female [egg-shaped] buttocks with the long body of a bird or bird carrying an egg."[57] Thus, the fertility of the female form is linked to the special generative powers of the bird, for "the water bird was an important source of food and consequently a symbol of well being."[58]

The Bird Goddess in the next picture (Figure 6) is a more complete and more differentiated standing clay sculpture, from 5,000 B.C., found near Moravia in what is now the Czech Republic. Gimbutas describes her as having a "pinched nose for beak, arm stumps for wings, small breasts, massive buttocks."[59] Thus I learned how ancient is the eros between human and bird.

Actually, long before the Blackfoot sweat lodge and my patient's duck, I had been courting—or courted by—the waterbirds. I was walking on the beaches of Pt. Reyes, and I couldn't take my eyes off the shore birds. Their slender bodies with long legs and wings in graceful flight weave together sea and sky. Against the pale seascape of winter the subtle grays of the Willet lifted my spirits.

---

[57] *Civilization of the Goddess: The World of Old Europe,* p. 235.
[58] Ibid., p. 234.
[59] Ibid., p. 83.

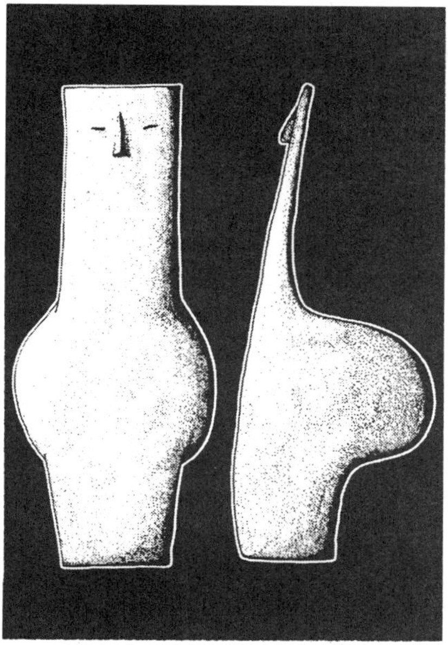

Figure 5

Figure 6

More than anything, it was the birds' movement that intrigued me. Lifting off gracefully, sometimes returning to lift again, effortlessly they float and sink. With the same ease of movement, they stay grounded or rise into the air. Will this one become airborne or not? Spontaneous in response, the bird waits till the last moment before taking off perhaps before its wings are completely unfurled.

The bird lifts off into the air and for a moment doesn't move but hangs suspended as if it belongs there. Another creature might perform this operation on preparatiion for flight, but this bird is already in the air. Then wings flutter, ruffle, stir intimations and desires, bringing the bird to life. Then the fluttering takes hold. The wind catches the bird and it sails.

How wondrous that a living thing can shift so easily between the elements, sea, land, air, ascend or descend so effortlessly, fly between spirit world and material world, between dream and reality, to take the living essence of the dream into life and back again? The dream world records our emotional change; feeling more self confident we reach out unexpectedly. The bird flies back and forth between this world and the other: from wintertime in the south, where it feeds, fattens, reproduces, then north to the farthest Himalayas—to the beyond.

This bird of transcendence does not fully reside in the material world. Rather it makes temporary nests to raise its young for flying northward. Nests for flying. Materials for flying. Body and soul. Imagine what the bird experiences at the moment of take-off for its northern journey, its heart beating to the accompaniment of the shaman's drum. It looks for its place in the flock, its own place in the universe.

Returning, there is a moment before the bird lands, in slow motion, its wings outstretched and slowly folding. Then ever so gently it settles, landing in the air above the intended ground before dropping, or stopping above the water which has created a space for it to float. My own landings are bumpier. When I return home from a professional meeting, I am agitated and out of sync. I have not caught up with myself, I have not found my place and so I quarrel with my wife, I can't settle into my work. The bird folds its wings and sits comfortably protected in itself, resting, nesting.

Suddenly the flock takes off, takes my breath away, is gone, then lands quickly further down. Why is it so hard for me to change direction? Or begin to move at all? And when moving, why is it so hard to stop and reverse, deciding against myself? Why can't I say no after I've said yes?

Such mysterious encounters with the birds heal my fear and isolation. In those Montana woods when I fled the sweat lodge because of pain, I had broken a sacred bond. I couldn't help it, but I did. The bond was to accompany the other men and women on the journey. Had I been raised in that culture, relationship would have been the centerstone of my existence. Joseph Epes Brown, a scholar of the Oglala Sioux and recipient of the teachings of Black Elk, explains the meaning of the words "mi taku oyasin":

> Established in "legendary time" is the custom of the men, when they had finished smoking the pipe together in a ritual manner, to say "mi taku oyasin" ("we are all related"). Here is affirmed the pervading conception of an essential and mysterious (waken) bond, binding together the people, the animals, the earth, and all that is.[60]

The pain in my chest drove me from the lodge and the warmth of the people and forced me to find something deep within myself. The charged nature of the atmosphere of the lodge made that discovery possible. I stayed with the pain just as an animal would. I suffered my pain. Release came with a marvelous image of the waterbird unwinding from my heart, wedding me to the intimacy I had experienced but not integrated.

---

[60] *Animals of the Soul: Sacred Animals of the Oglala Sioux,* p. 60.

Through the white egret that came to me in my solitary yurt, I learned what the poet Robert Hass calls "the wakefulness of living things."[61] Initiated by the wild animals, I was no longer isolated and this led me back to the warmth of the human world.

Geese

A man had this dream:

> It's winter in the far north—Canada or Alaska. Snow geese have settled on a frozen lake. Coyote spies the geese and stealthily stalks them. However, the ice is thin and coyote has to be careful not to get out further than the ice can support him. As he approaches, the geese fly free. Then as sometimes happens, coyote gets stuck in the ice and freezes there. Wolves, sensing food, find the coyote and eat him, leaving a leg frozen in the ice.

The crux of this dream is geese, geese set free.

Imagine geese of the north, spirit birds descending on a frozen landscape. These northern dream-geese are not ordinary birds, rather they come from another realm. They are birds as shamanic vehicles. The wild gander was the shaman's bird which carried him in trance, by magic flight, to ancestral lands. It enabled the shaman and later the yogi to bring back visions for the community. In the dream, the geese touch down on this remote arctic outpost to awaken a man, to remind him of the austere world from which they have come. What dreamer is in need of such inspiration? Who calls this visitation?

He is a friend, a colleague entering middle life—a scientist turned artist who had been brought up in the wilderness of the rural north. Both of his parents were artists. When this man was quite young, his father, before truly realizing his own artistic gift, committed suicide and his mother, following her husband's death, withdrew from life.

My friend's dream of geese escaping came at a time when he was forced to choose between his family and his mistress. Geese had long been special to the man, their breathtaking beauty in flight capturing his imagination. Seeing them fly free relieved him. He knew he had made the right decision to return to his wife and children, although he felt pain and sadness in having to give up his lover. The geese meant everything to him, and when he saw them airborne he felt released. The dream was not about the choice of a woman or the fear that he was being punished. The dream told him something deeper—that in the process

---

[61] "Happiness," in *Sun Under Wood,* p. 3.

of his quest to become an artist, he had found something for himself. The geese meant that for him. Other things and other people had meaning, but this was where he truly lived.

What part did coyote play? In winter, geese attract a hungry coyote, hungry enough to risk thin ice. The dreamer, too, is hungry, hungry to become the artist his parents could not. Being coyote-like, wily and roving, he awakens to emotional stirrings with a woman other than his wife. In the dream, too, he tries to capture the geese. This quintessential coyote in mythology occupies a transitional or liminal zone. Disruptive, he is always on the fringe of society, often satisfying his sexual appetite at the expense of others. Coyote is "a restless trickster, inquisitive, obscene, adventurous, and diabolically challenging,"[62] but he is also the bringer of new life. As coyote, this scientist-turned-artist would not willingly have given up the trick of having both relationships. What the man was unable to do, nature accomplishes by conspiring to get rid of coyote. First, the ice traps coyote who, full of folly, has made the mistake of going out on thin ice. He, of course, thought he could capture the geese and did not know that he would be trapped. He could not get what he wanted.

Frozen in the ice, coyote is finished off by the wolves who represent harsh reality, the return of the natural order. In this sense, the wolves are linked to the goose. They belong more to the stable elements in life than coyote does. The wolves might catch the geese, but they would not venture out on thin ice to do so. When the dream-geese return to the sky, the wolves reassert their power over the land; life returns to order. A healthy instinct puts things back in balance.

The man was excited about the geese flying free. In the moment it was the truth that he knew would hold for his whole life. He had to bring his life in line with this true experience or he was a dead man. No one needed to tell him this reality; it was visible in fiercely determined eyes and in his bodily movements. He had to become the artist that his father had wanted to be. Any other way of living was provisional. He needed to trust himself, trust the dream, trust his ability in his own nature to carry off this transition in his life.

The only disconcerting aspect of the dream was coyote's horrible end. The man, identified with coyote, experienced dismay at seeing the coyote's demise with his leg remaining as a fixture in the ice. But he was reassured because in the place where he actually lived, coyotes were reappearing. There had been several sightings of them. In the past, they had been killed off with pesticides

---

62 Joseph L. Henderson, "Psychological Commentary," in Margaret Schevill Link, *Pollen Path, A Collection of Navajo Myths*, p. 126.

that farmers had put out in order to protect their farm animals. The dream had to kill off this trickster side of life in order to ensure the protection of the newly emerging, more valuable life. But it does leave a leg of coyote preserved as a permanent fixture. It is a monstrous image, a specter, but nonetheless there is a mercurial aspect to it. Could it not symbolize the keeping alive of something that might othersie disappear forever? Who knows when coyote will come to life again?

Coyote, the man's youthful wily nature, was now replaced by deeper imaginative yearnings for the goose. He always carried binoculars with him to capture these chance geese sightings. The freedom of the graceful waterbird flying high frees the earthbound viewer to experience its exhilaration and momentarily to trust the bird as guide. The goose flies between heaven and earth, at ease in both, constrained by neither. In the old East Indian literature, the wild gander was known as "hamsa." Heinrich Zimmer, the scholar of Indian mythology, explains that the hamsa's song originates from the yogi's melodic breathing:

> The inhalation is said to make the sound, *ham*, the exhalation, *sa*, [revealing the gander's divine Self]. . . . The song of the inner gander has a final secret to disclose. "Hamsa, hamsa," it sings, but at the same time, "sa-'ham, sa-'ham." *Sa* means "this" and -*'ham* means "I"; the lesson is, "This am I." . . . I, the human individual" with a body, but also "I am He who is free and divine."[63]

Figure 7 (next page) depicts a goose or hamsa, from the Ajanta Cave in fifth-century India, painted in its winter home on water against lotus leaves. The bird points upward to its migratory spring and summer home in the Himalayas, thus symbolizing the Buddhist ascetic seeking enlightenment. This is the bird the shaman rode in magic flight between the worlds.

The sacred and indestructible spirit of the hermetic goose carries over to this day, as heard in the folk song "The Grey Goose" sung by Leadbelly:

> One Sunday morning.
> Lord, Lord, Lord.
> The preacher went a-hunting
> Lord, Lord, Lord.
> He carried along his shotgun.
> Refrain. [Refrain after each phrase]
> Along came a grey goose
> The gun went off baloom
> Down came the grey goose

---

[63] *Myths and Symbols in Indian Art and Civilization,* pp. 49f.

He was six weeks a-falling
He was six weeks a-hauling
Then my wife and your wife
They give a feather picking
They were six weeks a-picking
They put him on a pear board
He was six weeks a-boiling
and they put him on the table
and a fork couldn't stick him
and a knife couldn't cut him
and they threw him in a hogpen
The hogs couldn't eat him
He broke the hog's teeth out.
They take him to a saw mill
The saw couldn't cut him
He broke the saw's teeth out.
And the last time I'd seen him
He was flying toward the ocean
with a long string of goslings
and they're all going quank quank
and they're all going quank quank
and they held with the grey goose.[64]

Figure 7

The song expresses the spirit of the goose which cannot be extinguished. It survives anything that can be done to it. It calls to us as long as we live. On the other side, there is the expression "Your goose is cooked," or "I've got your goose," meaning you are caught and your game is up. It's the situation coyote found himself in. But my friend recovered his goose before it was cooked.

Another man, Japanese, was not so fortunate. His story comes from a sad but beautiful fairy tale about a man married to a nonhuman wife, a crane. Unlike the preceding story of the man who keeps his relationship to geese, the man in this tale does not understand the meaning of his crane wife and loses her.

A poor man named Karoku, living with his mother in the mountains, one winter day went to town to buy a futon [folding mattress] but instead ran across a man who had entrapped a crane. Feeling sorry for the crane Karoku bought it, then set it free. Returning home he explained to his mother that he had saved the life of a crane by using the money originally intended for the futon.

The next evening a beautiful woman came to Karoku's house asking if she

---

[64] *Leadbelly's Last Sessions,* disc 2, SF 40069, Smithsonian Folkways.

could spend the night. Soon she asked Karoku to take her as a wife, which he did.

One day the wife said to Karoku, "Please leave me in the closet for three days, and be sure that you don't open the door to look inside." So he left her there and didn't look inside, and she came out on the fourth day.

"You must have suffered in there. I was worrying about you so much. Come and have some food," he told her, and she ate a meal as he asked her to.

"Karoku, Karoku, please go and sell the material which I have woven in the closet for two thousand pieces of gold," she said to him. Karoku took the material to the lord. The lord said, "This is gorgeous merchandise. I would pay two thousand, three thousand pieces of gold for this, but can you make another bolt of it?"

"That I must ask my wife. I cannot give you an answer now," Karoku said.

"You don't need to ask her. If you agree, that will do. I will pay right now."

When Karoku returned home, he told his wife what had happened.

"Only if you give me enough time will I weave one more bolt. This time, keep me in the closet for a week. You must never peek inside during that time." With this, she entered the closet.

After one week, Karoku was so worried about her that he opened the closet door. Inside it he found a crane with nearly every feather gone, pulling the last fine feather and weaving cloth from it. The bolt was just completed at that moment.

"I have finished the material. However, since you have seen my true body you are surely disgusted with me, so I must leave this place. Truly speaking, I am the crane you saved. Please take this bolt of material to the lord as you have promised." She sat quietly facing the west. Then, suddenly, nearly a thousand cranes came and flew away with the naked crane.

Karoku received much money, but his feeling of loss was unbearable. Wanting desperately to see the crane, he searched all over Japan. When he came upon a beach he just sat there. Then an old man rowing a boat approached the shore. Karoku wondered where he had come from as there was no island in sight. As he was thinking, the boat reached the shore.

"Old man, old man, where have you come from?"

"I came from the island called Crane's Feather Gown."

"Please, would you take me there?"

"Sure." The boat arrived quickly at a beautiful white beach. When Karoku stepped on land, the boat and the old man disappeared.

Beyond the beach, Karoku saw a great pond. In the middle of the pond was a sand dune. There he saw many cranes gathered around the featherless crane, the queen of the cranes. Karoku was treated royally and feasted for a while. Then again by the old man's boat, he returned to his homeland.[65]

---

[65] Hayao Kawai, *The Japanese Psyche,* p. 106 (modified).

The crane's spiritual meaning is akin to that of the geese in my friend's dream. Traditionally, the crane—because of its longevity and the belief that it first brought rice to the land—is considered a bird of good omen.[66] This quality is also apparent in the crane fairy tale which begins with the hero Karoku living at home with his mother. He first exerts his independence by deciding to buy a futon, which suggests warmth for his house, an initial caring for himself.[67] He changes his mind, however, and uses the money to rescue a crane. Through this act he sacrifices a material possession for a spiritual one, and thus fosters his own inner life. In gratitude for Karoku's rescue, the crane, a nonhuman female, transforms herself into a woman and offers him marriage.

Instead of simply accepting the money for a bolt of cloth, Karoku becomes greedy and consequently loses the connection to his spiritual life. In addition he breaks a vow by not honoring the request of the crane to keep her identity sacred. Karoku cannot stand the tension of not knowing, so he breaks into the closet. Karoku needs to accept the mystery in his life. Then he would know that he was in his life, one that is meant solely for him, and he would know how to keep his wife.

In my own life the waterbird has helped to keep me faithful to myself. When my heart fluttered to the rhythmical beating of the bird's wings, I felt connected to the life around me. My body and its responses belonged to me. The poet Mary Oliver says it beautifully in "Wild Geese." She tells us that by tuning in to our body, we find our larger place in the universe. By connecting inside, we connect to the larger world. We don't have to do any more than that.

> You do not have to be good.
> You do not have to walk on your knees
> for a hundred miles through the desert, repenting.
> You only have to let the soft animal of your body
>   love what it loves.
> Tell me about despair, yours, and I will tell you mine.
> Meanwhile the world goes on.
> Meanwhile the sun and the clear pebbles of the rain
> are moving across the landscapes,
> over the prairies and the deep trees,
> the mountains and the rivers.
> Meanwhile the wild geese, high in the clean blue air,

---

[66] Ibid.
[67] Ibid.

are heading home again.
Whoever you are, no matter how lonely,
the world offers itself to your imagination,
calls to you like the wild geese, harsh and exciting—
over and over announcing your place
in the family of things.[68]

The egrets I came to know seemed to drop out of heaven itself onto the marshlands in harmony with the tides. With their white color contrasting sharply with the earth tones of celadon, gray, brown, they become a study in stillness, a standing meditation, to quiet the heart. Enriched, I become at home with my inmost crane who represents beauty, the animal element that thrives in mystery, that resists capture and control. The more creative person waits with interest to see what life will bring. In relationships, too, there is always a secret or mystery which requires honoring. If one does not allow room for the other to respond naturally, spontaneously, something vital withers.

Karoku suffers the fate of one who breaks into the mysteries. He loses his crane wife, but awakened to her true meaning, finds partial redemption. By letting go of his affair, my friend came to his own realization of what the geese meant: the mystery of his artistic gift.

Duck, Goose and Heron

Now our focus on the waterbird moves from air to water. Instead of examining a man's spirituality in flight, we learn about a woman's sexuality in water. We witness the awakening of the instinctual world and immersion in the animal world. Water is the medium. Osprey dive for fish. Long-legged shore birds, herons, egrets stand like stilts in the shallows. The Greater Yellow Legs and the Oystercatcher show off their colorful legs. Long legs of the Curlew and Whimbrel match their long bills, legs for wading, bills for probing. These graceful creatures inhabit water's edge, the fertile intertidal zone where waters ebb and flow. Feeding shore birds move to higher ground as the tide moves in and then scurry down as little crabs become exposed again. The mudflats are the ooze from which creation springs.

For the birds, water is full of possibility, sustaining the many activities of their lives. For us humans, too, immersion in water invites change. Water mixes, messes, washes, cleanses. Refreshed, we emerge invigorated, inspired. We relate, adapt, mold, submit, love. With liquid soul, we kiss. Water eases intimacy.

---

[68] Mary Oliver, *New and Selected Poems,* p. 110.

This is the kind of immersion in water that came to a woman who really needed it. This is her story. All her life she had lived through other people, cut off from her own feelings. No matter who they were, friends, family, teachers, students, her role had been to help them realize their potential. When she was a child, her feelings were not reflected back to her, rather they were sacrificed for mother and family. Now she is in a difficult situation, for she has fallen in love with a man whose life circumstance makes it impossible for him to be fully present to her, yet this love has awakened her. It has awakened her to the power and value of her inner life. It has awakened her passion. She is a nymph carried off by a duck. She is still a girl. She doesn't know whether to trust her feelings. Indeed, even to find out she has feelings is a revelation. "Is this me," she asks, "or am I just being what he wants? How can I tell?" So there is the possibility of an initiation. She can have a life of her own. She no longer needs to live through others. Here is her initiation drawing. She calls this bird "My gentle duck."

Figure 8

What does it mean? She sets out on the waters of life. She has a chariot, a creature that is instinctual but gentle, a creature that is at home in the place where she's going. There is an element of surrender, too. She is entrusting herself to the fluid and alien element, the external force that sustains a human life.

She is like Gretel in the Grimm Brothers' fairy tale when she and Hänsel free themselves from the old witch and begin journeying home. They come to a great stretch of water they cannot cross. Gretel cries out,

> Little duck, little duck, dost thou see,
> Hänsel and Gretel are waiting for thee?
> There's never a plank, or bridge in sight,
> Take us across on thy back so white.[69]

Throughout history women have ridden waterbirds on the walls of temples, carved into the sides of cliffs and even on the cover of *The New Yorker.* We have seen how a girl, a maiden who is lost, needs to discover an authentic connection to life. To do this, she needs to turn to the realm of the spirit-bird, the winged goddess, trusting that she will be supported.

Figure 9
(British Museum, London, England)

Aphrodite was a daughter of the sky, yet she was born from the sea and is the goddess of love and sexuality. In an ancient Greek image of her on a goose (Figure 9), she is being taken on a journey. She is seated on the goose much like my patient riding her duck. The goose enthrones her, cushions her. Large feath-

[69] *The Complete Grimm's Fairy Tales,* p. 93.

ery wings surround her. She is pillowed, safe and snug. The feathers are soft and inviting, sexually opening her, and the goose has a phallic quality. Aphrodite, being experienced, rides a goose while the girl rides a duck. The bird's long neck and feathery wings equip it to soar.

Sappho, a sixth-century Greek poet, describes Aphrodite riding on a car drawn by birds: "And birds, beautiful and fast, led you over the dark earth, whirling quick wings from the heaven's ether through the middle-sky."[70] In another Greek image of Aphrodite on a goose (Figure 10), she is upright.[71] Instead of being a passenger, this sculpted Aphrodite appears to direct the goose; she is in charge. Her vertical body and high cylindrical headdress suggest that she belongs to the spirit world, between water and sky, far from the stolidity of land.

Figure 10
(470-460 B.C.E., from Tombat Camirus, Rhodes; British Museum, London, England)

[70] Beverly Moon, ed., *An Encyclopedia of Archetypal Symbolism,* p. 147.
[71] From Erich Neumann, *The Great Mother,* plate 137.

The magical realm between water and sky is attractive to a man because it seems feminine, dissolving his link to his work and its pressures. Meditating on these geese bearing women I am led to even more archaic images, like the next two pictures of bird-headed goddesses. The first (Figure 11), is a black coal drawing from Pech-Merle, southern France (Upper Paleolithic Period, from ca. 23,000 B.C., Magdalenian Culture). Gimbutas describes it as follows:

> Female nude with pendulous [magical] breasts, wings for arms, and bird-head mask overpainted with "macaroni" . . . . motif, related to the symbol of flowing life or the water of life.[72]

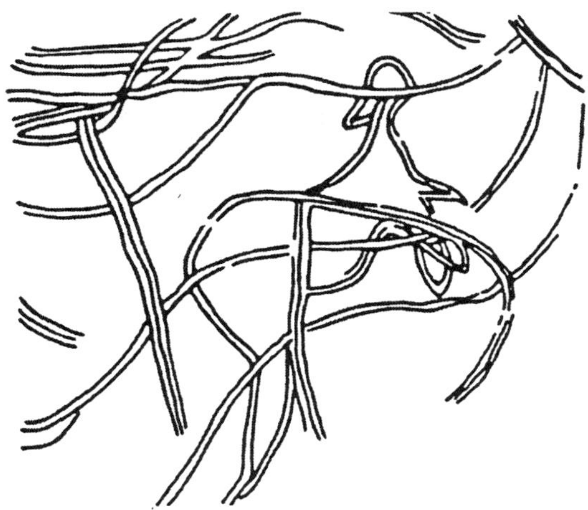

Figure 11

The second picture (Figure 12, next page) of a goddess from the Neolithic Period, 5900-5800 B.C., presents a more differentiated form. Gimbutas:

> Two views of the Bird Goddess's head with a massive nose, coffee bean eyes, neatly combed hair with a bun. Sesklo culture, from Arhilleion in Greece. Found in temple.[73]

Waterbirds from the Neolithic period enrich us with myths and fairy stories.

> Water Birds in fairy stories remain as magical birds, increasing or decreasing wealth and fortune. Water nymphs of European folklore who magically perform various kinds of women's work, especially spinning and weaving, appear as mortal

---

[72] *Civilization of the Goddess,* pp. 230f.
[73] Ibid., p. 231.

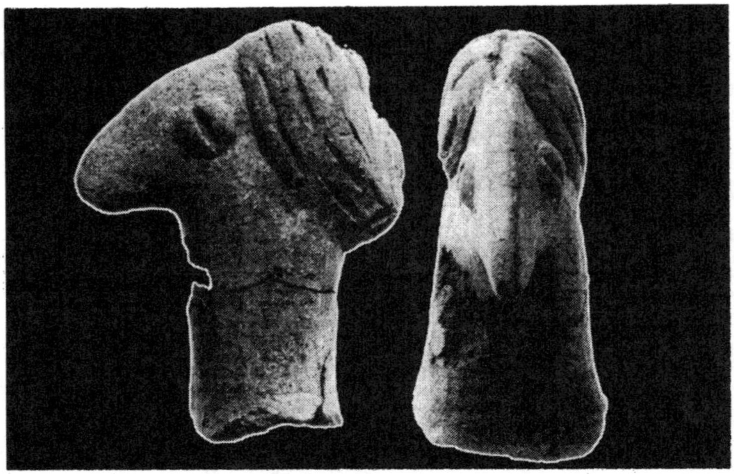

Figure 12

> women, naked with very long breasts. Sometimes they appear dressed, but one can notice their bird's feet and if their clothing is parted, there would be the body of a hen, a goose, or a duck. They work very quickly, without a moment's respite, but if angered, they can destroy everything.[74]

Birds possess a dual nature: as waterbirds, they are givers of life, and in the form of vulture, owl, raptor or carrion eater, they are bringers of death.[75] So too, archetypal woman has a dual nature: the two sides of the moon, the two faces of birth and death, the opposite feelings of love and despair.

Drawing herself upon the duck, my patient began to listen to her own feelings. As time went on, she began to trust her emotions. Her lively spirit flew about the room full of joy. She became like the bird that Mircea Eliade, the religious scholar, speaks of:

> All over the world learning the language of animals, especially of birds, is equivalent to knowing secrets of nature . . . . Birds are psychopomps. Becoming a bird oneself or being accompanied by a bird indicates the capacity, while still alive, to undertake the ecstatic journey to the sky and the beyond.[76]

She became herself. She said:

---

[74] Ibid., p. 234.
[75] Ibid., p. 230.
[76] *Shamanism*, p. 98.

> For the first time I have a sense of myself. I have "I am-ness." Something alive is around, a bird. There is hope, no matter what awful things are happening. I'll land on my feet and keep going. I used to apologize before because I didn't deserve good things in my life. Now I don't believe it as much. I can have it now and that feels good.

Carl Kerényi likens the Greek name of the stork *(pelargos,* mythologically connected to the source of life) to Demeter herself, founder of the eighth-century B.C. Kabirian mysteries, more archaic than the Eleusinian Mysteries. The tribal name of the Kabeiroi he also links to birds. He tells us that "the initiating priests and priestesses . . . belonged to the race of the first mystery priest 'Eum-olpos' which means 'good singer' " and was depicted on vase paintings with a swan, "regarded by the Greeks as one of the best singers among birds . . . although supposedly he sang only in his last hour,"[77] originating the familiar expression "swan song."

> The swan, the goose, and surely the duck, which is so often represented on Greek vases [5th century B.C.], form a group of [short-legged] water birds, out of which . . . the mythology of the divine mother and her daughter, expressing the destiny of woman, of the soul, and of all human beings, was molded in archaic times. . . . Stork, heron, and crane . . . suggest the existence of a long-legged group.[78]

On a second set of vase paintings were depicted uninitiated Kabirian males, phallic dwarfs or pygmies, wringing the necks of cranes. The cranes, symbols of the feminine spirit, are being devastated by the unrestrained phallic impulses of these dwarfs, even as they are being fertilized by them. The mission of Demeter and the feminine principle, says Kerényi, was "to open the path . . . . to the source of life, to the almost metaphysical roots of our being."[79] The function of the mysteries was to initiate these wild and crude men, who were more primitive than the trickster figure, and to educate them about the meaning of spirit as embodied in the feminine winged waterbird.[80]

The wooden sculpture of a fledgling and unhatched eggs (Figure 13, next page) is associated with the Egyptian creation myth in which the Great Cackler "laid the primordial egg from which the sun god sprang initiating all life and cosmic existence. . . .Its shrill cackle announcing the end of Nothingness."[81]

---

[77] The Mysteries of the Kabeiroi," in *The Mysteries,* p. 52.
[78] Ibid., p. 54.
[79] Ibid., p. 58.
[80] Ibid., pp. 56f.
[81] Egyptian Museum, Cairo, Egypt; Tutankhamon Catalogue no. 620 (1).

Figure 13

The Egyptians highly valued their animals, turning them into gods and goddesses. Often animals and human forms were combined. Egyptian scholar Henri Frankfort tells us that animals were valued for

> their inarticulate wisdom, their certainty, their unhesitating achievement, and above all their static reality. . . . The animals never change, and in this respect especially they would appear to share—in a degree unknown to man—the fundamental nature of creation.[82]

The final image of the waterbird is a stunning bronze and wood sculpture of the god Thoth as an ibis, together with the goddess Maat (Figure 14). More frequently he is depicted with a human body and an ibis head. As the god of arts and sciences with the knowledge of divine speech, Thoth performed the function of scribe to the gods. Because he is self-begotten and because of his connection to Osiris, he is compared with the Greek god Hermes, capable of creating the mysterious. But here he is a lunar deity.

> The ibis has a bill that resembles the crescent moon and its gait suggests the movement of the moon. . . . Plutarch has written that the alternating black and white feathers of the male ibis are reminiscent of the dark and light phases of the moon. . . . Like the god Thoth, the ibis was hostile to dangerous forces and a model of purity and good sense.[83]

---

[82] *Ancient Egyptian Religion,* p.13.

[83] Moon, ed., *An Encyclopedia of Archetypal Symbolism,* pp. 82ff.

Figure 14

Like the ibis, the woman dreamer was learning to trust the mysterious lunar thread, both in herself and in the deepening relationship with her male companion. This marked a transition from sea and sky to land—to mammalian warmth and the closeness of relationship. She had a dream in which she and her man were climbing a hill:

> As we near the top I see a large brown animal begin to get up out of the grass. At first I think it is a moose or elk but as he stands up I realize he is a camel. I am in awe at how beautiful the camel is and how beautiful the scenery is. This sun is beginning to set and the dusk settles. There is a pond or lake or some kind of still water that reflects the light.

She had grown up in the place of moose and elk. But in this new land of relationship, a camel sprang forth from the two lovers who had climbed rocks together in the desert. Her lover reached out his hand to her. The dromedary could carry them over long distances without water through harsh terrain. What difficulties would they have to endure?

In fact, the man was married. He became mired in guilt about leaving his wife. In response, his lover had the following dream which took her back to herself, to her bird, as if to reaffirm herself against the doubts of the relationship.

> I am in Alaska talking to some people about a belt buckle which is made of whale bone. I look at the belt buckle and see that there is a an image carved on the buckle but I can't make out the symbol. I know that if I can make out what it is then I will understand something important to me.
>
> Suddenly I see a beautiful bird flying against a cold icy background in Alaska. It is a heron with a large beak and long legs, its legs tucked up with its feet visible at the back. It is huge and beautiful with a large wing span, a blue-gray body and blue head. The light is reflecting off shore so the bird is surrounded by light. Then I realize it is the same image on the belt buckle.

She said that whales are special to her and the whale bone is intended to be a message. Migrating underwater mammals bring her an older knowledge; their majestic presence makes them magical, bigger than life. She identifies the whales as being female, and in her associations, she understands them to be good instinctual mothers with babies.

The belt is to be worn. It has a large buckle image carved by an artist. The woman likened the carving in the dream to sacred art made by Inuit and other indigenous peoples. Someone had carefully worked on this important piece, making it special.

As she talked she began to understand that the dream was integrating something spiritual as represented by the winged blue-headed bird (the patient has bright blue eyes) with the reality of life embodied by the female whale. But she became sad and when I asked her why, she replied that she felt lonely. She says that people are only interested in surface things and when she reflects these superficial values she is included, but not for her deeper self:

> People don't want to do things as I do, so I feel lonely because I can't share them. In meeting their needs I neglect mine. I have lived this way for so long that now I am afraid I can't really be myself with others, so I don't try.

Though she feels she is always pulled back to her old way, she can share real things with this man. "He is interested in some of the same things as I am and it's fun"—so she hangs in there with him, even though a deeper involvement does not seem possible.

The dream takes us back to a waterbird moment. Through being in this littoral zone she has found her true emotional response to life. She is beginning to be instinctual. What is happening may not look right to the outsider. People are likely to disapprove. There is something a bit scandalous about this which transgresses personal values. Discovering the waterbird forces her to leave the tribe. She has outgrown it. She is in a waterbird world between sea and sky that has no solid base. Later she will return enriched, but for now Aphrodite's erotic goose has taken her.

What captivated me about this woman was her vulnerability and her courage, how far she was willing to step into danger. Where was this duck taking her? In continuing the relationship with this man, she was going against all reason. Her feeling was the only important thing in the world. It was beautiful and I was afraid for her. How could she do it, I wondered. She was going against all she had learned, as well as risking her professional standing in the community. Yet it continued. There was at bottom, I could feel it, the animal that knew something beyond human knowledge. She was risking her life. Was I supporting her? If I were a woman analyst, I wondered, would I try to be more realistic with her? I knew that this might remain an unconsummated relationship, and that I would have to live with the tension also.

Together we followed the duck gone from the earth. I myself no longer had any guidelines. This was new for me too, I couldn't really counsel her, only follow the animal, follow the dreams; we were too far into it to turn back. We charted an uncertain course. As her analyst, the most I could do was to help her trust in the zig-zag course of her own waterbird way.

Frog

From the world of sky and water we descend to water's edge. Mythologically, we make a transition from the spiritual or psychic mother to the earth mother. Her body is fertile, regenerative. Instead of the shrill cry of the bird, we hear the throaty resonance of the frog. From flying we now leap about with hands and feet. We are in a spring moment with spring fever. Young girls open their hearts and bodies to their lovers. Frog spawn clouds the surface of the pond. Discover the frog.

This is the amphibious realm between water and land. Mud and slime, reeds and ponds. A pair of staring eyes protrude from the surface, then disappear. Intrigued, I create a break in the reeds. I squish toward the pond, my toes sink in ooze. The croaking stops, slender frogs fly out laterally—elongated—hind legs extended, splash, plop. Schools of tadpoles dart. The air is heavy, pungent, sticky, with no wind. There on a rock in the middle of the pond sits Prince Frog, motionless. He has finished his pushups! He meditates. He waits. His tongue flashes and he swallows. He is content. I am content. We are both still, quiet. He plays his flute. I am at peace and happy.

I fall into a trance. I am soft, warm, open, sexual. A striped red and yellow water snake undulates nearby. Floating lily pads open to translucent wings of dragon flies. Water scooters skim the surface. A yellow warbler perched tenuously on top of the reeds sways back and forth. Nothing seems solidly attached, everything is tentative. Animals are here and gone; from reed to shallow water; they submerge, reemerge, disappear, reappear. Frogs, tadpoles and dragonflies move continuously. Have you ever held a frog cupped in your hands, jumping, spitting, tingling, pissing, ready to leap?

"Breedeep, Breedeep." I once had such a pond, a spring-fed pond 2500 feet above the Petaluma valley floor. A row boat was tucked in the reeds. As I approach water's edge a hundred living things disappear. Then quiet—shush quiet. Individual animals reemerge—the loud cacophony begins. The red-winged blackbird's sonorous call pierces. Flycatchers darting between tall cattails dissect insect whorls. Lizards with long tails, short legs and grabby little feet move like lightning, then stop stone dead. Turtles sun themselves, heads poke out, bodies still, then slide into water, climbing over one another back onto rocks. Orange salamanders become creepy crawlies underfoot. Why do we feel happy? The inner life, too, pops out unexpectedly. Hypnotized we listen to life creating itself—listen to ourselves. Evening descends, frogs croak. I feel safe. Magical pond, where are you now? A voice responds:

> O pond, O pond.
> *The Wind in the Willows* pond.
> Who needs more than a pond?

All over the world the frog is disappearing. Environmentalists believe this is a bad sign, because the frog is an indicator species: what happens to the frog foretells the future of other animals in the wetlands. No frogs, no ponds. The croaking will be heard only in stories, myths and dreams. The millions of frogs that were brought to life when the yearly flooding of the Nile turned the land into swamp may no longer exist, but hopefully Hequet, the Egyptian fertility goddess to whom the frog was sacred, will continue to inspire fertility dreams. One young woman blossomed when she dreamt:

> I am standing in a shallow pool of water with multitudinous numbers of frogs. I catch some but unintentionally I squash others by stepping on them. So upset by having done this and wishing it had not happened, I try bringing them back to life by piecing them back together.

As this woman tries to bring these frogs back to life, she is transformed, tadpole to frog, girl to woman. She is a seventeen-year-old anorexic girl who hardly talked as a child. One day she bought a terrarium and put one frog and two newts in it and then decided it needed another frog. Only then did she remember her dream. The following day a boy invited her to a school prom. She had never thought of herself as attractive, someone in whom a boy might be interested. She was never asked before and she was so shocked that before she could think to refuse she said, "yes," then bought a new dress. She moved from dream to actual frog, to prom, to prince.

Her story brings to mind "The Frog-King, or Iron Henry," a fairy tale in which the frog plays a curious transformative role. It begins in a forest. The youngest and most beautiful daughter of a king is playing with a golden ball which falls into a well. As she weeps in loss the ugly head of a frog appears and says he will recover her golden ball, but asks what she will give him in return.

> "Whatever you will have, dear frog," said she—"my clothes, my pearls and jewels, and even the golden crown which I am wearing."
>
> The frog answered: "I do not care for your clothes, your pearls and jewels, nor for your golden crown; but if you will love me and let me be your companion and play-fellow, and sit by you at your little table, and eat off your little golden plate, and drink out of your little cup, and sleep in your little bed—if you will promise me this, I will go down below and bring you your golden ball up again."
>
> "Oh yes," said she, "I promise you all you wish, if you will but bring me my ball back again." But she thought: "How the silly frog does talk! All he does is sit in the water with the other frogs, and croak! He can be no companion to any human being!"
>
> The frog returned the ball, but when he asked for her promise she ran away and soon forgot him. The next day, "splish splash, splish splash," the frog creeped up to the door and asked to be let in. When the princess opened the door and saw the frog, she slammed it shut. Her father the king asked her what the frog wanted and she told him the story. Then the king said, "That which you have promised must you perform." So she opened the door, lifted him up beside her, ate together from the same plate and carried the frog, whom she was loath to touch, up to a corner of her bedroom. But when he insisted that she put him under the covers with her, she became terribly angry, and took him up and threw him with all her might against the wall. Splat! To her surprise, lying on the floor was a prince with kind and beautiful eyes. He then told her that no one could have rescued him but her. They married and returned together to his kingdom.[84]

In this story the princess's golden ball falls into the deep watery elements and into the hands of a cold and clammy frog, the "old water splasher," far below the princess's lofty tower. Her father, sensing it is time for her to embrace the slimy ugly-headed frog—meaning time for her to grow into full emotional and sexual

---

[84] *The Complete Grimm's Fairy Tales,* pp. 17ff. (modified).

maturity as a woman and marry—encourages her to accept him. The princess, until now protected in her father's kingdom, reluctantly agrees to her promise, short of taking the slimy frog to bed. In hurling the frog, even as she is fulfilling her promise, she is asserting herself, rupturing the link to her passive girlhood. Simultaneously, she is breaking a witch's spell, transforming the frog back into a prince. Through a burst of emotional fire she heats something archaic, the watery cold-blooded frog, into human form to be loved.

Though the frog required the girl's powerful touch, he contained within him the animal's inherent power to transform. This power is sacred, for it underlies our hope for healing. Through the animals of our dreams and myths, we humans too can break the bad spells of our lives, shedding old skins, bursting out of constricting forms, to become more fully ourselves.

In fact, the frog was one of humanity's early images of the self. The frog's little hands and feet resemble human hands and feet, making it a kind of mannequin. Striking human and frog images appear on pots from the Mimbres culture, which existed in the southwestern United States ca. 1050-1250 A.D. Painted pottery (Figure 13) shows the likeness between the frog and the human body with staring eyes and a pointed head.

Frogs jump with excitement. They teem; they squirt uncontrollably. The woman who dreamed of them can no longer stop them. The frog breaks her isolation. The great Japanese poet Bashó had this to say about frogs:

> An old silent pond . . .
> into the pond
> A frog jumps,
> Splash! Silence again.[85]

This haiku could go in many directions. At one level, it's about presence. Everything is as it is. There is no need for anything to be other than what it is. If a ball disappears, it just disappears. If a sound happens, it just happens. Going in another direction, the haiku could stand as a metaphor for the girl jumping into life. She drops into water not only her ball but her whole life, and out comes a prince. We all remember our first sexual awakening, when our being came to life like the earth around us. We squirted all over. Our skin, like animal skin, grows sensitive to touch. The intoxicating fragrance of the other person invites us in. We can't help but respond. The frog plops into the water. We skip, we dance, we are immersed. We multiply. We become frogs.

---

[85] Peter Beilenson and Harry Behn, eds., *Haiku Harvest,* p. 22.

Figure 15
(Mimbres culture; Heard Museum; Phoenix, Arizona)

The little beasties grew out of the water. Before they came to land, before there was land, there was just sky and water. There the slender waterbird unfolded its wings and took to the sky. Cleansed in the water, it flew free. It flew home to itself, to you and me. Thus, the world began. Then mammals evolved.

Dolphins

As we move from amphibian to mammal, from cold blood to body heat and fire, we turn to another creature of the margin. It joins water and mammal, humans and ocean. The dolphin is between land and water in a different way than the frog. As a mammal that went back to water, it symbolizes a human who, in returning to sea, reconnects to psyche. This half-mammal, half-human, is a Merperson, one who prefers the sea.

As we enter deep water, we see a dolphin arching. He is trying to lead a woman away from pain—away from an unbearable wound—away from her family and out into the ocean of life. He came to the woman just as the animal in myths would come to the young initiate in primitive societies.[86]

"How I wish mother could have stayed," the pained woman laments. She was abandoned by her mother at age seven and almost left to die of pneumonia. Her mother dissipated her own life; she followed her impulses, her whims, finally

[86] See Joseph L. Henderson, *Thresholds of Initiation,* pp. 154f.

destroying herself. For fear of ending up like her mother, the daughter, intuitive by nature, was terrified of trusting. Terrified of following her feelings, she cluttered her life with rational thought. She became a workaholic, a slave to achievement and to detail, while inside her inaccessible heart was crying. Her life dried up, then she opened a crack, only to become locked into a doctoral dissertation. "When I have finished, then . . ." but her life was going by.

This motherless young woman came into analysis when she left a man who was treating her badly. Even though she had made the decision to leave, she felt abandoned. On the rebound she met another man, but she was afraid to open her heart for fear of being hurt again. Confused by her feelings for the two men, she had the first of several visions and dreamt of dolphins. It began with the image of two men in two separate boats. Fearing they would leave her, the young woman began to cry.

> Then the head of a dolphin appears, laughing, and in so doing, transforming my "let down" despair. If I love them [the two men], they'll leave me just like my mother did. When the dolphin throws his head back to laugh, I can see that the scene is not taking place in the outer world but rather inside of the dolphin (me). The dolphin allows me to dive deep into the water under and between the two boats, and then into the air above (consciousness). He laughs at the scene. He is playful and allows me to laugh at myself in the "outer" predicament.

As a child the dreamer rarely had a chance to play. As a tot, she danced for joy in the barn to cheer herself up; her mother discovered her and in response whipped her legs. In order to heal her wounded legs after her mother left, the young girl turned to dance. "I'd always loved it," she said, "and danced before she left, to express my feelings and to experience my connection to something larger—a natural and sacred dimension." As she entered adulthood, she became a dancer. But her heart stayed closed; she danced to sadness.

Then the graceful dancer of the sea, the dolphin, appeared to her in the above dream. This rescuer of lost souls tried to get her to follow him. As steed of Eros and guide to Aphrodite, he tried to open her heart. This mercurial silver fish, who plunges so deep and leaps so high, linking together sea and sky, tried to help restore her intuition. This playful mammal who speaks several languages tried to teach the woman how to communicate feeling, to help her connect to people. But she refused.

She told me he had come to her before, that years earlier she had had an intense visualization of a dolphin swimming in a small pond. She said to him, "I know you can't be real because dolphins swim only in the ocean and not in small ponds." He stood vertically on end, out of the water, looked her straight in the eye and responded, "I am here just for you." But this overly intellectual woman who analyzes and interprets stays above the experience. She is cut off. Something is wrong with her perception. The animal makes a demand the woman cannot meet. He demands too great a leap. The dolphin that comes to rescue her seems wise, but he has a trickster feel to him. There is a problem with the animal, with the mystery. Is this the right animal for this woman? Which animals are uncertain guides?

How can you teach play? My wife was relieved to see our ten-year-old son begin playing because it meant he was coming out of his depression. He had become worried about school work and had lost touch with his friends. Women who are connected to their emotions notice people being playful. "He's too serious, he never smiles," or "I like him because he makes me laugh." These playful women who laugh, enjoy, relate, tease, remind me of a sculpture of a nude Indian goddess playing with balls as they roll down her arms and body to her feet. "Come play with me" is the message. She is life inviting the god Shiva to come romp with her.

I once saw a woman, a resident in psychiatry, who was married and had a child but, like the dolphin woman, could not play. She was identified with achievement. Although she was the outstanding resident of her class, she decided to take a year off from the program because, as she put it, "I need to get back to my life." She was losing touch with her child, her husband, her garden, her house, her love of literature. Her focus had become too narrow. Both her powerful father and the chief of psychiatry were furious with her. As often happens when one's conflict resolves, she stopped analysis. (We often see patients through their difficulties and then never learn what becomes of them.)

The sleek elegant creatures leaping out of the water, rescuing people, communicating like humans, inspire joy. Life is to be lived. The journalist Wendi Kallins in a newspaper column wrote about dolphins helping her overcome her fear of water:

> The crowning glory was not amid the coral reefs but farther out in the deep water. These were the spinner dolphins who frequent Hookena bay [Hawaii] and came twice during my stay. We swam out to play with them, and I marveled as they swam beneath us and circled around us, one group diving one way, another school dashing the other direction.
>
> Those particular dolphins are like whirling dervishes. They leap up into the air spinning around and then tuck themselves under and dive back in. You can almost feel them shouting with glee as they jump in pure ecstasy, and I would shout for

them screaming "Ya-hoo" and "Yippee" every time another would emerge from the depths. I am no longer afraid of the water. Now it holds a new fascination for me, the majesty of its power, the beauty of its secrets, and the playfulness of its creatures like the dolphins, whose magic touched my spirit.[87]

Ancient Greek images in stone depict playful dolphins encircling Dionysus, as in Figure 16. This dark god of the underworld, associated with the vine and sexuality, could awaken my motherless patient with a closed heart. She dreams again of dolphins and her father. This dream begins with her following her old pattern of achievement. She is in school, in an old-fashioned building, meaning she's stuck in the past. She sees "a huge truck full of cut branches trying desperately to mount a hill, in danger of falling backward and jack-knifing onto itself because of its sheer weight." She is loaded down with dead wood; it is killing her. Then the dream goes right to the heart of the problem:

> When I return to the dorm, I put on a summer dress with nothing on underneath it just to lounge around in my room. My stepmother and dad then knock on my door, inviting me out into the hall for a walk. I go out, mortified by the fact that my naked bottom is hanging half way out from under this tiny short dress. It's indecent to wear in public, let alone around my father. They don't seem to notice, however, and we walk down to the back door of this building (not the real one facing a sweeping driveway, but a modern one, opening out to the ocean at the back). I am stunned to see the level of the ocean waves when we open the door, and yet they come crashing just at the foot of the tiny beach a few steps from the door!
>
> More amazing still are the teeming numbers of dolphins that are leaping playfully through the waves. I feel a strong urge to join them, but worry about the dress I'm wearing, thinking that I might be better just to take it off altogether and join them in the buff. Then I remember that my father is there and that other students might see me naked as well and I pause. At that moment, I see my father take several steps toward them and disappear under the water, fully dressed but oblivious to that fact, so mesmerized is he by this nearly magical show of natural beauty.

This woman's problem is very grave because not only was she abandoned by her mother, but her father molested her when she was a girl. Now all the pain she experienced with him is starting to break up, to dissolve, because he too is attracted to the dolphin. He no longer needs her; he has an animal who can help lead him to his own development. Here we see the problem begin to solve itself, for while the outer father goes his own way she can heal the dream father. The dolphins are helping her do this.

---

[87] "Return from Paradise (again)," in *Point Reyes Light,* Jan. 7, 1993, p. 5.

Figure 16
(Hellenic era; Greek archaic period; Munich: Mus. antiker Kleinhunst)

Whales

The dancing dolphins, these musical fish, point the way to their lumbering cousins, the whales, largest mammal of all. Like dolphins and porpoises, whales are cetaceans. Early in mammalian history they adapted to the sea, but kept their warm-blooded traits of developing their young internally and giving live birth at sea, nursing the young with milk, possessing internal heat control mechanisms. Their young have hair. They have given up their vestigial limbs. Because they know both realms, they symbolize a way to move from the water world to the mammalian world and back again.

When we encounter the whale, we become embodied. This huge mammal that inhabits the fluid, watery world of change, brings about profound change in those of us who live in the more solid element of earth. A giant form within the formless, the whale helps us humans to more fully inhabit our own form, to truly become *of the earth.*

An Old English term for sea is "whale road." This is what being a mammal is about, really: finding one's right path, one's right place in the world. A woman I know had not yet come down to earth and taken form, She was in the air, so much so that she needed the biggest mammal in the world to help her find her grounded body. She had this dream:

> We are in Vermont: Mom, me, my brother, and some girl. I go outside to see the stars and in the sky I see a whale—its body shimmering. It floats over me slowly and then plunges suddenly into a body of water in the distance. I go back inside to tell the others—only my mother comes out to watch. Two more whales float over us. They do not dive into the water but disappear into the distant sky. We find a poster for the "event" but there are no words. Was it real, we wonder?

This woman had moved out west after graduating from a prestigious art school. She was teaching to support her life as an artist and taking Tai Chi classes, where we met. She encouraged me to try new things, to get me up in the air with her. "Neil," she would say, "you work too much." The last time I saw her she had opened a small school, teaching children to draw.

Although she said she had no idea what the dream meant, she was intrigued by this big movement coming down into the waters of the earth to meet her. I think she saw herself in the whale, that the whale might represent the possibility of her life becoming more accessible to her. I urged her to write the dream down for me, because I was collecting animal dreams. In recording it, however, she had omitted a crucial detail which only emerged a month later when we discussed it further: the plunging whale swam into a bay enclosed by a circular ring. This huge wild animal let itself be contained.

I wondered if at least a third of her divine inspiration might become realized. She was so mercurial, so evocative, giving the impression that anything was possible, that I was never quite sure where she would land. Who has ever seen a whale in the sky? A few years after the dream, I ran into her when she was on her way to France to visit her mother. Her life had changed. Not only was her school a success but she had published her writing in conjunction with her art work. An animal had embodied her life in a way that D.H. Lawrence would understand, for the whale brings the hot breath of the psyche into cold reality:

> They say the sea is cold, but the sea contains
> the hottest blood of all, and the wildest, the most urgent.
>
> All the whales in the wider deeps, hot are they, as they urge
> on and on, and dive beneath the icebergs.
> The right whales, the sperm-whales, the hammer-heads, the killers
> there they blow, there they blow, hot wild white breath out of the sea!
>
> and Venus among the fishes skips and is a she-dolphin
> she is the gay, delighted porpoise sporting with love and the sea

> she is the female tunny fish, round and happy among the males
> and dense with happy blood, dark rainbow bliss in the sea.[88]

Lawrence's whales stay warm in the cold sea. Their mammalian heat energizes their tremendous movements and supplies them with love of relationship.

Play is a part of the mammalian world, even for the most gigantic of animals. I remember as a little boy reading the picture-book version of *Jonah and the Whale.* Inside the whale's belly was Jonah and I was there with him. It was exciting to be inside this large dark cavern staring at the whale's ribs. I wasn't afraid because I was with Jonah, God's errant disciple, put there by God because he was disrespectful, so I knew God would get us both out, and I was right.

Then there was Pinocchio, the little wooden marionette who became a human boy. How I loved Pinocchio! His ever-lengthening nose, reminding me of Rudyard Kipling's story of how the elephant got a trunk, was a wonder. How I wished that when I did things wrong I would be punished in this miraculous manner; then I might have developed in a more straightforward way. At the end of the story, he and his father are both trapped inside a whale, just like Jonah. Heroically, Pinocchio leads his father.

> [They went] up the stomach and through the windpipe. Then they went the length of the tongue and climbed over the three rows of cruel teeth. Before making the great leap into the sea, the marionette said to his father. "Now get upon my back, clasp your arms tightly round my neck, and leave the rest to me." Gepetto did so, and the brave Pinocchio threw himself boldly into the water and began to swim.[89]

Some years ago when I was walking at Pt. Reyes National Seashore along North Beach, which has a sharp drop-off, I felt a sudden exhilaration in my chest, as if my whole being were expanded to almost infinite proportion. At the same moment, out of the corner of my eye, I saw a long shadow beside me in the water. From a higher dune, a man pointed and yelled, "Whale, close to shore!" I felt ecstatic. A tremendous energy permeated my whole body. As I continued to walk along the beach I enjoyed a deep feeling of well-being, free from the usual concerns. It stayed with me a long time and I felt whole.

Children and whales, children and elephants. The littlest people belong to the largest of animals. Who can understand it? Now we move from the largest sea animal to the largest land animal, the elephant, and then other land animals.

---

[88] "Whales Weep Not!" in *Complete Poems of D.H. Lawrence*, pp. 694f.

[89] Carlo Collodi, *Pinocchio,* pp. 223f.

5
Initiation by Earth

Who rides on a tiger can never dismount;
asleep on an elephant, that is repose.
—Marianne Moore.[90]

Elephants

When I was little, I used to go to the zoo and feed peanuts to the elephants. I watched their mysterious long tubes with two funny-sided lips curl up from my hand to their mouths. In the presence of these majestic beasts, I imagined myself a king, riding an elephant all beaded and decorated. I knew that this riding would take some getting used to: one huge leg moves and then the other and a whole mountain rolls underneath.

These elephant encounters, both real and imaginary, occurred in the town of Erie, Pennsylvania, an hour and a half drive from Youngstown, Ohio, where we lived. My mother wanted to see her brothers and their wives; I usually wound up staying with my Aunt Fan, who would tyrannize me when I spilled milk on her new carpet. Aunt Fan considered us inferior relatives, and perhaps we were, but while feeding the elephants I had no deficiencies. What would they care about Aunt Fan's carpet? What would they care about Aunt Fan? With Aunt Fan, I had to be neither seen nor heard. Admiring the elephant, I let myself be visible in my body and enjoyed it. The elephant and I were not dependent on Aunt Fan to grant us existence and enjoyment in the world. Magnificence means you get to do what you want. Who's going to fool around with an elephant?

When I was with the elephants, they seemed to talk to me and calm me. With them, I could be present, I could be myself. It didn't matter what I looked like or what my status was. Here in front of me was an animal as big as a house, barely fitting into his cage, and his soul seemed to me as big as his body. He wasn't embarrassed or ashamed. I would look into his twinkly eyes and laugh. I would watch him unself-consciously move his big body around. I could do that too. Now, as an adult, I am still warmed by the way the elephant brought out the curiosity and love in the child I was.

---

[90] *The Complete Poems of Marianne Moore*, p. 130.

At my brother's funeral, I overheard Aunt Fan, who hadn't seen me in thirty years, remark that I was no better looking now than I had been as a child. Fortunately, by that time I was finally discovering the elephant within. As an adult, I wrote a little poem entitled "How I Prized and Adored the Elephant":

> You were so big and I so little.
> You took your space while I tried to hide.
> You were so unusual. I tried to fit in.
> You poked your trunk through fence holes, asking for peanuts. I ate when no one was looking.
> Your trunk was wondrous and magical. My Jewish nose was an embarrassment.
> Your cries traveled great distances. My tongue was tied; I stuttered.
> You moved determinedly with great strides. I hesitated and retraced.
> You were huge, yet careful where you walked.
> You were the body I never had.
> I worshipped you.

Children and elephants; elephants and children. They belong together. They love their families and their eyes twinkle. They understand the same language. Feeling their way, they reach out, the elephant with its long trunk and the children with their little hands, for food, for whatever catches their eye—for life.

When a child starts school, is it any wonder that she may want to take the security of an animal with her? She stuffs her teddy bear into her bag, into the drawer of her desk. The boy asks, "Why can't I take my dog to school, Mom? He won't bother anyone, I promise."

A friend of mine dreamed of elephants and children. She was about to enroll her daughter in nursery school when she had this dream. It is the first day of school, and as she and her daughter enter the building, she is horrified to see stalls and stalls of elephants. Down the row, there is a baby elephant and she realizes that this is the stall where her child is to go. "How can this be? This is not what I thought," she says as she awakens confused. The entire school contains stalls of elephants. Each new child is to be assigned to a stall with a baby elephant. The woman feels that the dream might be a warning; why would her daughter be placed in a separate stall with an elephant? "The purpose of school," she thought, "is for children to learn by being with other children."

As we explored her dream over a cup of tea, her doubts were eased. The elephant is a huge animal with a big nose and big feet. He is not dainty and does not fit in. He will not overpower the little girl in an attempt to socialize her. He will simply be there for her—as a playmate. He is a friendly fellow with funny wrinkled skin and huge flapping ears. His legs are like tree trunks and his crinkly eyes don't see well. At the same time, elephants are renowned for stepping delicately; he will be careful not to tread on her. He can be jolly and playful. From his big body, he swings his long tube about, showing her the magic patterns of the world. This extended nose smells, examines, caresses, fondles, explores. The elephant will get to know the child's body through its trunk. The child will feel known and come to know herself.

This mother knows that however she might wish to, she cannot stay with her child in the strange new place. The dream of elephants reassures her that her daughter will be protected in a wonderful way. The important thing is that she will find the connection to herself, for she will have a live elephant that is always with her. He is large and stable, not easily pushed around. If she starts out with her elephant in the morning, she will wind up with him at night.

Wouldn't the world be a better place if we all could begin school by being assigned to a stall, our "home room," with our very own baby elephant? "Neil, you are assigned to room 102 and the elephant named Jake." It is not likely that Jake will disappear or be changed considerably, and if he does wander off it is unlikely that he won't be found. Here is my "Prayer to the Elephant":

> Stay–
> keep watch over this child
> hold up the world a little longer
> until she grows a trunk of her own.

The child trades in her mother for an elephant. The little girl goes to elephant school and learns the animal's way. They will grow up together, which means that her emotional life and her rational thinking will develop side by side. The animal will not be left behind. With his long winding trunk he will pick her up and carry her to class. Dignified and gentle, the elephant consoles the mother for the loss of her child. I imagine him placing his trunk on the mother's head to set her mind at rest. His presence also encourages the mother to look for her own elephant, to find her own unique way.

There is an ancient Hindu story about an elephant and a mother's son. In this story the elephant does more than support a child; he brings a child back to life. In return, the child adopts an elephant head and the mother rejoices. The elephant child's name was Ganesh. Of course he grew up to become a man with an elephant's head.

Ganesh had been conceived by his mother, Parvati, and his father, Shiva. Parvati, in order to draw Shiva out of his cosmic dance and into the world, gave birth to a child by herself. Shiva assumed she had been impregnated by another god and in his fury cut the child's head off. When Parvati explained to him what had happened, Shiva became remorseful and wanted to bring the child back to life. Parvati told him that in order to accomplish this, he would have to go into the forest and seize the first animal he could. Then he was to replace the human head with the animal head. Thus Ganesh came into being.

Ganesh grew up but remains always the Divine Child, playful, joyful, liking children's things. He loves candy and if you feed him sweets and keep him happy, then he will take care of you. There is the trickster in him, always playing pranks, trying new ways, comparable to our Western Hermes or Mercurius. Ganesh has a big belly that you can rub if you want to wish for wealth and prosperity. Most importantly, he can clear your path of obstacles. He does this by using his powerful trunk.

The Indian gods each have an animal they ride. Vishnu has an eagle, which is called Garuda; Shiva rides a bull called Nanda; Ganesh is the elephant who dances on the back of a mouse. There is a mystery to the huge earth-bound animal who with his great bulk dances on the back of a mouse. Do you notice, too, that many overweight people are light on their feet, as if defying gravity? Inside them there is an elephant who dances on a mouse. It is true. This is a mysterious truth about the biggest of big and the littlest of little.

A friend told me that while on safari in Africa he heard some rumbling just outside his tent in the middle of the night. He opened the flap and stared into a huge something inches away. He finally realized it was the knee of an elephant. It was munching on some grass practically right on top of the tent, and my friend was worried that the elephant might inadvertently step on them. They were afraid to leave the tent because, close by in a stream, there was a herd of water buffalo, which could also be dangerous. He became so frightened that he shat in his pants. The next morning the natives, unimpressed by his story, reassured him that the elephant was a regular visitor to the camp. "He's young," they said, "and easily chased away. Don't worry!"

How can something so huge and obvious be, at the same time, mysterious? The elephant is a *mysterium tremendum,* a living mystery. It is so big that we see only a part of it and don't get the whole picture. We often seem satisfied knowing only a sliver of the truth. Is it because we are too frightened to live in a world where we understand so little? If my friend could have identified the elephant's knee as something congruent with his reality, perhaps the bark on a tree, he might have gone back to bed. But an elephant in his bedroom is bigger and stranger than he bargained for. Some people are fortunate to have a friend, a spouse, a therapist or as in the Indian fable, "The Blind Men and the Elephant," a Rajah who helps them face things as they are.

> Six blind men who had never seen an elephant go in search of it at the palace of the Rajah. They find the elephant in the courtyard. Each man examines the elephant to learn about it. The first man touches the elephant's smooth side and pronounces the elephant "a wall." The second man feels the elephant's round trunk and announces "snake." The third man handles the tusk and thinks "spear." The fourth man examines its leg and thinks "tree." The fifth man rubs the elephant's ear and is reminded of "a fan." The sixth man fondles its tail and determines "rope." Then they argue about the elephant's nature, but they can't agree so the Rajah intervened. "The elephant is a big animal. Each man touched only one part. You must put all the parts together to find out what an elephant is like." They concurred with the Rajah. "Each one of us knows only a part. To find out the whole truth we must put all the parts together."[91]

In his hugeness, the elephant embodies the dialectic of known and unknown. Its trunk is a long dangling thing with a hole at the end, like a swaying phallus. It stretches itself out straight and long and then winds itself back up into a ball. It inserts itself into holes. It explores the wonders of the universe. It fascinates the young boy who feeds it and wants to take care of it. When will the young boy acquire a lingam of his own? He could learn about the phallus and its various symbolic manifestations from reading folk tales. In some, like *Pinocchio*, the long nose was a punishment; in others, a divine gift.

Rudyard Kipling took one such tale and made it famous in "The Elephant's Child," which begins at a time before the elephant had a trunk:

> One day an elephant child, who was full of curiosity, wanted to know, "What does a crocodile have for dinner?"
>
> After being spanked by his parents for asking such a ridiculous question, Kolokolo Bird told him, "Go to the banks of the great, grey-green, greasy Limpopo River, all set about with fever-trees." After many adventures, Elephant's Child arrived at the river to ask crocodile himself. Crocodile, hungry for dinner and seeing easy prey, grasped Elephant Child's nose and tried to pull him into the river. Helped by snake, whom Elephant Child had met along the way, he was able to resist, but Elephant Child's nose, locked in the crocodile's teeth, began to stretch and elongate until finally the crocodile let go. Although freed, Elephant Child was unhappy with his ugly nose until snake pointed out all the useful things Elephant

---

[91] See Lillian Quigley, *The Blind Men and the Elephant.*

> Child could do with it. He is able to kill a fly that lands on his shoulder, he can pluck up grass and put it in his mouth. He can suck up water and shower himself to cool off, he can pick boughs off trees. In short, he has acquired an unusual tool.[92]

Rather than the long nose being a punishment for Elephant Child, as it was for Pinocchio, it was a gift—a tool to help him explore his curiosity. The nose, and its extended form, the trunk that can sniff out hidden sources of delight, symbolize intuition.

Heinrich Zimmer tells us that that the elephant's "majestic appearance, irresistible strength, and gentle and calm temper . . . its grandeur, and intelligence, were [considered] virtues."[93] Perhaps that is why the kings of India regaled them in their courtyards. Zimmer writes that, except for his wife and children, the king's most prized possession was the elephant, "the priceless magical instrument whose presence in the royal stable was the kingdom's sole guarantee of rain, fertility and crops and the wealth of life."[94]

Paintings of Hindu mythology depict the elephant supporting the world on its back. In India, the elephant is the carrying power upon which the whole human race rests. Being the largest land mammal, it embodies the magnanimity of life, the largeness of soul. There used to exist a "Save the Elephants" movement composed of people who were not only concerned for the safety of the actual elephant, but who felt that in losing the elephant, the world was in danger of losing its very soul.

A woman friend of mine commented, "People shouldn't live alone, they should live in groups, like elephants." Presumably that is why the elephant survived the Ice Age: they are social whereas the more solitary mammoth died out. The elephants' heartfelt relationships to one another seem quite human. Each member is important to the whole, so the entire herd will move for the sake of one individual. They even care for the individual after death. For days after the leader's death, the remaining mature males linger near the carcass and in ritual manner they pick up the leader's great tusks, gently fondling them. It has been assumed that one of the differences between humans and animals is that humans are conscious of death, yet seeing the living elephants stroke their dead leader, one wonders about their feeling for death.

The idea of the elephant living in both this world and the world beyond is symbolized in kundalini yoga. The image of an ordinary black elephant is de-

---

[92] *Just So Stories,* pp. 60ff. (modified).
[93] *The Art of Indian Asia,* p. 161.
[94] Ibid.

picted at the root chakra *(muladhara),* the instinctual base, and the image of a supernatural white elephant with three sets of tusks, originally endowed with wings and descended from clouds,[95] appears at the throat chakra *(visuddha),* that of intuition and imagination. The night before the Buddha's birth, his mother dreamed of a white elephant, and she knew that she would conceive a divine child. A plate shows the elephant penetrating Maya's side with his trunk.

> Maya, the queen . . .
> Dreamed a strange dream; dreamed that a star from heaven—
> Splendid, six-rayed, in colour rosy-pearl,
> Whereof the token was an Elephant
> Six-tusked, and white as milk of Kamadhuk—
> Shot through the void; and, shining into her,
> Entered her womb upon the right.[96]

These opposites, natural and supernatural, are evident in the elephant's physical characteristics: its massive body houses the senses of this world, while its waving trunk seems to function by the wonder of intuition.

The apparently contradictory spiritual and sexual aspects of the elephant are symbolized in the dream of a young woman. At puberty she was molested by her brother, and the threatening elephant in the dream combines all the emotions that were split off because of the trauma. Since she is not in touch with them, they have turned against her:

> I am with my current friend Greg in a town which feels European [where he comes from], in the middle of a wide old street near what feels like a fountain, or some piece of public art where street artists are selling their work (in a hub of communal life). I am showing Greg around. He is a tourist. Suddenly, to my right, at the end of the street, from around the corner comes a huge elephant. Greg is in the midst of an interaction to purchase something, a card or gift, so he doesn't see the elephant. I am instantly convinced the elephant is going to attack Greg and kill him. My feeling is that because Greg has thick, elephantlike skin, the real elephant will be angry at this usurper, will want him dead. I tell Greg to be careful, that the elephant is coming, watch out. I put myself in front of him. And sure enough the elephant, rounding the corner of all-time, plods down the street, swaying calmly like always, his heavy feet sending up dust from the cobblestones, right up to Greg. Greg doesn't seem afraid of the elephant despite my warnings. I see the elephant is angry. I am terrified. The beast extends his trunk and touches him gently, to sense

---

[95] Zimmer, *Myths and Symbols in Indian Art and Civilization,* p. 106.
[96] *Symbols of Transformation.* CW 5, par. 490, and plate xlix(b).

him, clearly with no interest in hurting him. I stand there in the presence of this huge beast, awed and glad to be wrong. I realize my fear was irrational, not real.

She explained that Greg is very different from her; he deals with life in a straightforward manner. He is not afraid. She told me that when she was thirteen years old, she went away for a camping weekend with her older brother, her brother's friend, with whom she was in love, and another girl to whom the brother was attracted. When the brother's friend became involved with the other girl, the brother in desperation and frustration turned his attentions to his sister. This devastated her. She lost not only the young man but also her brother, her one ally in a totally dysfunctional family. That incident became a negative turning point for her, cutting her off from her deep self. She ran away from home and began acting out sexually, burying her real emotions. Greg, then, represents that part of her that is connected to life. She explains:

> My fear is that I am too thick skinned, like Greg, like the elephant. I will be in danger of attack from the elephant. My fear is that I cannot carry this energy without being cut off from the true source, the real elephant. That to embody it means certain retaliation, death. My instinct will do me in: this goes back to the wounding with my brother. So I have been afraid my whole life. That it will turn on me. The way I was feeling then, at thirteen, with so much of my budding sexuality and instinctual energy bubbling up, to be so filled with feeling for my brother's friend, and to have it stolen by my brother—the usurper! That if I reconnect with this part of myself, the feelings of love, the psychic potency, the sexuality and instinct all combined in me, that it will be dangerous and cause certain retaliation by my own deep life, those very energies embodied in the elephant. My fear is that somehow it is too big, too ancient, too deep, to be synthesized into my psyche. The elephant walks instinct into intuition, trumpets intuition into instinct. The dream brings to me the dynamic of my fear, what keeps me from containing my life energies in the thick skin of this massive body of psychic energy, the fear that keeps me from grounding in that instinctual place.

After she told me the dream, she gave me a poem entitled "Elephant Rocks":

> Here and there,
> at the edges and marges,
> a bit of elephant surfaces—
> a dome and a dip, a haunch
> or an aspect of head—
> some worn-away soft and yet
> angular hump of the
> shambling elephant armature,

up through the earth—a bump
or a knob with the elephant signature.
The ancient, implacable creature
comes ambling back; a bulge
reemerges, that sober, that
giveaway gray. The dirt
rubs away from the treasure
too patient and deep to be lost,
however we've hurt, whatever
we've done to the beasts,
whatever we say.[97]

By giving me this poem, she was telling me that she can be healed. She is more conscious of her real fear in exposing her feelings. In fact, she is now in love with a man but is afraid to be intimate with him. She tells me, "If he stays in my house, he will see me for who I am. I don't know that I can let someone into my life now. I don't know how to do it. He will be in my kitchen, in my bed inside of me. How can I be myself with someone else present?"

I reminded her that, years ago, he did stay with her for a week and it went well. She started to cry and tremble. She responded, "But I wasn't in touch with my feelings then. I admired him, but I wasn't present in myself." She missed out on the socialization process of growing up. When her brother molested her at age thirteen, that was the last straw and she gave up. She still fears connecting to her emotional life as a young girl. However, she has done the hard part of therapy, she is connected. She is alive. That is the important thing.

D.H. Lawrence, in capturing the fullness of feeling that elephants display to one another, lays out what the little girl, by keeping her relationship to the elephant, might experience as she matures:

The elephant, the huge old beast,
  is slow to mate;
he finds a female, they show no haste
  they wait

for the sympathy in their vast shy hearts
  slowly, slowly to rouse
as they loiter along the river-beds
  and drink and browse

and dash in panic through the brake

[97] Kay Ryan, in *Elephant Rocks,* p. 84.

of forest with the herd,
and sleep in massive silence, and wake
together, without a word.

So slowly the great hot elephant hearts
grow full of desire,
and the great beasts mate in secret at last,
hiding their fire.

Oldest they are and the wisest of beasts
so they know at last
how to wait for the loneliest of feasts
for the full repast.

They do not snatch, they do not tear:
their massive blood
moves as the moon-tides, near, more near,
till they touch in flood.[98]

Lawrence's elephants seem to understand what their life holds for them, and they know how to take pleasure in it. They savor the richness of their sexuality. Lawrence compares the largeness of these beasts with the largeness of the life they enjoy; implying that their large bodies have large souls. The poem says to me that we humans haven't a clue about how to live; that we are always trying to make the reality of our life into something else.

These social animals with big hearts have many ways of staying in touch, both real and imaginary. In fact, they can communicate over long distances. When the females are in heat, their cries can be heard by the male over a distance of twenty miles; the males' trunks reach high in the air and pick up the female scent. This feature of elephants comes through in the dream of a mother who enrolled her daughter in a school with elephants. In the dream each elephant had a vibrating plate in its forehead which was used for communication. So even though the elephants were isolated in separate stalls, they could touch.

My intuition about this dream image is that the vibrating plates express the same notion as the third eye in some Eastern religions, a place of psychic openness. I don't know if elephants do, in fact, have vibrating plates in their foreheads, but their massive cousins the whales do. I learned from a woman who studied whales in the St. Lawrence Seaway that they have a "melon," a rounded mass of blubber found between the blowhole and the end of the nose. She said

---

98 "The Elephant Is Slow To Mate," in *The Complete Poems of D.H. Lawrence*, p. 465.

that the melon is used for communication, that whales can change the size and shape of the melon depending on the distance they want their signals to travel. This determination is based in part on the configuration of the body of water and the number of whales in the pod.

Whales and elephants do stay in touch with other members of their community. They take care of one another. The elephant, with its warm family bonds and concern for the world, imaginatively touched another woman's heart. She had fallen in love with a man, hoping the relationship would lead to marriage and family. He cared for her too, but since his first marriage failed he had been afraid of commitment. After two years, he finally told her that although he loved her and did not want to lose her, he did not want to marry again. She dreamed:

> We have an elephant that is really lonely. It is missing its family. We walk around the countryside, going from circus to circus, looking for other elephants but can't find any. The circuses and zoos are filled with tired, dirty looking animals.

The animal in the woman had been well attended to in her relationship with the man, but now it did not feel cared for. Her problem was that she didn't know how to attend to this inner animal on her own. She attended well to work, but she seemed incapable of nurturing herself. Although she liked her house, she never spent any time there; she seemed unable to just hang out and relax. She didn't garden or leave much time for reading. She would rarely fix a meal for herself, but she could do everything for her mate. That is why she invested so much energy in this relationship, too much. She said, "I wanted so desperately for this relationship to work that I thought if I were able to be perfect, then it would." Now that the relationship is over, she is learning how to take better care of her emotional life, and is also experiencing relief at not having to work so hard. She can reclaim her life. As her self-image improves, she realizes that a man can like her just for who she is; she doesn't have to perform.

Another uncared-for elephant turned up in a female student's dream. In the dream, the elephant had enormous shits and this woman was stuck with cleaning up the mess. What led to this shitty job was that at some earlier time she had joined a religious group led by a talented and charismatic man. Initially, this leader showed an interest in her and encouraged her to become a teacher, but when a new girl caught his eye, he dropped her. This became a pattern, instilling anger in the students who were discarded. When the woman confronted her teacher about the fact that he was carrying on seductive relationships with women and that there were power drives in the community that had nothing to do with spiritual practice, he denied it, blaming her instead. She dreamed:

> I'm in a house—some sense of just waking up or coming to awareness. This is a house I share with (unknown) others. In the living room there is a long neatly molded brown pile of shit, a mountain of shit four feet high by six feet wide. It stretches from one side of the room to the other. I'm puzzled. When I go outside I see that this pile starts again at the corresponding place on the exterior wall and stretches eighteen to twenty feet across the lawn. At the edge of the lawn there is an elephant with a man on it. The man had given us the elephant without telling us that she had been ill. If she had not shat within the week she would have been in danger. The man has not been honest with us and is a bit untrustworthy. I think how unnaturally worked the manure is. It is smooth and uniform in shape and what a big clean-up job there is ahead.

So the immense size of the elephant can be both awesome—in a reassuring and inspiring way—or overwhelmingly negative. Families of alcoholics refer to the "elephant in the room" that everyone pretends not to see, a metaphor for the problem that has become the family secret. The dream-elephant shit in the room of the living ("living room") is something dirty that is not being acknowledged. The shape of the excrement is unnatural, suggesting there has been an attempt to make it, by nature unpleasant, conform to a correct social persona or attitude The group leader cannot accept anything negative about himself.

Ordinarily we think of the immense dignity and majestic quality of the elephant, but it has a comic aspect too, with its huge derrière and enormous turds. Sometimes this comic aspect can turn dangerous, as in a story my son told me. He believes he read it somewhere, but he doesn't know whether it is actually true or not: A veterinarian was treating a zoo elephant for a blockage in its gut. If this week-long blockage were not cleared, the animal would die. When the vet reached in to loosen up the blockage, out came a volume of shit with such velocity that it knocked him against the wall. He hit his head on the wall and blacked out. Buried in animal shit, he suffocated. Here the comic aspect and the numinous immensity of the elephant come together in a horrible way.

All elephants are big, but we don't realize how big until we are confronted with the problem of moving them. This challenge arose for an overly responsible New England woman who dreamed she was returning home to take a teaching job in the local school. But there is a catch, says the postmistress:

> "If she wants this job she has to take the elephant." I have no idea what she's talking about—an elephant? in Wentworth? Everyone sees my look of surprise and they all start telling me at once that this elephant appeared in town one day and they can't seem to get rid of it. They don't know what to do. So it seems that if I can relieve them of this huge problem, they will give me the job.

The dream is attempting to help the woman be more conscious of just how big is the load she takes on as the dutiful daughter. Though the elephant can give us a majestic ride, it can also become an immense burden.

Sometimes all aspects of the elephant—the grand, the majestic, the sacred and profane—do come together, as they did in a marvelous beast who existed in our San Francisco office building. He was a psychiatrist and in many ways did not fit into a conventional mold, which I suppose is why everyone loved him. I always thought of him as another part of myself, my animal other, my elephant brother in San Francisco. Years ago, as psychiatrists, we each had offices on the first floor in a Victorian house. He occupied the back room while mine faced the street. A long narrow hall connected the two offices with a waiting room for patients in the middle. This house, which had survived the 1906 earthquake and fire, was built in the 1880s and 1890s. Made from wood, it creaked in the wind, rolled with earthquakes, and vibrated when people entered and left.

Promptly at 3:15 every afternoon, when he had finished with his last patient before his break, my friend would depart from his back office. Taking exactly six huge elephantine steps; he would arrive at the front door. (Wasn't there a game that we played as children when we took so many "elephant steps"?) When I thought of him, I always thought "elephant." Physically he was fleshy, roly-poly, and even though he took large steps he moved rather slowly. He was like a lumbering animal coming down the hall. Lord knows what would have happened if he had encountered a patient in the way because this large mass of body was unstoppable. Reaching the door he opened it and in one gigantic motion leaped down the four steps to the sidewalk.

In my mind's eye, I actually pictured him as an elephant with his trunk swinging from side to side, hitting the walls as he made his escape. From the walk it was only a step to his car, which was parked on the corner, across two crosswalks. The car was ticketed daily by meter maids who came to know him personally, and would leave him notes along with the tickets, such as: "Dear John, sorry to do this—can't you find a legal spot at least one day a week?"

He would drive to the elementary school to pick up his children, then deposit them at home and return to park his car in exactly the same spot, leaving the ticket on the windshield in hopes that a single ticket would satisfy his friendly ladies. Then he would charge through the gate and leap up the four steps with a crash. Even the windows rattled. Once through the door, he would push off against the walls, propelling his large body down the hall to the waiting room to greet his 3:30 patient. The elephant had returned.

My friend's thunderous roar down the hallway shattered my image of professional medical comportment. I was just starting my practice and worked right from the book. How could I let an elephant crash through all I had learned? We were supposed to be quiet and restrained. We were taught to let the patient's projections heap themselves upon us until we were no longer identifiable even to ourselves. This animal psychiatrist coming down the hall was giving himself permission to exist in his own way. He was tending to his own needs. He was the elephant of the six blind men, with all the different parts not fitting together, yet he was able to make them all work. His practice was the busiest in the city. You couldn't get an hour with him. Often, while traveling through the building, passing the doors of offices, he would hum this traditional folk song his grandfather taught him when he was a boy:

> I went to the animal fair.
> The birds and the beasts were there.
> The old baboon by the light of the moon
> was combing his auburn hair.
> The monkey he got drunk.
> He fell in the elephant's trunk.
> The elephant sneezed. He fell to his knees.
> And that was the end of the monk,
> the monk, the monk, the monk,
> the monk, the monk, the monk.

His lumbering action partook of the mysterious. It ordered my life and the lives of patients. Listening to this gallop from inside my office, its reverberating vibrations were inexplicably reassuring. Knowing that an animal so full of energy could meet life's expectations gave hope to my patients and to me. This elephant barreling down the hall broke through the timid queries, the endless fears, the unending doubt.

One regular patient of mine, quite used to all this, would time the ending of the telling of a dream to the elephant's return. Then we would settle down in the quiet to investigate and explore. The dream and its meaning were forever intersected by the elephant. Sometimes the explosion of energy at the beginning of the romp would help her recollect a dream. When she had to change the time of her hour to one with no elephant, she never again reported a dream.

For three years we enjoyed elephant life together until this man moved to another state. Neither my patients nor I could adjust, so we, too, had to move to another house with a different set of "goings on." But my elephant friend and I have become closer over the years, and now we exchange letters and read each other's writings. When I think back to those early years, I miss the mid-afternoon explosions that would enliven the post-lunch slump.

The irrational had lumbered in. It taught me that life is bigger and more various than I had thought. There were people who operated in the world differently from the way I had been taught. My Freudian supervisors pounded into my head a technique to be followed in the doctor-patient relationship. The only correct interventions were either in response to resistances by the patient or as interpretations whispered from above. Now I didn't feel I had to know all the answers. I could let the animal in. It was mysterious. Where did dreams come from? They were unpredictable yet deeply relevant. Something bigger than me was running this show. There was at bottom an elephant, something marvelous but preposterous. It does seem as if it were created with an absurd sense of design. No psychiatrist's building would ever have allowed one of its occupants to shake both its foundation and the solemnity of the analytic hour to this degree. It couldn't happen. But sometimes the irrational does lumber in, and it can't be ignored. It's the big life. It's a big deal.

There is another powerful animal that intuitively finds its way, not with a trunk but with antlers that reach upward toward the heavens. That animal is the elk, along with its more delicate cousin, the deer.

Deer and Elk

We look through the eyes of the deer into the other world. When their big brown eyes look back at us, they beckon us to follow. Man to animal, animal to the mysterious; we touch the wonder of the universe.

The doe brings her twin spotted fawns into the backyard. Between nibblings of grass, she lifts her head and extends her long velvet tapered ears. Then she poises, on the point of taking off. She can leap great distances, her feet touching the ground only here and there. The doe comes and goes so quickly, so shyly, so elusively. I think that she is a visitor from another world. When I write, she appears; when I look for her, she is gone. She is as hard to catch as feelings that appear unannounced and disappear abruptly, stirrings of the heart, recollections of things past. When she leaves, I feel suddenly empty, as if something has been taken from me and, for a moment, I panic for the loss of that gentle soul and that ability almost to fly.

Fairy tales depict the deer changing into a goddess and then back into a deer. In one story, a man follows a deer to shoot it, then it transforms into a goddess.

Woman and animal change back and forth, as in a divine wedding. They share the same soul.

So it is for a middle-aged poet, who sought therapy to dissolve his writing block. His heart opens first to a goddess, then to a deer. He dreams:

> I come to a tent in which a goddess is living. It's a desert tent, small but upright and square. The flap is open and held up on stakes, as an entrance. A man enters the tent, goes to the back, and starts making love to the goddess. A woman at the entrance explains what's taking place. She says the man is really making love to a doe. Excited, I look in and see that the goddess has fallen below the man's embrace so that he's lying on a dais with her image instead of her. There are silken sheets and sumptuous bedding that resemble a dazzling cloudscape. Then I see the deer, numinous and magnificently beautiful, lying on the ground. She seems slain, or helplessly pregnant. But she's alive and quivering in anticipation of love.

The dreamer is a large, shy, introverted man with a lot of feeling; he needs loving, needs to be accepted for himself. In his loneliness he approaches the tent of the nature goddess Artemis. Passing through the door, he experiences his heart opening, the way a curtain opens or a pupil of the eye dilates. It is a physical thing, this opening of the heart. As his fear drops away, he finds himself in the arms of a goddess. But she is a goddess, he is a man. She is an archetype, he lives in the real world. So she gives him a doe, her living embodiment, the real feeling that would bring him warmth and comfort so he could accept himself.

The dream helped this man to feel more related, first to himself and then to other people. After it, he began to care about himself. He moved from an isolated house in the mountains to a nearby community. The same week, he contacted a woman he had known for a long time, and they began a relationship. Now they live together. He had never enjoyed a sustained relationship before.

Jungian analyst Linda Leonard links the symbolic meaning of the reindeer, a messenger of transformation, to the human heart and compassion. She tells us that in many cultures, when people find the way to the deer's heart, their own heart is opened. "In the Sami creation story, the shamans help the people find the way to the reindeer doe's heart, buried deep in the center of the earth. There, by the doe's heart, the people discover all of creation's gifts and treasure."[99]

In the man's deer dream, this innate spirit present in animals and man is made visible by a numinous light surrounding the deer, and is known as the *light of nature.*[100] It is pagan. A figure who embodied this earthy spirit was the Greek

---

[99] *Creation's Heartbeat: Following the Reindeer Spirit,* p. 46.

[100] See "Paracelsus As A Spiritual Phenomenon," *Alchemical Studies,* CW 13, par. 148.

singer and prophet Orpheus. His lyre tamed the animals, quieted the souls of men and even appeased the gods so much so that they allowed him to try to bring back his beloved Eurydice from the dead. Through song, Orpheus gave voice to the spirit of nature.

Analyst Linda Fierz-David interprets the Orphic rite pictured in the Villa of Mysrteries:

> Orpheus taught while he sang and played the lyre, and his singing was so powerful that it mastered all nature; when he sang to his lyre the birds flew about him, the fish left the water and sprang to him. The wind and the sea became still, the rivers flowed upward . . . . It did not snow and there was no hail. Trees and the very stones followed after Orpheus; tiger and lion lay down near him next to the sheep, and the wolves next to the stag and the doe. Now what does this mean? It surely means that through a divine insight into the meaning of natural events . . . nature's happenings become harmoniously ordered from within. Everything becomes light and all creatures are appeased when the mediator, in the act of worshipping, represents the light of nature. Orpheus is an embodiment of devotion and piety; he symbolizes the religious attitude that solves all conflicts, since thereby the whole soul is turned toward that which lies on the other side of conflict. . . . And as he does this, he is truly Orpheus; that is a good shepherd, his primitive embodiment.[101]

Alone in the deep forest, one can sometimes experience the secret magic of Orpheus. By day, the music of Orpheus rustles through pine and grass to the accompaniment of animal movement. Dragonflies, butterflies, darting insects, make patterns in the air. Little unseen birds, bushtits, wrentits, hop inside a bush. Busy ants crisscross under foot. Woodpeckers hammer away, crows caw, jays yak, song birds sing their melodies. Overhead, noisy squirrels jump from branch to tree. Color delights; the orange of sticky monkey, blue of iris and lupine, light purple of thistle, dark purple of huckleberry and coffeeberry clustered under dark green foliage, red of poison oak.

When I go alone at night on a forest path, there is a stillness, a hush and inner quiet. Nothing moves, yet all is alive. Animal eyes peer out. Trees communicate; rustling, murmuring. They tell you what secrets the little underground animals have picked up, what crows and jays have screamed by day. They tell you about the little things, the unimportant things, the things life is made of.

Sometimes I think of my nightly walk as a moment to relax, to reflect. But it isn't exactly relaxation that I feel. My skin becomes sensitive. My ears perk up,

---

[101] Quoted by Henderson, "Ancient Myths and Modern Man," in Jung, ed., *Man and His Symbols,* p. 145.

the hair on the back of my neck stands up. Even though nothing moves, the whole forest is alive. It demands an emotional response.

Then I go deeper into the night forest and feel simultaneously drawn and at risk. It's just for a few more minutes, I tell myself. Why does it have to be a challenge? Why can't I walk as if it is day? There is no hurry, I am not sleepy. There is even a little moon. I won't get lost. What is the fear? All the living elements, pine needles on the path, hanging moss, overhanging trees, soften sound, absorb sound. It is dead quiet. Suddenly a large animal explodes out of a thicket. It leaps as though endowed with a spirit to carry it whither? Its quickness and agility take my breath away. The quiet is shattered. The deer and I have surprised one another. As the deer bounds upward into the night sky, I follow. I understand and I am no longer afraid.

A deer like this appeared unexpectedly in a woman's dream and changed her life. She had earned a Ph.D. in science at a prestigious university. When she married and had a child, she lost interest in pursuing a career, but nevertheless felt guilty when colleagues offered her plum jobs. Much to her surprise she became pregnant with her second child and three months later she had this dream.

> I am asleep with a baby, my son, and also my two sisters as babies. I awake, feeling something crawling on me. It is ants. They are on my son too. We brush them off. I fear that they've gotten into my ears.
>
> I call to my husband to help us. We are in a backyard of some kind. He does not respond. He's not next to us as he should be. I get up and look around.
>
> I find him seated with two of my old high school friends and rivals, participating in some vegetation/nature ritual. They are seated to the front and back of him, wearing masks made of leaves and lettuce. He is seated in front of a deer head or antlers, decked out in furs and leaves.
>
> I am furious that he should be with them, helping them with their ritual, and not being with me where he belongs. I'm jealous too. He looks sheepish as he realizes I've discovered him.
>
> I awoke from this dream feeling bad, vulnerable. The house felt strange, full of odd shapes and noises.

The dream moves from mother with babies to a mysterious initiation rite involving a deer head or antlers. The woman's husband is the initiator in this ritual, perhaps a shaman. The initiates are wearing vegetation masks. What could it all mean?

In telling this fertility dream, the woman suddenly began to sob uncontrollably. She was shocked by the fact that she was jealous of her husband for participating in the vegetation/nature ritual.

> It's an older-than-patriarchs, natural-rhythm-of-life ritual that he's entered into here, and I am furious to be left out. Maybe my husband could be my guide into maturity if I weren't so busy being jealous and indignant.

Her dream begins with ants. They are hard workers. They are industrious. They construct things. They are busy, busy, busy. The woman is busy also, with her child and with the myriad tasks that life demands. Because she and her mother were so different, the mother handling things of this world, the daughter intuiting the patterns of the universe, the daughter never felt affirmed by her mother. In the dream, the ants represent her irritation at being run ragged by work while her husband is away from home successfully enjoying his career. If she and her mother had been closer, she would have been able to enlist the help of the ants, who have the ability to sort things out.[102]

This woman needs a ritual so the value of mothering doesn't get lost. She is not being nourished by the mystery underlying birth. She needs to replace the compulsive negative aspects of the ants' work with the spirit of an animal, which would give blood, warmth and vitality to her day. Also, she needs to find a creative outlet that would take her out on her own in the world.

Pagan rituals complete with stag horns are still performed. The rite of spring was celebrated by people gathered together at Point Reyes National Seashore. The local paper headlined the story, "Too Many Pagans, Park Service Says."[103]

> Stag horns on an altar. Women dancing topless with flowered wreaths in their hair. Men planting a Maypole.
>
> It was all a bit much for the Park Service, who issued a $100 citation to the priestess of a pagan group celebrating at Limantour Beach last week.
>
> Apparently, there were too many pagans gathered in the park—more than the 25-person limit—without a special-use permit.
>
> But after interrupting the ritual and urging the women to cover their breasts, rangers allowed the group of about 70 to continue their Beltane celebration, a wiccan ritual symbolizing the fertility of the earth and the union of the sexes.

The deer dreamer had left such lusty passions behind in her quest for knowledge. She did make a stab at entering this world when she began a doomed affair with her married instructor, but feeling shamed and awkward she went back to her studies more committed than ever. What made her story complicated was the fact that her interest in academic studies was not fundamentally genuine. She had inherited an ambivalent attitude toward achievement from her mother who

---

[102] See Erich Neumann, *Psyche and Eros.*

[103] Stephen Barrett, *Point Reyes Light,* May 14, 1998, pp. 1, 3.

held the opinion that, while that it was dangerous and wicked to be an ambitious woman, if you didn't get out there and "make it," you live with a sense of failure and jealousy. The two women rivals in the dream, who in fact were ruthlessly competitive back in high school, capture her husband's attention.

She comments on the dream.

> This is who I am. I am A's wife. I am my child's mom. I struggle with household chores, I enjoy my warm women friends, I take naps. This is me. I'm giving up trying to be something I'm not trying to justify myself. I might try to strive but it will be something out of who I am and not something I'm striving for that's not me. It's simple, who I am is right in this moment. I don't need to go out and accomplish things in the world as my husband has done. It's not an extroverted thing that needs doing but an introverted one. I need to take my authority into hand. I am so often presenting myself too apologetically, too weakly, in a subordinated way, and then feeling frustrated and furious when I am treated as weak and subordinate. I need to not be afraid of my own power.

There is a strength that comes from being connected to the source of life, to the mystery of growing things. The woman's mother, who had lost touch with this feminine knowledge, allowed her authority to be carried by the woman's father. But now the woman, initiated by a fertility rite that includes reverence to deer horns, is getting in touch with her own authority as a woman. The deer's yearly new horns are the headdress honoring the regenerative powers of nature. With these horns the deer can stake its territory and claim its space. These sprouting horns could empower the woman and transform her negative jealousy into a confident attitude.

Emma Jung and Marie-Louise von Franz write about the symbolic meaning of the stag as a God or Self image:

> [The stag] knows the secret of self-renewal, for . . . when, from time to time, it is feeling old it swallows a snake and from the venom of its bite loses its antlers and grows itself a new pair. Thus, . . . we also should put off the 'horns of pride' and renew ourselves. . . . He [the stag] is a god of vegetation and of death, of the communal meal and the intoxicating drink through which communication with the other world is established.[104]

The animal endowed with its ever regrowing antlers would be the animal of animals to heal the wound transferred by her disconnected mother. In the past, because the woman was not in touch with her own deepest longings and frustrations, she could not express herself in a way that was understood; therefore, she

---

[104] *The Grail Legend,* p. 258.

became stubborn and rebellious. The antlers, designed for attacking and defending, would represent an expression of assertiveness that is not split off from nature. The ever-renewing antlers suggest that her directed interests do not have to become fixed, but can change according to her need. The antlers symbolize a spiritual attitude and, in mythology, "point the way as a guide."[105] Overall, the stag represents "an urge toward individuation."[106] Further:

> According to many local Germanic legends the stag was supposed to have caused springs to flow, or to have pointed out healing springs to men. More often it shows the hunter the way to his beloved, with whom it is secretly identical.[107]

The antlers, combining the feminine curve of the horns with the masculine spike, impart to the woman both a sense of relatedness and the natural ability to seek what she wants.

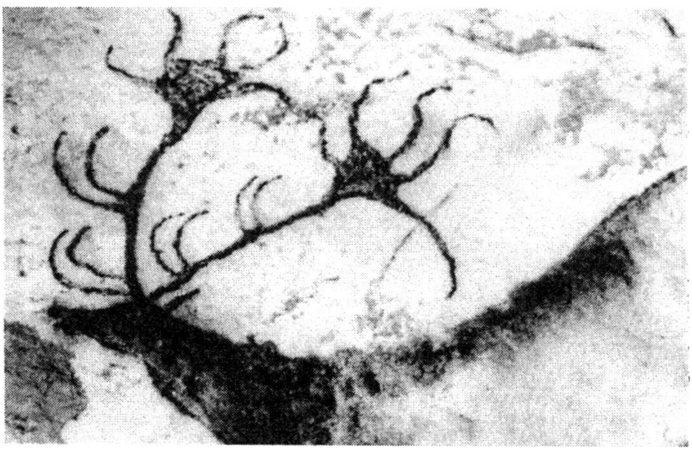

Figure 17

This beautiful stag (Figure 17) is from the Paleolithic cave of Lascaux.[108] The animal's power is visible in its extraordinary antlers. The upper ones, appearing much longer than they could possibly be, reach out like the points of a star, like fingers reaching to the sky. There is something numinous about this stag. It draws our gaze, as it drew the gaze of the artist who painted it eons ago.

---

[105] Ibid., p. 260.

[106] Ibid.

[107] Ibid., p. 259.

[108] From Joseph Campbell, *The Way of the Animal Powers,* plate 96, p. 63.

Our own familiar stag is the European red deer or North American wapiti, commonly called elk. It belongs to the large, ruminant family of Cervidae, including deer, elk and moose, and which are distinguished by their solid, deciduous antlers.[109] Appendages of the skull, antlers are composed of a solid bony core and serve as sexual ornaments and weapons. Attaining their maximum size at summer's end, they fall off following the mating season, and grow back.[110] Through this remarkable feature of the body, the stag comes to symbolize the cycle of death and renewal.[111]

Common to all deer are the antlers, the powerful racks that fight and claim turf, that can break through worlds and open up a life. With its yearly growth of antlers, the stag heals our wounds and opens up our heart. It did so for a patient of mine whose heart was broken twice over, first when his biological mother gave him up for adoption, and later in his teens when his aunt, a young woman in her thirties, suddenly died. His story is the story of the elk.

The man was adopted. He was pulled away from a clan, a people who for generations had made their home by the sea, who with strength and guile had risked their lives and wrought their living from the cold of the North Atlantic ocean. Some of the family members could neither read nor write, but they knew how to read the water to tell where the fish lived, and how to cut the ice from their boat so it wouldn't sink in winter storms. These were a hardy people; they lived by their instincts. The man was touched by this rough and primitive life as a young baby when he lived with his mother before she gave him up.

He kept the smell of it in his blood, yet because he was yanked out of this rigorous environment at so early an age, he could not claim this vitality in his new home. He was like a wild animal inside, stuck down in strange walled surroundings. Yet he was not connected to the wild part of his nature; he kept it in chains because he was frightened and did not understand how he was supposed to live. He learned to rely on vigilance, closely observing people.

Being perceptive and intelligent, he did well, but his endeavors were not from his heart, so the success he readily achieved was a false one. It didn't satisfy; he was restless. He yearned for something but didn't know what. He had affairs with women, seeking emotional connection; he piled up large business successes with prestigious cultural benefits, but he came up empty. "Something is missing," he would say.

---

[109] Ronald M. Nowak, *Walker's Mammals of the World,* vol. 2, p. 1209.

[110] Ibid., p. 1198.

[111] See Emma Jung and von Franz, *The Grail Legend,* p. 258.

I often found it hard to sit with him. Even though we would hit on the right meaning in the moment, it all seemed to disappear into a void. What was missing was the human element, that emotional ingredient that allows us to take something in, respond and emit. Even after the most moving hour with him, I would experience a cold draft leaving the room, the cold draft the patient must have felt when he was abandoned by his mother. There was no living animal in that man. I had never experienced anything like it, even in psychotic patients.

After years of suffering with his pain of not feeling connected, a remarkable thing happened. He had a dream of an elk. It spoke to every cord in his body. He took in every detail like a starving man, like a man who for the first time in his life had seen something that he had to have. The elk became the most important image he had ever seen. Everything he said about the elk was what he needed to experience in himself. He needed to be this powerful elk: then he could be real, he could have his life.

His encounter with this dream elk began when he applied for a passport renewal. After several weeks, he unexpectedly received a phone call from the Federal Bureau of Investigation ordering him to appear immediately in their office. When he asked why, the agent wouldn't say. When he asked if he could call his lawyer, the answer was, "Yes—but if you are not here in sixty minutes, we'll issue a warrant for your arrest."

When my patient arrived, the agent asked him, "Who are you?" "What do you mean who am I?" my patient responded. "We mean just that, what is your real name? Where were you born? Where did you go to school? Who is your mother?" Profoundly flustered, my patient repeated his name and told them, "I know I was adopted. What is the problem?" "You have a fake birth certificate. There was no such person born by this name, on this date, at this hospital or anywhere in this state. If your mother is alive, we suggest you have this straightened out." My patient countered, "My adoptive mother is dead. I never asked her about this."

Further investigation turned up legitimate adoption papers, revealing that he was born in Canada and had a Canadian birth certificate under a different name. He was cared for by his birth mother for a few months before being turned over to an orphanage for adoption. Within two months he was adopted by parents in the United States. Those babies in the orphanage for whom parents could not be found by the time they reached the age of one year and older, were killed and buried in the back yard in butter boxes. Years later when this horrific scandal was discovered, over a hundred babies were unearthed, known as the "butter box babies." The year of the patient's birth was 1949.

How he was brought across the border without citizenship papers remained unknown. After the border crossing, the boy's adoptive father called the governor of the state, a friend, to help him obtain a United States birth certificate. A counterfeit birth certificate giving the boy a new name, with a fictitious time and date of birth from a local hospital, was issued with an official state seal.

The Immigration and Naturalization Service, I.N.S., working with the F.B.I. on this case, gathered the information and arranged for a federal court date. The judge, satisfied that the facts were authentic, swore in my patient as a naturalized citizen. The judge then asked him if he would like to ask any questions. The patient had the presence of mind to ask to see all the papers, which revealed the names and locations of his biological parents.

Traveling north into the country of his birth to a remote Canadian island in the Atlantic ocean, he discovered three families that had intermarried for several generations. When he located his birth mother, she was in a state of disbelief and asked him to bare his arm where the tell-tale birth mark identified him. The members of the family, all of whom looked exactly like him, welcomed him. Then he began the painful process of trying to discover what had happened between his fifteen-year-old mother and his eighteen-year-old father, who had parted just after he was conceived. Apparently they had quarreled, but the reason was kept secret.

He did learn from his aunt, his mother's older sister, that she had had a child at the same time as his mother, and had offered to take him and explain to people that she had twins, but the mother declined. Fate intervened: the day after his aunt gave birth, typhus struck the aunt's household which then had to be quarantined for two weeks. The aunt believes to this day that if during that crucial period of bonding after birth, she had not been housebound and had been able to be with her sister and the baby, she could have convinced her sister to let her keep the child.

Now, my patient has a more open relationship with this aunt than with his mother who remains quietly angry and withholding. His aunt sends him a birthday card each year, but not his mother. Once when he called to thank his aunt for the card, his mother was in the room and his aunt asked him if he would like to speak with his mother. His mother said to him, "I'm sorry I didn't send you a card." He responded politely but in recounting the conversation to me, he conveyed his anger. "Why do I need to hear that my mother won't recognize my birthday? I feel after talking with her like I don't exist. Why wasn't she interested in where I went or what I was doing? I feel like a stranger."

Soon after the court hearing and the renewal of his U.S. passport, he applied for and received his Canadian passport. Now he has two passports from two different countries, with two different names. "Which one is me?" he asked. Not only did he have a fake passport, he felt like he had a fake life. He said, "I see in other people what I don't have. It's an 'I am' identity. They know who they are. I want to be like everybody else. I have a life, but I created it; it's artificial. When my mother gave me away, I couldn't bring that life with me. Something was interrupted. What got cut off is what I see in other people. It's like in surgery, when you cut a large vein you tie it off. The blood in that vein is not going anywhere. That's me. A friend asks me, 'Why can't you just be yourself?' I can't be. I can't relax."

As he continued to explore his identity, his biological father developed cancer and soon died. It wasn't until the patient's name was included in the obituary acknowledging him as the oldest son, that he really felt himself to be a member of this original family. He was deeply moved and felt for the first time in his life that he really belonged. Then he dreamed.

> I'm in the front living room of the apartment of my teen-age years looking across the street at another house. At first there appears to be an auction but later I realize that there is a funeral for someone.
>
> The crowd's attention turns to me and newspeople are peering through the window trying to take my picture or do an interview. I walk to the back of the apartment to the bathroom. On the counter is a picture of my Aunt Sara [his adoptive mother's sister] but she is alive. I look toward the door and a full-sized elk walks by. I look into the mirror and see a sick old man with sunken eyes. This scares me. I look for the elk again and when I look back into the mirror, the image is me.

The dream begins with death. The patient was auctioned off. That was his first experience of death. Then his adoptive father, a feeling-type man, the parent who wanted a child and initiated the adoption process, to whom the boy was closely attached, died of facial cancer when the boy was four years old. He remembers a man with facial bandages. Observing the face of his father slowly disintegrate must have frightened the little boy. He had frequent dreams of having killed someone and feels a murderer's guilt. Then there was the death of his grandfather at age nine, and most significantly the death of his Aunt Sara at age sixteen. She was the younger adopted sister of his mother, a sexy and emotionally expressive woman who loved my patient and to whom he experienced erotic ties. When she died, he lost hope. From that time on, he became self-destructive.

Seeing his Aunt Sara alive in the dream filled him with ecstasy. But he was even more awed to see a full-sized elk walk by. With reverie, he described the elk as "statuesque, powerful, wild, beautiful, perfect. Its nose was black and its tall antlers went all the way back up. The forelegs were powerful and well shaped. The elk's fur was gray and brown, each hair lying down as it was supposed to, presenting a shiny coat. The chest was powerful and there was a grace in the way it walked." Like the other deer animals, the power of the elk with its tall antlers is linked to the heart of this Aunt Sara and the renewal of feeling.

The sick man in the mirror was a composite image of both his adoptive father, whom he loved, and his biological father. The dream's replacement of the sick father figures with his own image helped him let go of his identification with death. Now he could feel alive. The elk is a creature that can shed a powerful part of itself, and then renew itself—just as he himself felt renewed after the dream. When he saw his own face in the mirror replace the face of his father, he exclaimed, "I don't have to be my father anymore. I could be me. I knew it wouldn't happen again. It wouldn't change back. Something happened. It's a milestone. The fear is ugliness. Now it's over with death, old age and cancer."

Then he talked more about the animals. He said, "The animal is healthy. I don't think a lot of people have seen unhealthy animals. Paleolithic man drew these big powerful images on walls of caves. That's how they showed power. They didn't draw mice. They didn't draw these animals because they were afraid of them. They drew them because it was nature, because it was power."

"Why the elk?" I asked him.

"It is the animal that for me represents Canada," he said. "That's where I was born. That's who I am."

The elk is the strong yet agile animal of the land that befits this strong coordinated man. Its antlers point toward the heavens which guide the elk and can restore the man's spirit. This adopted man had the strength he needed to power his way through life, but he wasn't connected to the stars. He didn't know where he was born or who he was. Identified now with the elk, his heart, body and spirit are of one intent. He has dignity and his strength serves a purpose.

From the graceful deer and elk, we move to another powerful animal with horns, not with many points that reach upward, but with tusks that bore straight ahead. We move from an aesthetically beautiful animal, one whose strength is connected with spirit, to an ugly animal whose power is seemingly devoted to itself. Instead of bounding over earth with bugle calls, we are grounded in earth grunting.

Boar

When I was struggling at a particular juncture with this book I had a dream that I was looking at myself in the mirror. Instead of being self-conscious about my large nose, I noticed two symmetrical rounded protrusions on either side of the median line of my upper lip. In the dream I thought they were too large to go unnoticed and I couldn't quite understand why they were there. I had never noticed them before. "How will I explain these?" I thought. Upon awakening, I realized that the dream bumps were in exactly the same place as tusks would be on a boar. "Tusks," I thought, "yes, tusks. That's exactly what I need." As with any challenging task, one needs strength to achieve completion.

The boar is known for its strength. The boar is also ugly. It is short, stubby, squat, whiskered. Its powerful but unappealing neckless body stands on funny little legs that can run like the devil and ends in a pig head complete with snout and little eyes. With its sawed-off nose, the boar is opposite from the elephant with its long searching trunk. Yet, even an animal of great dignity like the elephant can become boarlike when it goes into "must." The boar's strength and ferocity made it one of the favored beasts of the hunt. Its ugliness is linked, mysteriously, to its strength.

This connection is found in myths and fairy tales. Gnomes, earth spirits who live under the earth, are dwarflike and physically deformed, often hunchbacked. They are powerful little creatures who guard secret treasures. One such figure in the Grimm Brothers' collection is Rumpelstiltskin, a hunchback who by spinning straw into gold saves a miller's daughter, but in return demands her child.

Hephaestus was a deformed Greek god with lame legs, twisted feet and dislocated hip. His mother, Hera, ashamed of him, cast him out of heaven into the netherworld where he became a blacksmith and fashioned everything in the Greek pantheon from Zeus' golden throne to the armor of Achilles. Like a boar, he had a powerful torso.

Perhaps the most malevolent figure in English literature is Shakespeare's hunchbacked King Richard III who, realizing that he cannot succeed because of his physical deformity, turns villain. His shield is engraved with the animal image of the boar. Another literary figure, this one benevolent, is Victor Hugo's Hunchback of Notre Dame. He lived in the underground sewers of Paris and came to represent the harshness and brutality suffered under Louis XI.

If it's true that ugly people are strong, how did they become so? Not reflected by the warm smile of society, they have had to struggle on their own and are the tougher for it. They are not dependent on other people for approval and validation, but rather, being self-reliant, are free to discover and explore their innate abilities. Like gnomes, they have acquired self-knowledge. The Greek word *gnome,* meaning "moral aphorism" or "proverb," might well apply to these resolute folk. There are many examples of self-taught people considered homely who have contributed something original to our culture. Henry David Thoreau took to the woods to present his individual viewpoint. Abraham Lincoln, perhaps America's strongest, most independent-minded president, kept our nation together. They combined ugliness with strength.

Fierceness and tenacity have always been highly valued. From the beginning of time, humans tested their strength against the strength of the animal. Visual records of the hunting of the boar date back to 30,000 B.C. The boar is among those animals painted on the wall of the Palaeolithic Altamira cave in Spain. Scholars assume that boys were made to crawl through the narrow passageways into the caves as part of their initiation rites to become men and hunters. Inside, the cave paintings of animals of the hunt were illuminated by torchlight and must have been as magical to these young initiates as they are to us today. There, the shaman of the hunting tribe, revealing himself in magic flight, would have provided a needed image of transcendence to the new hunters.[112] For, as Joseph Campbell tells us, each hunter would have to face the mystery of death,

> both for the beasts killed in the hunt and for himself. And the answer found was "Nothing dies; death and birth are but a threshold crossing, back and forth, as it were, through a veil."[113]

Becoming a hunter meant transcending ordinary reality, and this empowered a man to act freely without fear

A later myth, which focuses on the tooth of the boar, is found in the planting culture of the Neolithic period, 6,000 B.C. to 2,500 B.C. This mythology extended into pre-Hellenic Greece and saw an elaborate development in the Malekula people of Melanesia. There the king, wearing a boar's mask with tusks, was symbolically sacrificed to the Great Mother in an annual ritual to ensure the growth of new crops honoring the lunar cycle of the goddess (Figure 18, next page). The boar's tooth was shaped like the crescent moon, curved to fit the shape of the breast of the woman. In this mythology man's initiation was not yet separate from the earth mother. "Life is merely being detached from the earth's womb; death is returning 'home.' "[114]

---

[113] *The Masks of God: Primitive Mythology,* p. 342.

[114] Mircea Eliade, *Patterns in Comparative Religion,* p. 253.

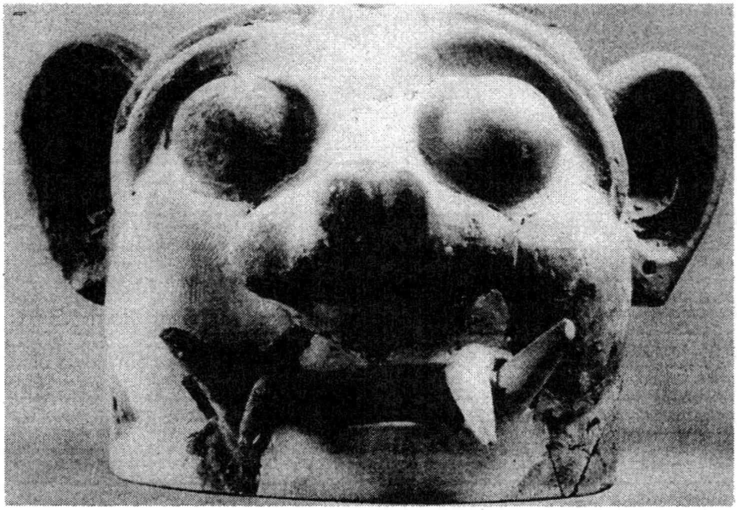

Figure 18
Terra cotta boar mask; Hellenic era, mainland Greece, ca. 700 B.C.

> Throughout Melanesia the tusked boar is the principal sacrifice in rites of the men's secret societies, and . . . associated with these is a lore of the mysteries of the afterward, to which the deceased gains entrance only by virtue of his spiritual identification with a ritually bred tusked boar—his "death pig"—which is sacrificed instead of himself to the guardian goddess of the fiery gate.[115]

The role the boar plays in a young boy separating from his mother is told by John Layard:

> The Malekulan boy's first ritual act, undertaken at the age of about five or six under the guidance of his father, is the sacrifice of a pet boar, at which time he gives up eating with his mother and joins the older boys in a special house for bachelors, where he is given more boars to rear and sacrifice. The effect of such repeated rites at this early stage of life is a conquest in the developing male child of his infantile dependency on the mother: the mother as a protecting, but also as a retaining, "devouring" mother, and himself as a mother-devouring child. The youngster's feelings of dependency and affection are transferred from the mother to the boars, which are male and yet also food, like the mother, as well as eaters of food, like the boy himself. And when the cherished pig is then sacrificed, the system of dependency that it stands for and supports is overcome and transcended, the "ghost"

---

[115] Joseph Campbell, *The Mythic Image,* p. 452.

> or "spirit" of the boar going into the sacrificer and he incorporating in himself the support formerly sought from without.[116]

Through the ritual slaying of the sacrificial animal, a man attains life after death. Henderson discusses the psychological meaning of these Malekulan "rites of vision." Developmentally, the young man's experience of the mystery of death and rebirth follows the earlier phase of separation from his mother. This initiatory rite of the "myth of emergence served to commemorate man's emergence from the unconscious state of at-oneness with nature."[117]

In our contemporary life, too, there are rites of passage. I met a tall, elegant man who was struggling desperately to give birth to something new within himself. He had been referred by a younger friend of his, also a patient, whom I had helped get launched in life. Before even meeting the new man I happily thought I could help him too. It would be a cinch. At the initial meeting, I found him very congenial. His young friend had been feisty, "in your face," leaving me little time to to reflect. The new man was more to my liking—cooler, more contemplative, and he had already achieved a level of success in his professional career. His difficulty lay in his relationship with women. After several years of marriage, his wife was leaving him, and the more I heard about this wife, the less I thought the problem resided in my patient. It would be clear sailing.

Things seemed to go well at first. He understood how his failure to express his feelings to his wife, the failure to stand up to her, had contributed to the failure of the marriage. He gave her nothing to grab onto, nothing to fight about. He withdrew, leaving her angry and frustrated. He was missing an intrinsic masculine strength. Several months into analysis he had this dream:

> I am in a boat and I meet my current girl friend and a trickster figure. My girl friend has a boar's tooth which she hides under her breast. Because the curve of the boar's tooth exactly fits the curve of the breast, only a woman can hide this. The trickster figure has a deck of cards which he can bring together and separate like an accordion. The cards have runic symbols on them, like those seen in the Tolkien books or similar to astrological signs.
>
> I steal both the boar's tooth and the deck of cards. When brought together, they have tremendous power, a power to move things around. The three of us go to an outdoor garden restaurant. The waiter there seems to be a sinister type of character and I feel uneasy about him. I also begin to feel guilty for having stolen the boar's tooth and the deck of cards, and I end up telling them that I stole these two things.

---

[116] *Stone Men of Malekula,* pp. 255ff. and *passim.*

[117] *Thresholds of Initiation.* p. 147.

> They respond by telling me that I have a better use for them than they do and that I should keep them. It turns out that the waiter is a great person and we become friends. With this new power that I have attained from the boar's tooth and the deck of cards, I am able to help the waiter with his training. This involves weight lifting and other strengthening exercises.
>
> Then another sinister figure comes in and slashes my friend with a knife, opening him up.
>
> Then I am walking down by a different restaurant and I see a building under construction that, strange as it seems, is in the process of constructing itself. But I see through the cornice that the evil person is doing the work. No one else can see him. Using the power that I now possess, I realize that I can see through buildings as well as track the evil person. But I also realize that I cannot completely contain this power, and some of it leaks out. The evil person was equally able to track this leakage and discover my friend. I feel bad that by not containing this leakage, I put my friend in jeopardy.

As a boy of twelve, this man had been given a boar's tooth by a Portuguese hunter who had killed the animal. The hunter befriended the boy, gave him a whole jawbone of another boar, but it was the tooth the boy kept all these years as a reminder, as a link to the time when he too could be initiated into manhood. This will to live, this tooth, the tooth of the boar that can bite, tear into flesh, snare, is not to be used but hidden under a woman's breast, subsumed by the man's need of nourishment from mother's milk—hidden under the crescent moon, just as the king, in Malekulan fertility rites was symbolically sacrificed annually to the mother goddess. The boy's power, now the man's, is held by a trickster, a false magician, a psychopath. He cannot do it on his own. He is afraid of his own shadow. Where was his father?

His father, hard working and successful, had been consumed by his professional career. He expected his children to do well and from time to time fired salvos of criticism from afar. The patient's mother, frightened and needy, felt inadequate to the task of raising her many children. She manipulated her son through Catholic guilt into becoming her confidant, her man. He closed down, burying his feelings. He withdrew into his art, into his own beauty. He became moody, passive-aggressive. He leaked out his power.

The man is sensitive, intuitive, intelligent, attractive to both women and men. In his late twenties, having already achieved his professional goal, he takes a wife but cannot keep her. She tries to relate. He is afraid of her and withdraws. She can't find him, so she leaves. What has become of his energy? A real man can be fierce. He can build up his body, his masculine strength. He can charge straight ahead like the boar, toss off his secret mother-lover with his great horns, decimate her with his fierce energy. To seek his fortune, a man can test his strength against the might of the world. A man can make his life.

Psychologically, this man is still a boy. He needs the strength of the short ugly boar to become a man. He dreamed of the boar, but it eluded him. The animal was too smart for the likes of this aesthetic, indecisive Hamlet. He needs to develop the ugly strength, the fierce determination of this short-legged charging beast. He needs to make these tusks of the male killer pig his own. That would take him into the land of the heroes, the world of power, the masculine world. It is the dark world in which enemies sometimes hold the power. There is no room for fear, inertia and self doubt. Men doing battle in this way are still trying to prove themselves, in sports, in combat, as hunters. One man who wrote about the heroic quest was Ernest Hemingway. In the final moments of his short story, "The Short Happy Life of Francis Macomber," the hero faces a ferocious buffalo that charges like the boar. He succeeds, only to be murdered by his wife.

Hemingway's men are either finding their strength or have just succeeded. They are still fighting heroic battles; they speak in monosyllables and tend not to have great relationships with women. Only after a man succeeds in his heroic quest can he relate easily to women. Feeling solid inside, he no longer finds women threatening. In mythology, the man has to slay the dragon in order to rescue the woman. In the movie *Chariots of Fire,* the runner marries the woman only after winning his Olympic medal. My patient was a sort of failed hero. He entered the battle only half-heartedly.

There was a haunting, tragic quality about this willowy young man, so intuitive, with so much promise; one's heart ached for his spirit god to be realized. After his divorce he immediately attracted a young singer with a lovely lyrical voice who fell in love with him. Together they shared an intense erotic relationship, two sensitive souls vibrating on the same frequency, connected to life by a tenuous thread. Then his old mother problem set in and he longed not just to be on his own, but to do things in his own way. He should have lived first on his own after the breakup of his marriage, but he wasn't strong enough, nor was the singer. They were both too needy. Watching the breakup of this relationship was very painful. Each would tentatively reach out for the other in a way that couldn't possibly work. In the end she went off with a destructive man and he settled for someone convenient.

This man lived poetically, and when he had the dream of the boar's tooth I thought he might find the strength to realize his intuitive nature. He reminded me of the failed hero in the movie *The Deerhunter,* directed by Michael Cimino. It is a love story of an aesthetic, tentative young man who does not have the strength to commit to his beautiful fragile lover. Instead he clings to the confident older brother figure, the hunter played by Robert DeNiro. There is a poignant scene in which the young man, now a soldier in Vietnam, tries to call his lover but can't connect so he gives up. Such a tenuous thread. It might seem to the viewer or the reader that with a little encouragement the soldier in Vietnam or my patient could strengthen their connection to their women, but the harsh reality of their old parental complexes was too strong. I felt helpless.

Staying in touch with the limitations of our work keeps analysts grounded, keeps us more focused on where the difficulty lies, what is missing in the patient that keeps him from healing, and forces us to look within ourselves to see how we might have contributed to the failure. Can a therapist, over time, draw a boarlike strength from the ugliness of failure?

Horses

Another animal that can lend transformative strength is the horse. However, unlike the ugly boar, the horse is elegant. From its inception, the horse brought with it a restless and high-spirited energy. It can travel over great distances and when humans learned to ride it the course of civilization was changed. Waves of nomadic Indo-Europeans on horseback invaded and overcame the rooted matriarchal planting cultures.[118] The Trojan horse that conquered the older matriarchal Troy came to symbolize a new Greek patriarchal order. The horse had stirred things up; life was no longer stable.

The long history of the horse also invades the dream-world. Its restless energy infused the life of a female patient of mine. You could feel her ride her horse from morning till night. She never dismounted. She even rode her horse furiously in her dreams. In childhood, she had been raised by horses. They cared for her, watched over her. They must have known that she was abandoned. As a little tyke accompanied by her dog, she would scurry out to the stables holding her blanket and follow the horses about. Much of the day, she recalls, would be spent walking behind them, keeping close to their back hooves. Her grandmother was terrified that a horse might inadvertently kick her, but the woman's father said the dog would protect her.

Imagine what it must have meant to her, a little wisp of a girl following the

---

[118] John Weir Perry, *Lord of the Four Quarters: Myths of the Royal Father,* pp. 112f.

hooves of these large powerful animals. Where were they taking her? What did she experience?—the whinnying, their sweat and warmth, their smell, the large droppings, the stamping feet, their sudden gallop when anything startled them, the blowing of hot air through their nostrils onto her face, mingling with her own breath. Did they nuzzle her? She told me that once she whispered in a hairy sorrel's ear, "The main thing is to stay alive."

Horses are big-bodied animals with small brains. Because their hooves do not feel the earth, they are in danger of stepping in holes and breaking a leg. They are unstable, unwieldy, shy. They are also beautiful and fleet. Did the horses know that this little girl, lonely and fearful, would develop a feeling of independence from riding them, that she would learn to control them, absorb their energy, feel their power as well as her own power in controlling them? They must have known because they accepted her, perhaps realizing on some wordless level that she could supply the mind they were missing. Their big unwieldy bodies would feel better with a bigger brain guiding them. It was a good match, the skilled rider fitting the need of the horse. At the same time, the woman's big brain was in danger of running away with her, so riding the horse grounded her.

There are times when the human brain is a liability, out of balance, and then the powerful body of the instinctual horse kicks in. This is illustrated in a story that Jungian analyst Jane Hollister Wheelwright tells in her book about growing up on the family ranch near Santa Barbara. She would watch the ranch hands return home on horseback after a Saturday night out drinking. They were so drunk that they could not sit up in the saddle, but each time they would begin to fall, the horse would suddenly adjust itself to keep the man in the saddle.[119] This is in contrast to my woman patient with her overworked brain. The drunken men had impaired their big brains and the horse supplied an instinctual knowing.

What events led up to my horse-woman developing an over-reaching brain? She was the second-born of three children and grew up on a ranch with horses. The ranch was quite isolated, and although she was her father's favorite he was rarely home. He was a successful engineer with an artistic flair who invented things and painted murals on the children's walls. But there was trouble in the marriage, and her father's emotional needs were met elsewhere. Stuck out in the middle of nowhere with no interest in the land or horses, her mother became depressed and began drinking. She slept all the time, avoiding her husband and their marital problems. The father would tell his daughter that she must be good,

---

[119] *The Ranch Papers*, pp. 130f.

since "your mother is sick and not feeling well; she may die." One day the three-year-old girl went to her mother's room in the middle of the day and, seeing her mother lying very still on the bed, thought she was dead. She later attributed many of the fears which haunted her throughout her life to that moment. In the aftermath of this experience she turned to her older brother and their dog, the peacefulness of the barn, the strength of the horses.

One day, after a steer threatened to break through the picture window in their living room, the mother called it quits and moved with the three children to the city. The twelve-year-old girl lost her father and, more importantly, the barn and animals were taken away. This was a devastating loss, and tragic also for her father. After he remarried, neighbors reported seeing him secretly returning to the ranch after it was sold. Even though the patient modeled herself after her father, becoming powerful, imaginative, versatile—"I wanted to make things happen like my father"—he lost interest in her. As she grew older he couldn't acknowledge her many gifts and accomplishments, including a doctorate in science from a prestigious university.

She is an example of a pattern that is often seen in "fathers' daughters." The daughter begins as the apple of her father's eye, then comes puberty and she becomes her own person with her own interests. She no longer fits the picture of her held by the narcissistic father, who has all along projected onto her his own needs for a creative anima. She may continue trying to please him and win his approval, but his interests often shift. Since something of the old fiery emotion remains, he can become critical or difficult. His pulling away often has the effect of taking away a daughter's confidence. She continues looking for a father in another man, seeking to win his approval for her creative ideas or career. It is a sad story because often the women are brighter than the men they choose, and so the relationship becomes frustrating and deeply draining of their life energy. Although the women see the problem, they have trouble leaving these men.

It is not unusual for women to form strong bonds with horses. I have several patients who own horses, ride horses, show them, love them. They spend part of each day riding and caring for them. But they differ from my patient who spent her early years with horses. When she talks about them, you feel the horses' presence inside her, as if they are at home. They are not exotic possessions, nor did she always take perfect care of them. She had a family-like intimacy with them, informal, with no showing off, no acknowledging, really, that they were even animals. They were a part of her being. As a young woman she was thrown by a pony whose mother was a kicker, reminding her of her own mother. But that didn't stop her from always having horses.

When this woman first came to see me, she spoke so rapidly, jumping chaotically from one thing to another, that I had trouble following her and thought she might be suffering from the flight of ideas characteristic of manic-depressive disorder. The inner visions of the patient's horse came into the room through the dynamic rhythm and cadence in the patient's delivery of words, echoing the beat of horse's hooves. Her fast-paced vocabulary couldn't keep up with her galloping mind. Thundering hooves, reverberating words, made the earth vibrate. The spirits were awakened. We were no longer in an ordinary therapy office. The beating of the hooves, like a ritual drum, carried us off.

Being in the room with galloping horses reminded me of the description of the shaman's relationship to the horse in the Paleolithic period. The horse's spirit was captured in the shaman's drum, carrying him into another dimension of consciousness. Mircea Eliade tells us how drums echo the horse's hoof-beats, enabling the shaman to make his ecstatic journey to the world beyond:

> The iconography of the drums is dominated by the symbolism of the ecstatic journey, that is, by journeys that imply a breakthrough in plane and hence a "Center of the World." The drumming at the beginning of the séance, intended to summon the spirits and "shut them up" in the shaman's drum, constitutes the preliminaries for the ecstatic journey. This is why the drum is called the "shaman's horse" (Yakut, Buryat). The Altaic drum bears a representation of a horse; when the shaman drums, he is believed to go to the sky on his horse.[120]

Riding with this woman's high spirit in the analytic hour was like being on an ecstatic journey. Her intuition moved like lightning; who could keep up? She could see when things needed doing and possessed the necessary "know how" but she could often intimidate people, anticipating things down the road that they didn't see. She typically tried packing four days into one. Only a horse's energy could accomplish the many tasks she set herself. She thought she was a woman in a horse's body. I liked the energy. What was so refreshing about her was how her horses spontaneously moved about. We were always chasing after them. Sometimes they would charge at me and I welcomed the challenge. To keep up with her horse I had to ride my own. I felt myself spring to life. To sit all day and be suddenly confronted with horses spontaneously alighting was refreshing. Where would we go this hour? So we learned to ride together, she leading sometimes, and sometimes I. I was able to ride the Sorrel she was afraid

---

[120] Eliade, *Shamanism*. p. 173.

of and she rode horses I had never seen before, horses in water and with wings.

How I hated for the hour to end! How I longed to stay with the rhythmical beat, the passion, the adventure. Where would we travel next? I rode horses depicted on the walls of Paleolithic caves. I experienced the intensity of Leonardo da Vinci's horse drawings. I could see the blacks, whites, sorrels, buckskins, gathered together in the center of the earth in Black Elk's vision.[121] These horses had the power to take you somewhere. I was too caught up with the patient's spirit and my own to want to come down to earth. No ordinary horses for us! My countertransference threatened to get the better of me. I realized I would have been more helpful to her had I been able to authenticate her spirit, to make a relationship with it, bring it down to earth, rather than being carried away with the horses myself. I needed to help her find some sustenance, not in words but in the living of her life.

So, gradually I gave up my horses for hers. I imagined myself to be a horse only in relation to her horse and the process of healing in therapy to be like following a horse's hooves. As I learned to follow her and we developed a healing relationship, she was able to settle down. About six months after she began analysis, she had a dream about her problem with intimacy.

> I am standing alongside the haunch of a horse. I am afraid of being kicked. The scene changes, and I am in the back seat of a car, face to face with the horse, nose to nose. The horse is curled up around me, so that the horse cannot kick me, and he is no longer dangerous.

In the dream she settles down in the back seat of a car, nose to nose with a horse that is cozily wrapped around her so he can't kick. A warm relationship becomes the antidote for fear. This dream was followed by many dreams of horses, probably a hundred or more during the years of analysis, always around the core issue of intimacy. Her close proximity to, or distance from, the horse expressed the ambivalence about human relationship. The animal still symbolized her unresolved need for love which caused such fear in her. This theme was always dramatized by how well she was able to care for her horses.

As she began to trust the analytic process, other animals came into the picture—large wild animals that opened her up to still deeper layers in herself. This is her dream that brought the animals:

> She is taking care of a baby in a small house and sees a parade of animals coming down the street. She is momentarily distracted and cannot find the baby. She is

[121] See John G. Neihardt, *Black Elk Speaks,* chap. 3, "The Great Vision," pp. 20ff.

> afraid that somehow it might have crawled outside the house and is in danger of being run over by a car. She finds the child, and no longer afraid, becomes excited by the parade. She wants the child to see all the animals, so they go outside. The animals leading the parade are familiar and domesticated: dogs and horses, followed by giraffes, elephants, lions and tigers. There is much excitement.

After this dream she felt herself letting go of fear and self-doubt, her life energy returning. She associated the dream to the following story. When she was three or four years of age, there lived near her ranch a man who was a retired lion tamer from a circus. In retirement he kept his lion at home. She and her older brother would visit him and he would let them pet the lion. When their grandmother got wind of this she tried to stop it, fearing they might be attacked by the lion. So she called the lion tamer to tell him that her grandchildren were not to visit any more. Because the lion tamer liked the children, he told them they could continue their visits so long as they kept them secret. The canny grandmother found out, however, and reported the lion tamer to the authorities. The lion was taken to the zoo. The man was given permission to visit his lion there, but the children were not, and the little girl lost this magical companion. Now the magic returned in her dream.

She had no association to the baby, but its age corresponded to the amount of time she had been in analysis. The dream begins as usual with a doubt or fear undermining the gains she has made in her analytic work. Yet the parade sets new life to marching. There are all the animals, two by two, as in Noah's ark. They are the horses parading around her corral, oblivious to her mother's stupor. She is again following the animals who have not lost stride, are happy and proud, calling out to her. The parade is led by animals she knows, ones that have been an integral part of her life. These familiar creatures are followed by large wild animals, which represent the deeper instinctual layers of the unconscious.

The horse is domesticated; we can make it go where we want. That is why young girls like to learn to ride them; they want to know how to direct this powerful energy in themselves. But lions and tigers are wild. Even lion tamers are never quite sure when the big cats might turn on them. They are nature in the raw, and this rational, scientifically-trained woman always operated out of her thinking. Her mind was everything. So for her to allow an emotional center in her to open up, one that had no connection to her mind, was quite a shift. Some deeper life was emerging. She no longer needed to be in control. This "wild" nature would infuse her with a new emotional energy that would better nourish her and help her to feel more connected to her life. She had always complained about being so caught up in her work that she didn't know where she was when she got home at the end of the day. She was disoriented within her larger life—but her dream was orienting her to the totality of her personality.

As a child, this woman's dog and the horses protected and affirmed her, and then became a bridge to the larger life, to the whole animal kingdom representing life itself. Now that her magical lion is beyond the grandmother's interference, the child, who was almost lost, can open up to nature's wonders. The animals have been restored and parade for all to see. A reconciliation also took place when she invited her mother to see her ride her favorite horse. The mother said, "I see it's true that horses are important to you."

Predictably, following the tremendous breakthrough of the dream, the woman had a regressive dream. She approached a horse and asked herself, "Will this be a safe horse or not, something I can ride? Is this an opportunity to be with this horse? Should I take care of it?" She responds to her own question, "I don't think I can—maybe I can. Did I take care of this horse? Did I feed it? It's going to starve to death. It's lost its lead lines. I am with the horse." Then the horse becomes smaller, the size of a dog. "It's too small for me. How am I going to look on this horse?"

Not long after these two dreams, she came into the session complaining of loss. For some reason, during a recent visit with her sister, she couldn't be with her in the way she wanted. "She expects things of me. I am supposed to have all the answers. It's unrealistic. I think she is jealous of me being my father's favorite. I don't trust her. I don't feel support from my family. My brother and sister were taken care of by my mother's family but not me. I was left out." She bemoaned the fact that she felt as if she had no family. Since her father's death several years previously, she said, there was no center within the family. This is what she must have experienced as a twelve-year-old when her father left the family. In the same breath she asked, "Will there be any horses in my life? Will I, or do I, have a family?" So the horse is equated with family.

After her marriage ended there were periods in her life when she had a horse stabled nearby but never went to visit it; she let hang in the stables an expensive saddle which eventually disappeared. Her neglect of the horse became the expression of her self-neglect. Now she felt bad about it. Horses require care. They are needy like her mother and herself. They wreak havoc. A friend asks if she would like to ride again and she considers. "How dangerous is this? Are the horses out of my life or not? Are the men out of my life or not?" In response she has this dream:

> I am standing on the front porch of a weather-beaten white farmhouse. There are people in the house and a white horse comes up the porch and through the front door. I jump up and start to go after it because horses aren't supposed to be in houses. I go to the front door but don't go into the house. Then the horse comes bolting out of the house and passes me on the right, charging down the stairs. I say "Oh shit" and put out my hand as I start to go after him. The horse twirls around and comes half-way back up the steps near me. It decides to stay.

In reality this woman hates white horses, but this one was sweet, not scary. Reddish-brown horses are those of her childhood, and she was sometimes afraid of them. Although this dream horse is not originally to her liking, he is safe and responsive and offers the possibility that he won't hurt her as the past has. The horse comes right into the house rather than waiting for her. She has had trouble taking care of her house, putting things in order, getting plants or fabrics to make a pleasant living space for herself and friends. She blames this neglect partly on her being a workaholic, but actually she doesn't value herself and feels frustrated, afraid to create a more personal life.

Soon after this dream she bought some plants and a filing cabinet instead of storing things on the floor. In the dream she is on the front porch, halfway between outside and inside, meaning that she has probably never really adapted to a life away from the animals and outdoors. But the horse comes right into the house so that people, herself, and horses will now relate. She said that when riding a horse her mind was focused and she was entirely in the moment. "That's what I used horses for, to relate but also to control. I have to be with them so as not to split off [dissociate] or go somewhere else." Horse and rider go together; they symbolize our life that points to the same fate, heroic man coupled with animal instinct.[122]

However, as important as horses were for her, she had difficulty keeping her horse on the ground. She lived high up in the stratosphere of consciousness, long gone from the earth. She had become the heroine, the one classically identified with Apollo as creative animus, riding the horse's power all the way to the sun. She rode the power of the horse to the sun, fulfilling the wish of every adolescent boy who soups up his car with extra horse power.

The horse symbolizes a person's life energy. It needs to be ridden, otherwise it falls back into the unconscious. Upon death, an old ritual from the Upanishads decreed that the horse be led to the grave and slaughtered for the use of the rider in the world beyond. When Narbona, the great Navajo chief and grandfather of

---

[122] See *Symbols of Transformation,* CW 5, par. 421.

Hosteen Klah, was killed in 1849 by Colonel Washington, military commander of the New Mexico Territory, his two favorite horses, a palomino and a gray stallion, were killed and the saddles and bridles were chopped into little bits.[123] As Jung notes, "When the horse is sacrificed the world is sacrificed and destroyed."[124] A remnant of this custom still exists in England. At a military funeral, the horse is "led behind the coffin with the dead rider's boots hung reversed on either side of the saddle."[125] In this country John F. Kennedy's funeral procession with the riderless white horse following the caisson symbolized the life that was taken.

My patient, too identified with her scientific mind in a masculine way, shied away from making women friends. She was too sensitive and temperamental to expose her feelings. She had been so wounded by her lack of mothering that it was difficult for me to find a way to talk to her about the problem, and when we did she was unable to stay with it for very long. The mother problem intruded in her life in other ways, such as an eating disorder. When she would return home after a crisis-oriented, ten- or twelve-hour work day, there was never anything healthy in the house to eat. She never seemed to have time to buy groceries, so she would stuff herself with whatever was at hand, always accompanied by large quantities of alcohol. Or she might take herself out for a big dinner, justifying such gorging because she had worked so hard. She didn't drink during the day, but her alcohol consumption in the evening was excessive. Typically, she would get to bed late, awakening in the morning in a bad mood, dragging herself out of bed. She was a large, good-looking, well-proportioned woman who was definitely overweight, but she carried it well.

She had a dream which shows how uncomfortable she becomes in a relaxed intimate setting with friends and what she does to spoil it:

> Friends gather for a picnic. The faces are warm and related, the food colorful and appetizing. It is an ideal day, but suddenly chaos erupts. The reserved picnic space is not honored and strangers enter without permission. Then horses begin running wildly around the perimeter, disrupting things.

The panic the temperamental horses experience when they are frightened and then bolt is the same panic my patient experiences when she begins to relax in social situations and experiences other people accepting her. She is too afraid, too skittish. Her emotional life cannot hold. Her horse rears. In fact she had a

---

[123] Franc J. Newcomb, *Hosteen Klah: Navaho Medicine Man and Sand Painter*, p. 41.
[124] *Symbols of Transformation,* CW 5, par. 658.
[125] Barbara Hannah, *The Cat, Dog, and Horse Lectures,* p. 114.

dream in which the horse maintained a rearing position as if it were walking on its hind legs. Rearing horses frighten people. She moved like a horse, bolting, skittering sideways, and avoided nuzzling.

Because of this woman's workaholic nature and her inability to take care of herself, she was prone to illness. Her immune system was worn down. She lived in a narrow window between frantic overexertion and illness. Whenever she had recurrent bouts of flu, sinus infections and back problems, she would feel as if her life was turning against her. During one severe episode of influenza she became quite upset that she was missing so much time at work where people were dependent on her. To combat her depression, to rescue her spirit, her psyche sent her a fantastic dream horse made of clouds. Was it Pegasus, the divine winged horse of Greek fable that is said to have sprung from the trunk of the gorgon Medusa when Perseus cut off her head? Is this the symbol of what could carry this woman into a new era of her life? Here is the dream:

> A tall mountain of dark boulders appears before me. As I step onto the first boulders, a fantastic white horse made of clouds appears under me (I'm riding). He lurches from rock to rock. His neck, with a very heavy white mane, is close to my face. I'm grateful and afraid. Can I trust him? I anticipate him twirling and dropping me on the rocks. I try to balance and urge him forward while I want to slip off to greater safety, to crawl alone over the piles of boulders I know will grow bigger under my hands. I am suspended in place without a bridle. Am I willing to ride?

This flying dream-horse comes to carry her out of difficulty. How can she resist? She needs him but she can't trust him. She has no bridle and no control of him, and with his mane in her face she can't see. His hooves land on boulders. He may drop her at any moment. The situation is not so different from when she was a little girl and the horses came to rescue her. She could have been kicked in the head, but she wasn't. She had no choice then, as she doesn't now. She doesn't know how to get down; she still has no control over her life.

The dream pictures how she experiences the harshness of her working day when she is tired and sick. She is suspended between a phantasmagorical animal made of clouds (her intellect, much of which she has little control of, because *it* takes her) and a hard dark mountain of boulders (the reality of her life). She is on the edge between being out of control and depression. There is no human place where ordinary mortals can live in communion with others, sharing work and enjoying a personal life. She is disconnected. She saves her large brain for her work. Fear and anxiety govern her body. She cannot care for herself, so she becomes sick all the time. On the same night she had another dream:

> I'm searching through pastures looking for my horse. Hilly pastures with trees, ups and downs, leaves, dirt, sometimes tall grass, leaves under the trees, roots of trees, creeks; I look in many places, no horse anywhere. Later I see horses. One is mature, the right color, sorrel, but I don't recognize her as mine. Perhaps it's been so long that she has grown and matured to look different.
>
> Finally I go into a small protected place and find my dog curled up. I'm glad to see him, but he looks very ill. A voice behind me says, "He's dying." I realize it's true. I feel sad and helpless, but glad I found him.

Her feeling about this dream was that she was reconnecting to something vital earlier in her life. But the horse that she knew then has matured, indicating that she has to face the fact that time has passed. Knowing this makes her sad. And her dog is dying. What does that mean?

There was a further regression toward the end of our work when she became ill yet again. She couldn't find her horse, so she became *like* a horse, but in a negative way. There was a sad feeling to this dream.

> I go into a barn. There are partitions, stalls and lots of straw but no horses, no horse poop. After I'm inside I'm aware of myself charging around.

Two years after this, she died from the medical treatment and complications of a highly unusual brain tumor. Because the location of the tumor was life threatening, her doctors prescribed an intensive course of radiation and chemotherapy. Two weeks after being discharged as cured, she died.

Her illness interrupted our analytic work together. It is hard to know what lasting benefits she might have realized had she lived. Just months prior to her illness she had begun to see me less frequently. Her back was hurting again and she often traveled out of the area to see body-work specialists. With the extra time off, she began to read more and became interested in cognitive therapy, in which she could more clearly see her own psychodynamics. Did this new interest point to the value of analysis in sparking a desire to better understand herself, or was it an avoidance? She followed up this interest by finding a charismatic teacher who led marathons on weekends. He was more rational and confrontational than I. With him she could display her mind, congratulating herself on being able to challenge and interest her teacher. She didn't stop seeing me; rather she would come in proud of the insights she gained, wondering what I thought of them. But she developed signs of becoming hyperactive again.

Soon after that, she began developing symptoms from her tumor. The onset of the symptoms was fast. During a session in the office, I watched her mouth droop and noted other troubling neurological signs, so I called her doctor.

In looking back at this woman's last two dreams, in which her horse is gone and her dog is dying, I wonder if they were prognostic. Did they indicate that her life force was disappearing? Everything she said or did was always in reference to a horse. She rarely came to me without a horse dream. Horses were permanently stamped in her psyche.

Over the five years that we worked together, I could feel the horse bringing her into life. I could feel as well the original horsepower in her that as a child had saved her from being consumed by her mother's alcoholism and depression, her father's departure, and later carried her through university. That horsepower also supplied the energy she needed to run her scientific business. But her horse wreaked havoc on relationships. By the end of our work together she seemed to have settled down considerably. She was growing out of the horse to a new way of being. As she began tentatively to reach for new relationships, she had a clearer idea of how she wanted to live, even though she couldn't yet implement it. She had definitely changed.

I was saddened to hear of the tumor that would end her life. It seemed so sudden. She was so full of energy, so involved in work projects, so verbal. I couldn't imagine life being taken from her, or my life without her. As her analyst, I was disappointed to see our relationship prematurely aborted. I would have been interested to see the effect the analysis would have had on her in the long run. And what would it mean to me to live without horses—not to be challenged to the very brink of my capability—not to have the wind and beating of drums instill the room with spirit?

I miss seeing her. I always looked forward to our sessions, even though her hour followed my lunch hour and I sometimes had to hurry to finish a sandwich. Now, I'm not in such a hurry.

For an elderly friend of mine whose death was imminent, horses in a prescient dream took part in a funeral procession. Like my woman patient, he had a long relationship with horses and a deep intimacy with the land. Horses had been a bridge to his whole life. The family had large holdings in the Sacramento Valley and as a young boy he rode down the valley to attend school near Santa Barbara. In our last meeting, he told me of a dream foretelling the death of his mother who had actually been dead for some time:

> My mother is riding her Mustang—a horse who after a full day of riding still had plenty of energy. She leads it out to the edge of her property and says good-bye to it. Then she walks up three steps through a trellised gate and disappears.

My friend had been close to his mother. He was in his sixties when his mother died, and that particular summer we went backpacking together in the Sierras. One night over a fire I expressed my condolences. He laughed and said that a man in his sixties ought to have let go of his mother. He had, indeed, been greatly influenced by his mother, especially by her spiritual intuition. In many respects he had followed his mother's horse into Jungian analysis and now he himself was preparing to follow this horse to another world.

Just as the horse was a bridge for my woman patient, this male friend became a bridge for my relationship to the land. He was particularly important to me early on in my professional life. Typologically, he was what Jungians call a sensation type, that is, one with little intuition but rather a connection to the land and to physical reality. In the early part of the century, his father had developed a working ranch on the top of a ten-thousand-foot pass in the northern Sierra mountains. As a young boy, together with the regular ranch hands, every summer he would lead the grazing animals up to feed at higher pastures. He had ridden everywhere in the mountains so he showed me the land firsthand, from the valley floor upward.

Yet he had never been backpacking. When I suggested we go, he jumped at the idea. We both made out lists of what to take and his included, of all things, a carton of fresh eggs. My first response was to laugh, but I questioned him instead. He said that they always carried eggs in saddle bags and never lost one, so why couldn't we carry this extra weight? Pretending we were horses with saddlebags, we carried the fresh eggs and had them every morning along with fresh coffee from the little percolator he carried. I could feel the poise he must have showed when riding horseback: it was expressed in way this percolator perfectly balanced at the edge of the fire.

He was a staunch Republican and an environmentalist before there was such a word. Conservation of values and of the land was vitally important to him; he embodied stewardship. One day a Forest Ranger appeared where I was standing with fishing pole and angler's paraphernalia hanging out of my pack, and I hadn't bothered to get a fishing license. This was not only going to cost me a hundred dollar fine but I expected to be embarrassed in front of my friend. Although getting a license had crossed my mind, I thought that being in the high country we would not meet anyone for five days. Now, here we were, face to face with the law.

My friend took over, greeting the officer with: "How come you guys aren't protecting the land like we used to?" and explained how his family had always taken care of the property and now that the land had been appropriated by the

State, they at least ought to care for it as well as private owners had. The officer replied defensively and my friend said he should do such and such and by God get this word back to his superiors.

I asked him later why he had been so harsh with the Ranger. He said not only was his family going to lose the land at the end of the ninety-nine year lease, but he paid good tax dollars in support of this protection and so expected responsible results. In my friend's mind, the government and this officer worked for him. I had been brought up to be afraid of the law, as being authoritarian in a negative way, and tried to get away with whatever I could. Thank God this land had been cared for by my friend and not by me. I didn't ask him if he had a fishing license; better left alone. We did catch trout one morning and that delicious breakfast seemed to set the tone for the rest of the trip.

We took several backpacking adventures together. Around the campfire, high in the mountains, I journeyed with him in spirit all over California on horseback. The horse wasn't just an imaginary animal that carried my friend and his mother to the beyond; it bore me into this great land and ushered in a new way of living. I think in many ways the horse symbolized something similar for him. It was his connection to the land, his great love; the vitality of the earth carried his spirit. He told me that when he was in France in World War Two he became depressed, not only because he missed his family but because he was separated from California and the land. Both my friend and my woman patient had horse dreams which foretold their deaths. In her dream, the woman could no longer find her horse; in his, his mother says good-bye to her horse. The horse is life.

Having emphasized the powerful aspect of the horse, I want to close with a lovely poem by James Wright, as a way of honoring the lighter, more delicate, feminine aspect of the horse. Horses don't always symbolize power and libido, and they aren't always masculine. Those in Wright's poem are playful. They are tender and shy in their feeling for one another. They reflect the softness of the grass. They are frisky as young girls can be when meeting someone they like. In this poem, they are light as feathers:

> Just off the highway to Rochester, Minnesota,
> Twilight bounds softly forth on the grass.
> And the eyes of those two Indian ponies
> Darken with kindness.
> They have come gladly out of the willows
> To welcome my friend and me.
> We step over the barbed wire into the pasture
> Where they have been grazing all day, alone.

They ripple tensely, they can hardly contain their
happiness
That we have come.
They bow shyly as wet swans. They love each other.
There is no loneliness like theirs.
At home once more,
They begin munching the young tufts of spring in the
darkness.
I would like to hold the slenderer one in my arms,
For she has walked over to me
And nuzzled my left hand.
She is black and white,
Her mane falls wild on her forehead,
And the light breeze moves me to caress her long ear
That is delicate as the skin over a girl's wrist.
Suddenly I realize
That if I stepped out of my body I would break
Into blossom.[126]

One of the horses in Wright's poem is female and points to the opposite constellation in man, his relationship with his feminine side. This is the delicate intimacy, "delicate as the skin over a girl's wrist," often hidden in men, but here very feelingly brought out in comparing the horse to a young girl.

Most of the horse's brain is devoted to its musculo-skeletal system and to its sensory awareness. Little is devoted to cognition. The horse's powerful strength can take the rider over mountains and rivers into life. It is a force to behold. Its sensory neurons alert the horse to ever-changing conditions underfoot, so it can fly at the slightest provocation. In this sense, the horse is extremely sensitive, feminine, almost psychic say many horse lovers. The rider often visualizes the image and the horse responds.

The deeper meaning for my woman patient, for my male friend and for Wright is the same: the horse connects them to something mysterious in themselves, something that will transform them if they let it in.

From the horse, we now go to the beyond.

---

[126] "A Blessing," *Collected Poems*. p. 135.

6
Initiation by Fire

Man is nothing, if not on fire.
—C.G. Jung.

Imagination and Transcendence

This chapter is about the fire of transformation. First, we were initiated by water, now by fire. After immersion in the cool bath of water, we are tempered in the heat of fire. Water and the waterbirds baptized us. Water dissolved our fear and rigidity and opened us to love and sexuality. It eventually brought us to land and to the animals. So, from flying and water, we have come down to earth, to the warm-blooded mammals, to flesh and blood. After we have landed on solid ground, after we have taken on form and become involved in earthy matters, things need to get loose again, need to become mutable. We have to face transcendence, death and eternity. It is not enough to be grounded; we have to look at eternal things. This chapter is about becoming heated up, so that the spirit can be released. This is purification by fire.

In early societies a spiritual quest often followed a ritual of initiation. The puberty rites or initiations that marked the transition from adolescence into adulthood,[127] as well as the initiations of the medicine man or shaman, included three stages of development: separation, transition and incorporation. Through separation from the mother or seclusion from the tribe, the initiate faced his dead ancestors, the creation gods and his own death. A ritual operation or other physical ordeal often accompanied the initiate's transition from the profane world to the sacred.[128] The final act of incorporation was completed by the initiate's identification or union with the gods.[129]

The purpose of the initiation then as now was to help the initiate to acquire objective self-knowledge, enabling one to stand on one's own and ultimately to face death. Psychoanalysis today is considered a kind of modern initiation. The separation or seclusion phase in analysis begins when our mask or social persona is revealed and we enter into a dialogue with the unconscious. An example

[127] Mircea Eliade, *Rites and Symbols of Initiation: Mysteries of Birth and Rebirth*, p. 2.
[128] Eliade, *The Encyclopaedia of Religion*, vol. 7, pp. 230f.
[129] Henderson, *Thresholds of Initiation*. p. 84.

of this stage is seen in Thomas Mann's *The Magic Mountain,* in which the young hero is removed from life to a hospital high in the Swiss Alps to heal his tuberculosis. He turns inward to examine his life. From this detachment comes the ordeal of confronting oneself. If successful, one gains a certain amount of objectivity and wisdom that may then be contributed to society. Because a long period of time has elapsed and the outer world is no longer as it was, the initiate must reenter life wherever he finds it. Mann's hero, after being healed, comes down off the mountain to pick up a gun to fight in World War One. This return to life is illustrated in the last of the famous Ten Ox-Herding Pictures of Zen Buddhism, where the enlightened man comes down from the mountain into the market place, carrying candy and gifts for the children (Figure 19).

Two of the examples in this chapter follow this spiritual progression. One is the story of an elderly woman who dreams of her death dragon awaiting her. The other is my own story, about my confrontation with two fires, one inner and one outer, and the tremendous energy that was released. Eliade tells us that

Figure 19
Entering the City with Bliss-Bestowing Hands.

mastery over fire and acquiring inner heat were often part of the initiatory ordeal in shamanistic practice.[130] "He who obtains magical heat vividly demonstrates that he belongs to a superhuman world."[131] Fire in the initiation rites was controlled, but fire breaks out in the analytic process spontaneously. We can't make it happen and when it does, it transforms everything we have worked on and makes it real. Fire incinerates, heats things up to such a pitch that we are awakened, never to sleep again. The animal in us stirs and torments us, forcing us to live out our nature whether we want to or not.

Fire Dragon and Unicorn

Wood burns, changes into smoke and ash. Burning passion, anger, rage—if these fires are contained and made conscious, they can change the form of our life. A young man with a raging inner fire practically burned my building down. He would come in all smiles with a need to please and then, without skipping a beat would explode. He reminded me of a patient on the adolescent ward at Napa State Hospital, whose only warning sign before hitting someone was a broad smile. My patient, however, was not psychotic and through a carefully monitored heat control system, with fire extinguishers at hand, he was able to transform his rage and hate into a fire dragon, a creation of his own imagination.

This young man came to see me because his anger and hatred were interfering with his job and causing him such severe headaches that at times he couldn't function. Early on, I thought the headaches were caused by stopped-up energy, anger and pain from childhood that he seemed unable to release. I don't think I had ever seen anyone as angry as he. He was paralyzed by it. No matter how hard he tried, he couldn't get rid of it. His rage would not respond to the ordinary therapeutic process of catharsis, insight and interpretation; nothing seemed to work. He was stuck. He felt like he was in a conflagration that was out of control. For years he'd carried inside a rage at his parents for so afflicting him with their emotional needs that he was unable to tend to himself. Unable to cope with the ordinary demands of growing up, he was besieged inside with the "screaming meemies" (his term) and he was in a panic.

At my suggestion he began to draw his rage. What was most striking to see in the early pictures was that he had no self-image or body image to contain this fire anger, no vessel that could temper or regulate the temperature, no furnace that could transform these fiery elements and so bring change. What he needed

---

[130] *Rites and Symbols of Initiation.* p. 85.
[131] Ibid. p. 87.

was a form that could contain and direct his undifferentiated anger. He started out trying to paint a fire dragon but wound up instead with an armadillo. He comments on his pictures.

Picture 1

> I am horribly stressed. I can't sleep at night because I am anxious, on edge and my brain is racing. It feels like something wants to tear out of my chest, out of my head. I get out of bed to paint how I feel. I paint myself, small and with a horn on my head. The horn is where the stress is coming from and I grab my hair to try to relieve the pressure. In the painting I am splitting in half at the horn and another me has grown out of the smaller me. I am a huge heart and no body and I am screaming with another horn coming out of my head. I try to paint the scream coming out and I feel that I want to paint a dragon. I paint and it looks more like a armadillo. There is yellow and red flame coming from its mouth. It has protective spikes lining its back. I feel defensive, disembodied, ungrounded and furious.

The lower half of this first painting is much like his earlier drawings (not presented here) in which his boyish self is portrayed with a disconnected body. In

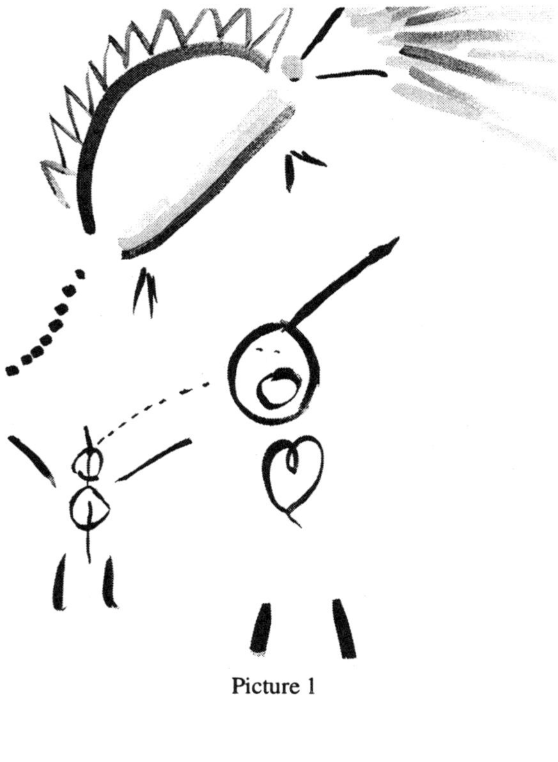

Picture 1

the earlier drawings his parents, playing a more active role, are often shown as stick figures shooting at him or dismembering him. Horror, anger, and fear scream out in this picture, as in the earlier ones. Sometimes he would draw a picture with just a screaming mouth, reminding me of Edward Munch's engraving, *The Scream.*

He explained that at age four or five he was racing and competing with the family dog, a German shepherd, to see which of them could reach the porch of their house first. He hit his head against the side of the porch, causing a wound which required many sutures to close. A scar remained, and it was from this scar that the dream-horn grew. He said the family dog, which was "too big for me" and with which he competed for his parents' attention, was really his parents' dog and carried the family's problem. He also competed with his brothers, all close in age, for his parent's attention, especially his older brother who picked on him and whom he hated. He described his mother as a moody and depressed woman, who often sank into anger and felt victimized. The patient had learned only two years earlier about his mother's secret, that she had been passionately in love with her first husband, a young Navy pilot who was killed while flying shortly after they were married. She never recovered from this loss.

Looking at Picture 1, the young man pointed to the horn on the small figure (bottom left), exclaiming, "That's where it hurts, where the stress is coming from. This is war. This is death. Everyone is cut apart—in bits and pieces." On the right there is a larger, less well-defined person, represented by an enlarged heart and screaming head that shoots out a large black projection. Two small lines, indicating legs, complete the image, which reveals an exposed heart, black, unprotected and uncontained, and a head that hurts. He said that as a child he was given no creative or emotional coping tools. He had to rely on thinking.

Then he tried to draw a dragon, a ferocious animal that would express his own fire power, anger and passion. But he was emotionally blocked, and in frustration he drew an armadillo (Picture 1, top). This creature reminded him of his father, who was obdurate, slow, without spirit. Unable to ride his fire dragon out into life, the son relied instead on his father's animal, an armadillo, which is heavily defended with armor plating. Significantly, his father's animal, unlike his own, does have a complete body. It is this father's body that carried him out into the world. To pay for his education, the young man found an administrative job—obsessive, compulsive, by the numbers—like his father's military job. But working dutifully like his father was giving him such severe headaches that I encouraged him to leave his job and to trust that he would find more creative teaching work closer to his heart. This he eventually did.

Although he was disappointed in his failed attempt to draw a fire dragon, he persevered. On the second try he decided to include the horn which spontaneously arose in the first drawing, and from that he got the idea to draw a unicorn. For the first time he expressed his own self-image.

Picture 2

> The next day I paint again. I want to paint a unicorn. I paint a large, colorful unicorn with a purple nose that has a snake's tongue poking out. It is a large horse, strong with a horn on its head, a powerful horn and the yellow flames from the armadillo have reappeared as a flowing golden mane of the unicorn. The unicorn is fast and can fly in the air; it is the part of me that cannot be touched or harmed by pain. Being spirit it remained pure from the horrible anger of my childhood. My parents were not able to touch this part of me, but until now I haven't been in touch with it.

Here the first drawing of a disembodied person is replaced by the powerful body of a unicorn. Its large upper part fills the page, indicating an animal whose size and thickness is several times larger than all the parts of the previous draw-

Picture 2

ing combined. The yellow flames of anger are transformed into a golden mane which reflects the sun's rays, symbolizing masculine spirit and intuition.

The powerful black horn matches the strong forelegs which carry the animal forward wherever desired. Black lines also mark the body, again suggesting power but also indicating something still too dark and heavy. A purple nose with a snake tongue darting out endows the animal with a natural instinct to sniff out the passions he might pursue, to relieve his mind from doing all the work.

In a chapter entitled the "Unicorn in Alchemy," Jung notes that the unicorn is a symbol of Mercurius, the transformative element in the psyche that can bring miraculous change. He explains that "Medieval tradition associates unicorn with lion 'because unicorn is as strong, wild, and cruel as the lion'. . . . This animal named 'lycornu' in France and Italy is evidently derived from 'lion'," and tells us why the unicorn is often found with the virgin:

> The virgin represents his [Mercurius's] passive, feminine aspect, while the unicorn or the lion illustrates the wild, rampant, masculine, penetrating force of the *spiritus mercurialis.*[132]

For the angry young man, the unicorn would be the animal that would free his dammed-up energy and direct it with a powerful new masculine "point."

The horn initially formed from the protruding scar of the wound becomes the focus for penetrating healing; new life sprouts from the old hurt. In the first drawing the horn splits in two, creating a second figure in which his long standing wounds are exposed. This self-healing function of the horn, generated from its own wound, now opens the long standing wound, a necessary procedure for any healing to occur. The wound has been transformed into the horn of the unicorn which, as Jung explains, signifies "health, strength, and happiness of the blessed."[133] In Picture 2 the powerful horn, given new authority, can direct and guide the animal's spirit.

This young man, most wounded in his imagination, could until now only follow the slow obsessive armadillo of his father. But the son's imagination breaks through with a fire dragon and a unicorn as if it were there all along, mysteriously intact, until one day it is given the opportunity to fill the space reserved for it.

In a similar vein, the poet Rilke describes how an image, if a space is left for it to crystallize, can be created out of the imagination. In the following poem the

---

[132] *Psychology and Alchemy,* CW 12, par. 518.

[133] Ibid., par. 519.

mythological unicorn exists as objective reality in the psyche. It requires nothing but love to nourish it.

> Oh, this is the animal that never was.
> They hadn't seen one; but just the same, they loved
> its graceful movements, and the way it stood
> looking at them calmly, with clear eyes.
>
> It had not *been*. But for them, it appeared
> in all its purity. They left space enough.
> And in the space hollowed out by their love
> it stood up all at once and didn't need
>
> existence. They nourished it, not with grain,
> but with the mere possibility of being.
> And finally this gave it so much power
>
> that from its forehead a horn grew. One horn.
> It drew near to a virgin, white, gleaming—
> and was, inside the mirror and in her.[134]

Through the wisdom of his own psyche, the young man's anger coalesced. He knew nothing of the unicorn's symbolic significance except that he felt it was a powerful animal. Keeping this tremendous energy locked up inside must indeed have made him angry, like a corralled horse going crazy because it can't run free. He reported, "The same night as the drawing I had a dream of horses flying in the air. I've seen them before. They fly and wheel in circles above me," reflecting the flexibility of movement he was beginning to enjoy.

The strength and power of the unicorn is similar to the horse. Jung shows a picture in which a horse's forelock is twisted into a stiff plait to make it look like the horn of the unicorn.[135] The imaginative unicorn and the earthy horse become interchangeable. The imaginative unicorn has become the animal of this world that heroically will carry him into life.

Picture 3

Now the dark heavy lines have disappeared and a light elegant animal appears. The lightening up of the darkness reminds me again of the Zen Ox-Herding Pictures, in which the Zen student encounters a black ox representing his own true nature, still unknown. As an awareness of himself grows, the ox turns lighter in color, until finally the distinction between the man and that

---

[134] *The Sonnets to Orpheus,* II, 4, in *The Selected Poetry of Rainer Marie Rilke,* p. 241.
[135] *Psychology and Alchemy,* CW 12, Fig. 244, p. 441.

which he seeks disappears, leaving the perfect and eternal fullness (or oneness) of the circle. When my patient talked about Picture 3, there was a lightness to his being, as if he could put down his heavy anger and begin to express himself in a quiet manner.

The unicorn standing on its hind legs points its horn toward a green harp, which brings back the melody of Ireland that was stolen from the young man. The old Celtic lore reverberates through his blood and he began compiling a family tree of his Irish ancestors as they emigrated west to the Spanish-speaking Americas. As his anger toward his parents gave way to his own true feelings, he was inspired to propose to the woman he had been dating. At the wedding he insisted on an Irish band, even though he had no money to pay for it. Looking at the picture we see that a guiding star appears between the unicorn and harp, as if he is now following his fate.

Picture 3

The unicorn conveys best the spirit of intuition, the psychic Mercurial element that can breathe life into the deadest of things, and then serve its master as if it were the most natural thing in the world. A poem by Marianne Moore entitled "Sea Unicorns and Land Unicorns" conveys the ethereal and elusive spirit of the unicorn, which can live unnoticed for long periods of time and then suddenly appear. Here is the last stanza:

> So wary as to disappear for centuries and reappear
> yet never be caught
> the unicorn has been preserved
> by an unmatched device
> wrought like the work of expert blacksmiths—
> this animal of that one horn
> throwing itself upon which head foremost from a cliff,
> it walks away unharmed;
> proficient in this feat which, like Herodotus,
> I have not seen except in pictures.
> Thus this strange animal with its miraculous elusiveness,
> has come to be unique,
> "impossible to take alive,"
> tamed only by a lady inoffensive like itself—
> as curiously wild and gentle;
> . . . . .
> The unicorn "with pavon high" approaches eagerly;
> until engrossed by what appears of this strange enemy,
> upon the map, "upon her lap,"
> its "mild wild head doth lie."[136]

Like the spirit of my patient which survived a brutal childhood, the unicorn can undergo severe trials and survive unharmed. The unicorn resting its head in the lap of the virgin symbolizes the spirit which has entered into earthly life. When my patient found his unicorn, he could at last relax. The war was over.

Picture 4

This picture shows a horse that the patient feels is his. It's a plain little horse with a horn. There is a sweetness and vulnerability in the lines. The smile creates a human touch, letting us know that this little green horse is to be ridden.

I could see myself in this man, equivocating and indecisive, and at a point when I was hesitant about following my own direction with this book, I had a

---

[136] *The Complete Poems of Marianne Moore,* pp. 77f.

dream that reminded me of the patient's plain little horse.

> Instead of attending a dinner at a professional meeting (which I am ambivalent about) I head out to a barn where John Wayne is fixing me a harness and bridle for my horse just like his. It is a little horse and two small stable boys kiss it on the mouth and the horse kisses them back. I suddenly feel strong and excited, looking forward to the riding. Will I ride with John Wayne for awhile?
>
> Then a young seal takes to the water, pursued by a strange-looking devouring water animal, but I see the seal can swim faster and will escape.

The dream supplies me with a horse to carry me forward, prepared by no other than the great American hero John Wayne. Although he has never been my style of hero, I did remember hearing, a few evenings earlier on the radio program "Fresh Air," Terry Gross interview Kirk Douglas. During the interview, Kirk Douglas talked about his relationship with John Wayne who told him to be tough, because viewers looked to them to carry that role. Much to my astonishment, I must have responded to Wayne's ideal of being tough and was able to return, reinvigorated, to my book.

Not long after the young man connected with the excitement that comes from having his own little horse, he had a disturbing regressive dream, which ended with his being rescued by a dog:

Picture 4

There was a man on the side of the road who shot things from the top of people's heads with a gun—I couldn't see the gun because he controlled it but wasn't firing it. The shots were coming from the woods behind him. He was angry, authoritarian. One man walked away. The angry man yelled at me—he asked me where the man went? I said I didn't know. The man who left was watching from above, trying to figure out how the magic was done. This made the angry man more angry.

Then I was one of the three people who was firing the guns from the woods. I was in on the secret. Then I was being chased and was captured by the police in front of my old home. I went to the bathroom and a dog came in. I couldn't get rid of him. He had come a long way. He had a message for me.

Picture 5

This dog is carrying a scroll in its mouth which represents all the paintings so far completed. Like Cerberus, the dog goes between the two worlds; he is bringing the young man everything he has learned to help him with his anger. This dog has wolf or coyote in him, something wild and free. Like the unicorn he is powerfully built and well endowed with masculine sexual organs. He has good sensing apparatus, a long nose to smell (intuition), big ears to hear (discern) and he makes direct eye contact. The man says that the dog is lighting a fire "under my ass. He comes at night like the raccoons to tease my dogs, reminding me of the wild life that is out there."

Picture 5

Though emotional fire was the dominant affect expressed by this young man, it was negative fire that was eating him alive. The fire needed to be made conscious, to be contained and regulated, so its heat could supply the energy to go forward in his life quests. His anger had transformed into the flame of passion.

Death Dragon

A seventy-seven-year-old woman patient of mine had an innately passionate nature. Her fire was her social energy, her charm, her animation. Passion had nurtured every aspect of her life, from intimate relationships to her pursuit of social causes. But she was coming to the end of her life. Now, as her life-energy is diminishing, her passion must take a subtler, more ethereal form.

Fire does transmute matter to a less substantial form; it purifies, releasing spirit. The form it takes in this elderly woman is not the immense fire dragon of the angry young man, but a dragon of death, transcendence and eternity. It appeared in a dream as a delicate creature that resides inside her ear. She senses that when it awakens it will kill her. But before that dream (which I will give here shortly), she faced death through her conflict over killing her cat.

Her aging cat had been diagnosed with diabetes. She considered whether to put the cat down, while at the same time she thought of taking her own life. She felt as though the cat were her sole companion, though in fact she did have friends and family. Her concern was not about injecting the animal with its daily required dose of insulin herself, but whether she could trust the caretakers to administer to the cat when she traveled. If the cat went with her she was worried that a maid might inadvertently leave a door or window open and her cat would disappear, leaving her with terrible nightmares. So the conflict narrowed to: "Do I want a warm cat to stay in bed with, or do I want to travel?"

Her daughter encouraged her not to put the cat down. Thinking through her daughter's attitude, she realized that the daughter thought that without her cat, she might take her own life. Feeling her daughter's concern touched the woman and made her aware that her daughter still needed her.

In fact she had given considerable thought to suicide. Her greatest fear was that she might lose her cherished mind by contracting Alzheimer's disease. "How will I know if I've lost it if I have lost my capacity to reason?" she asked. She had aged considerably in the last few years. She had a variety of worsening metabolic diseases which require an attentive balancing of medication. She complained of being frightfully exhausted so it took her longer to get everything done. She added, "I have some loss of memory; I start to lose an essential word or forget a first name." She has in the past been quite social, but as she has lost some voice she observes, "People can't hear me so I am no longer interesting." She had become quite despondent when she couldn't read because of cataracts, but since reparative surgery she was often her old self.

"The cat gets me up. I have to feed him, clean his box, give him a shot. I don't have depressing thoughts when I'm taking care of him." Due to the diabetes the cat is losing weight, just like its owner who is down to ninety-nine pounds. "He must be my animus," she laughs. She also enjoys being thin. "Now I can wear a size four," she smiles one spring morning, sporting a combination of soft pink and a subtle celadon green enhanced by simple jewelry. How could an underweight old woman with bony knees inspire the essence of spring? I marveled. Yet to me she did.

Here is her dragon dream, and another about death:

> There is a beautiful little dragon in my ear. It looks like an ancient piece of Chinese jewelry with enamel scales colored Chinese red and bright blue. It has a wormlike body with a fancy head. It's a handsome little thing. It's curled like a snake or uroborus with its head near its tail. It is asleep, and when it awakens it's going to kill me.
>
> I am in a room lying in bed next to a room in which my grandparents are sleeping. It is a plain simple room with a very flimsy door separating these two rooms. It was made clear in the dream that I am to join my dead grandparents. It seemed more familiar, less frightening.

In reference to the Chinese dragon, she told me that having lived in San Francisco, with its roots in Asian cultures, her parents collected Asian art which she came to admire. That the little dragon chose to reside in her ear was very reassuring, she said. It was a safe place for it to be, and it was comforting for her. She explained that she is becoming deaf because her ears plug up. "It's a bothersome old age." Especially when she hasn't eaten, her ears fill up. It is as if she has begun to starve herself to death.

She said that her ear represents her connection to others. "All myths spring right there in my ear. It's very ancient. The dragon represents fire and gold associated with meditation. It's part of my personal mythology."

As a younger woman she had been in Jungian analysis, which had been quite important to her. She knew that the Chinese dragon is a life symbol; its undulating movement and fire power invests all things with dynamic energy. In the West it often stands for the negative or devouring aspect of the unconscious which the young hero must overcome in order to realize himself. In her dream it takes the form of the uroborus, the snake that eats its own tail, an image not unlike the earrings she often wears, symbolizing the state of at-one-ness, the *unus mundus* or time before consciousness, and so might represent death. It is a paradoxical image because now in life the patient is awake and the dragon is asleep. Safely tucked in her ear, it supplies her with a vital relationship to her psychic life, but when it awakens she will fall into eternal sleep.

Moving to the second dream, she mentioned being quite fond of her grandparents, remembering how they cared for her and taught her things. Several generations back, her ancestors came to this country in the middle of the nineteenth century with the influx of Spanish Sephardic Jews. They made their money in diamonds so she had been brought up in wealth, privilege and private education in Europe. Being quite beautiful and enjoying relationships with men, she became a kind of cultural anima figure, attaching herself to well-known literary figures. Later on she also became somewhat of a political figure in Washington, a big money raiser in a national political party and a fireball fighting for liberal causes. Social graces were important; she had wit, intelligence, good taste, cunning, charm and quickness. When such a person with highly developed social skills ages and the very strengths that have supported her begin to fail, depression often follows. "People won't like me anymore," she said.

This woman had also developed an inward looking spiritual dimension, as evidenced by the dream-dragon in her ear. She had been fiercely independent all her life, and as she felt the ravages of aging she didn't relish becoming a social outcast. As well, her money was running out. "I gave it all away," she volunteered. The thought of killing herself was ever present.

Her struggle over whether to keep the cat alive contributes to a growing emotional maturity. Until recently she had always thought of herself as being much younger than she actually was. She identified with the age she felt inside, perhaps half her actual age, but now she feels more congruent with her actual age and feels good about that reality. She had had other dreams she felt spoke of her coming death. In one she was with her daughter in a lake created by the Buddha's lap, suggesting a quietness in her soul.

As she nears the end of her life she is trying to resolve a stormy relationship with her daughter. Deep down she cares for her, but when she tries to acknowledge this bond, emotional turbulence flies in from both her own unresolved relationship with her dead mother as well as from the daughter. Her daughter's recent concern about the cat led to a new level of feeling. She wrote a love poem, "My Dragon," which she dedicated to her daughter. Her dragon seems to represent intuition, a gift of the gods that has guided her life as well as her daughter's:

> As it is beautiful,
> I give it to you.
> As it is love,
> I give it to you.
>
> As it is that we only intuit,
> it is for you.
> For we share it—daughter,
> we share it.

As she is accepting the limitations visited by aging, she is facing her death.

> I have to finish my task in life before I can go. If life has any meaning at all, it's to solve some particular problem. I feel quite certain about that. My solution is growing. You have to be quiet enough to know that. I'm not blown off course as much as before. When life is finished, the little dragon curled up inside my ear will take me in. He's going to cause my death when he comes out, not kill me but rather he will engulf me. My consciousness will disappear.

We learn more about the dragon as symbol from Marianne Moore:

> If I, like Solomon, . . .
> could have my wish—
> my wish . . . O to be a dragon,
> a symbol of the power of Heaven—of silkworm
> size or immense; at times invisible.
> Felicitous phenomenon![137]

Moore's dragon seems to have all the attributes of a Self or God image, tiny or immense, visible or invisible, but certainly divinely happy. Spirit animals—stag, unicorn, dragon—are magical. They embody the power of transformation. They are incarnations of the spirit Mercurius that can take any form or shape. Psychologically, they represent the mysterious, what we refer to as intuition and imagination. Linking the unknown world to the world that we know, they bridge life and death. They convey the independent spirit that women often connect to in their cats, a certain aloofness, something that can't and won't be controlled by things of this world alone.

I asked a colleague with an interest in Chinese culture if she was familiar with Moore's dragon poem. She lent me a book by the Chinese scholar Wu

[137] "To Be a Dragon," ibid. p. 177.

Hung, who had researched a Chinese Han Dynasty inscription to the Yellow Dragon. It explains why the image of the dragon lives or dies. Unlike the woman's dream, the dragon dies when the ruler is not consciously alive.

> "The Yellow Dragon. It swims in a pond when [a ruler] does not dry up the pond to fish."
>
> *Textural references:* "The Yellow Dragon is the head of the four dragons. When [a ruler] does not dry up a pond to fish, his virtue reaches deep springs. [In response,] the Yellow Dragon swims in the pond. The dragon can [fly] either high or low, can be either tiny or huge, visible or invisible, short or long. It suddenly appears and suddenly disappears."[138]

In both the inscription and in Moore's poem, the dragon represents that mysterious elixir of life. Knowing this tells us that the elderly woman has understood something of the meaning of the dragon as it relates to her life.

Shortly after my patient struggled with whether to put her cat down, it died. As her medical situation continued to deteriorate, she began to have hypnagogic visions every night, or hallucinations as she called them, in which she either heard or saw a cat or simply knew that one was in the room. She said that when she tried to touch the cat, its body turned out to be a bedside lamp or became a table. She said that the vision of the cat was so real that she put out food for it. "The cat was there, it was very vivid," she emphasized. She continued to see it, but then it was not there. This upset the patient because to her it meant she was not connected to reality. When she first saw the cat, she thought it must be an alley cat, but where did it come from? At other times she saw different cats, black, white or tabby.

After some deliberation, she usually realizes that the cat is not real, but just in case, she says, "I'll put some food and water out. Rationally, I know the cat is not here. I know it is a delusion, but what am I do?" She feeds the cat as if it were real. Her cat has become a spirit. No matter that it no longer has an outer body or form. She continues to nourish the image inside.

The cat has always been an important symbol for this woman. As a little girl of seven or eight, she identified with the cat in Rudyard Kipling's *Just So Stories.* "That's me, I'm the wild, wild cat that walks in the wild, wild woods," she exclaims. When she told me this, I realized the cat was really her totem animal. She had never been without one; it was her living self.

I remembered a film I had seen many years before about an indigenous Sibe-

---

[138] *The Wu Liang Shrine: The Ideology of Early Chinese Pictorial Art,* p. 237.

rian trapper's relationship to his totem animal. The movie, *Dersu Uzala,* is taken from the diary of a Russian officer exploring Siberia at the turn of the century. He writes about his guide, Dersu Uzala, a direct descendent from the Goldi, a shamanistic tribe. Toward the end of Uzala's life, with his eyesight failing, he shoots a tiger, his totem animal, something one should never do, and realizes that his life is over. Without his eyes, he knows that he cannot continue to live as a hunter in the wild. But he also knows that the era of being a hunter is over. He says, "All round soon all game gone . . . Me think ten years, no more wapiti, no more sable, no more squirrel, all gone."[139] Soon after retiring to a small cabin in town, he dies. Like my dying patient feeding her spirit cat, Dersu Uzala would cook meals for his dead wife and children, an old tradition.

So, too, the woman's cat is her totem animal. Even though her cat is dead, she continues to see cats in the morning. It is possible that when she no longer sees them, the dragon will awaken and she will die.

As this woman's body deteriorates and her worldly persona fades, her intuition deepens and, paradoxically, she becomes more calm. She laughs more with her wry sense of humor. This old lady, whom I could hardly understand through her whispers, is heading out toward her death. Indeed, recently she dreamed that she was walking backward on a dirt path into a sunlit spring forest. She said, "The dusty path curves away beyond where I can see. When I get there, then I will see more." As she told me the dream she experienced "a shivering feeling in my spine." She felt she was letting go, that she was leaving. "I don't care as much and I feel the calmer for it. My heart is emptying out and I feel content."

About the time she dreamt of the fancy little dragon that would take the fire away from her, I was visited by fire dragons that practically incinerated me. They weren't the dragons of final death but rather those of a transitional death. A phase of my life was ending; I was entering a liminal zone. Whatever dead wood remained from old psychological wounds was igniting, but the new growth had yet to emerge. The flames of passion in me were so alive I could hardly stand it. The gods were stirring, creating winds of intuition. My world felt like it was coming apart. I hadn't yet achieved the serenity of this old woman.

The Phoenix and the 1995 Pt. Reyes Fire

Suddenly an image catches fire. It seems to arise from nowhere, when one's mind is on other things. It takes hold, becoming a burning passion. How it happens is a mystery. Rilke conveys this mysterious ignition:

---

[139] V.K. Arseniev, *Dersu the Trapper,* p. vii.

As on all its sides a kitchen-match darts white
flickering tongues before it bursts into flame:
with the audience around her, quickened, hot,
her dance begins to flicker in the dark room.

And all at once it is completely fire.
One upward glance and she ignites her hair
and, whirling faster and faster, fans her dress
into passionate flames, till it becomes a furnace
from which, like started rattlesnakes, the long
naked arms uncoil, aroused and clicking.

And then: as if the fire were too tight
around her body, she takes and flings it out
haughtily, with an imperious gesture,
and watches: it lies raging on the floor,
still blazing up, and the flames refuse to die—.
Till, moving with total confidence and a sweet
exultant smile, she looks up finally
and stamps it out with powerful small feet.[140]

Rilke's fire, which spontaneously combusts as his Spanish dancer's emotions heat up, seems out of control. But in the end she is its master. She comes to life, her passion ignites a relationship. Something changes and calm is restored.

In the second spring after my dog Moss died, and after I had returned from a trip to the southwest attending Hopi ceremonial dances, my own phoenix experience began. A personal fire had entered my veins. Suddenly and inexplicably I developed a projection onto a woman. She was tall and striking and occupied a position of authority. Being exceptionally good with languages, she was preparing to change careers and break into international trade on her own. Whether this anticipation of change was too far in the future or whether she was having difficulties in her marriage, she was not satisfied emotionally.

Her body radiated fire, which she both displayed and held in check, thus creating a most provocative tension. We arranged a time to meet without her ever taking her eyes off the computer. Because the sexual tension could not be contained long enough for a real relationship to develop, things quickly unraveled and I was left with a passion I could not still. I felt like the imprisoned panther in Rilke's poem related earlier. I didn't know what to do with it. Nothing could quell this fire, burning of its own accord. I couldn't talk to anyone about it. The

---

[140] "Spanish Dancer," in *The Selected Poetry of Rainer Marie Rilke,* p. 43.

experience felt sacred and deeply personal, belonging to me alone. A fire god was paying me a visit and I wasn't going to miss this encounter, even if it killed me. I did nothing with it but I was left with a shocking power from inside myself, the realization that something like that could happen to me. It was autonomous, involuntary, like a bird flying out of my chest.

Gradually this fire subsided and in its aftermath I was left with grief, but as the months went by it dawned on me that I could write about the animal dreams I had been collecting. I had never written a book before, only short pieces, and I felt unequal to the task. I told myself that I wouldn't think of myself as a writer but would simply share my interest in animal images. Deep down I wanted my dog back and I felt that writing about him and other animals might assuage my grief. My analyst often joked with me that I never used words to communicate; rather I would try to translate my feeling responses, often unsuccessfully, into a foreign language, English.

However, before the writing had begun, while I was still burning up inside, that following autumn, in October 1995, a forest fire destroyed over twelve thousand acres in Pt. Reyes National Seashore. From my little house I could see the entire ridge on fire behind the town of Inverness. I felt the fire god had now descended in literal form. A ribbon of gold and red lit up the night sky, reminding me of another fiery image from my boyhood in Youngstown, Ohio, when at night I would look down into the Mahoning Valley and see the great open-hearths of steel mills burning. But the fire on the Inverness ridge was not contained; it was threatening our houses and land, awakening fear and awe beyond memory or imagination. Something bigger than anyone could cope with had arrived. We tried talking with one another as if that would help and as we ordinarily did when community issues arose, but each of us was really alone in our own thoughts. We were at a loss as to how to respond. The presence of a fire god displaced our usual human interaction. Who were we, what were we about? If our houses went, we would have to rethink our lives, but our fears weren't specifically limited to our homes. One couldn't exactly put one's finger on it. Thinking straight felt impossible. Should we plan now what to take out of our houses or should we wait for the call to evacuate?

All night I watched the fire. Small explosions would flare up and die down when a new group of trees suddenly incinerated, and then the ribbon of yellow gold would return to its natural bed. In the evening the wind had died down and what little there was, was blowing away from us. So even though I was within a mile of the fire, strangely, I cannot remember the smell or sound; whether this was because the wind was blowing away or whether the awe blocked my hearing, I don't know. There was just the sight of it. Every time I awoke from sleeping on the deck there was this beautiful flare, firelight, which grew unaccountably reassuring. Some presence was keeping me warm, contained, comforted and loved. I must have felt this as a boy watching the mill furnaces burn at night, when I was lonely and in need of rekindling my heart. Experiencing these feelings now seemed a strange response, knowing that my neighbor's son had lost his house.

The general opinion was that if all else failed, the fire-fighters would make an all-out effort to stop the fire at the road. Instead of being relieved at this news, I must have tensed up, because while leaning over to tie my shoes I suddenly felt my back go into spasm. That morning, after having lain prone all night on the deck, I couldn't get up. No matter what position I tried, from whatever angle, I couldn't rise to my feet. Now that the wind had picked up, the fire looked truly menacing and it seemed to be coming straight toward me. I had no idea what to do. Finally, with a tremendous effort, I forced myself upright. Never in all my life did I experience such pain, and I thought I might have damaged my back muscles. Once up I managed some mobility.

For the first time I thought the house might go. I didn't know what to take. I hadn't ever really considered it. How could I carry anything with my back hardly able to carry its own body? I decided to take only the things I cared deeply about. First I chose a favorite book, an anthology of literature edited by Somerset Maugham. In it was my most loved short story, E.M. Forster's "The Celestial Omnibus." Then I took an old warm terry cloth bathrobe that my wife had sewn for me, now so worn she thought it should go in the rubbish heap. Next I managed to carry two large heavy Chinese ceramic water containers, beautifully and naturally shaped. I had paid $30 or $40 each for them in Chinatown in the old days. I saved two bronze candlesticks that had belonged to my grandparents, probably the only things I have from them and which my wife thinks are so ugly that she wouldn't have them in our city house. I lifted an Oriental painting off the wall, leaving a gaping hole that it covered. I removed two small flat-weave Afghan rugs that I couldn't live without. Then I wrote a note to the firemen explaining about the different water systems and tacked this message on the door.

As I walked outside in pain, a big bomber flew very slowly overhead, so close I thought I could touch it. It was several times larger than my house and suddenly the area felt like a war zone. A mixture of feelings surfaced—fear, awe, sadness, excitement, pain, and underneath everything, anxiety. The fire looked terrifying. How could I justify my feeling the night before of being contained by a warm god? Had I been out of my mind? When I came down the hill to the main road I ran into a company of perhaps fifteen fire trucks parked along it. When I arrived in Inverness a mile away, there were two more companies parked in a local store lot and along the roadside. These trucks with the fire fighters all in yellow suits and black hats were very reassuring. Overhead, helicopters were dipping big buckets strung on the end of long dangling lines into Tomales Bay, scooping up water and dropping it on the ridge above.

All these marshaled efforts made me think of what it must have been like for those involved in a great war effort. I remembered how in front of my father's drugstore, in World War Two, there was a big barrel for people to throw in tin foil or aluminum, and every so often I would bring the butcher next door a small coffee can filled with hardened fat and grease that my mother had saved for "the Boys." After weighing it he gave me a few pennies, which I was allowed to keep. He always smiled at me when he finished his calculations. Did he give me a little extra, I wondered?

In Inverness, hardly a soul was in sight except the firemen, a few reporters identified by their cameras, and some official-looking people. I did run into a big earthy woman who looked like she had been through it all. No doubt responding to my palpable fear, she told me not to worry. She said the fire was fairly contained and that's why they had begun dropping water now with helicopters. This was the first optimistic news in days. On the way out of town, at every intersection of roads descending from the ridge to the bay, there was a company of fire trucks. I had never seen anything like these. They weren't your ordinary city fire trucks. They were different shapes and colors and of every possible vintage. There were sturdy little trucks reminding me of "The Little Engine That Could," built for terrain other than roads, and specialized trucks with tanks and strange equipment. The fire fighters looked attentive but relaxed. I was never so happy to be part of the collective; my tax dollars were visibly proving worthwhile. People could be relied upon in this great effort and someone somewhere was organizing it. Who could keep track of it all? Later I read in the *Point Reyes Light* of the great unselfish contributions people made.

Should I have stayed there? Driving out of the area and returning to normal life, I felt disoriented at first. Gradually, calm returned. My house didn't go up in flames, and we rented it to my builder's family whose house had burned down. My back pain lingered a long time, and was finally cured by acupuncture.

My inside fire gradually subsided as the waterbird chapters evolved into a book. I had managed to contain the inner fire and had come out with something tangible. Now, in looking back at this period, I wonder what all the emotional fuss was about. I can't really remember the torment, I suppose, just as women forget the pain of childbirth. They have their baby, life moves on. The pain was part of the process and we are all on the other side. It's a memory we can write about; we don't have to live through it again.

The passion of the inner fire combined with the Pt. Reyes fire seemed to awaken a burning need to express my loss and recovery of nature. There is a time for our life to catch fire. We put everything on the burning pyre to kindle a renewed form of being. Burn the torch, kiss the fire. Then our fire warms and lights our path as the burning stars illumine the heavens.

Guerranero, Dream Animal

And birds, beautiful and fast, led you over the dark earth,
whirling quick wings from the heaven's ether through the middle sky.
—Sappho., 6th century B.C.

A dying woman's passion releases her soul and it coils into the air like incense smoke. Now, in an insubstantial, purified, ethereal world, she joins animals that live in a special mode of existence. Ether is not matter and is beyond the physical world. It belongs to the world of the mind. Animals that breathe ether, similar to the fiery unicorn and dragon, do not exist apart from the imagination. You cannot find them in the forest or the zoo. They live only in the world of the psyche, and when they appear in a dream they are visible only for a moment, leaving no scratch marks in the sand.

After my passion was awakened and I was consumed by fire, I took flight into the world of imagination. Images of writers whom I wanted to meet flew into my mind. New ideas descended into my waking life at the oddest times, as if sent by the gods. As I burrowed deeper into my book, I slowly withdrew into a world of psychic reality, making it the only one that existed.

When I first began writing, I had difficulty staying connected to the psychological explication of the case material. It was too much like work. Each time I sat down to write, I had to break through a barrier, but now I wouldn't come out for days at a time. Even I could see that I was impossible to live with. Without saying a word, I might rudely leave a dinner party to investigate a suddenly remembered reference. My research would stir a whirlwind of new ideas, sending me deeper into an ethereal realm, that rarefied atmosphere where other humans don't seem to fully exist. As I began to take wing with these images, I realized that all the imaginary animals after the fire were birds—spirit birds. I had begun to live in the spirit.

I embarked on this venture from the seashore, mesmerized by the waterbirds. I watched them, as real beings, fly in the air. I experienced them in my imagination as they unwound from around my heart and flew into the beyond. Although I occasionally flew with them, I remained on the ground. But now, the physical bird had transformed into a psychic bird, an animal that could not be tied down. As transsubstantiated animals, they came down to fetch me.

About this time I gave a lecture on the waterbird that included showing some slides of paintings by the Northwest artist Morris Graves. One look at his extraordinary birds tells you that they live in another dimension. Some of the titles of the bird paintings that indicate the supernatural are *Masked Bird Fishing in the Golden Stream, Ecstatic Gander, Moon Bird, Blind Birds, Spirit Birds, Wounded Scoter #2, Crane with Void,* and *Guardian*, a shamanic bird with antlers. Graves knew that in India the gander was a symbol of enlightenment. Its Sanskrit name, *hamsa,* comes from the word for yogic breathing.

When Graves painted *Young Gander Ready for Flight,* he depicted "the miraculous transformation about to result from the gander's rhythmic breathing," according to Ray Kass, a professor of art and friend of Graves.[141] Kass tells us that "Graves has remarked of this painting that the gander's lungs have been trained through concentrated meditation for the breath that will carry its flight to enlightenment." In another painting, *Gander Ready for Flight,* the bird is preparing to take off; its wings extend in a diaphanous mesh of fine white lines suggesting motion as it looks upward in anticipation of the transformation that is about to occur.[142]

Like Graves's *Gander Ready for Flight,* I too began to live more and more from this ethereal realm. As my psyche brought forth more images, I felt surprisingly reassured. Looking upward like the bird toward future experiences, I recalled that the mistakes I had made in the past no longer bothered me as much. However many life possibilities I had cut off, life offered itself anew. A mysterious essence had called up these spirit birds and I was free to soar with them, in the moment, without looking back, without looking down, without always checking to see where I was. The reality of the psyche had taken hold.

---

[141] Ray Kass, in *Morris Graves: Vision of the Inner Eye,* plate 41.
[142] Ibid., plate 92.

But before I enter the zone of the purely imaginary, I find I have to backtrack. I return instead to my origins, to a different kind of bird, to the humble chicken—the animal of my mother and of my Jewish heritage. As children, my friends and I would taunt one another with, "You are a chicken shit," without ever really knowing anything about the timidity of chickens. Do chickens back down? I didn't know then about cock fights. To this day, I have never understood the chicken. It rarely comes up in people's dreams, at least in those of my patients, but in fact for millennia it served as a healing image, used first by the shaman and later taken over by the Jewish mother. The shaman would transfer the patient's illness to himself and then to a chicken. The Jewish mother would take chicken soup and stuff it down the throats of the sick and dying, sometimes yanking people off the street if they looked the slightest bit anemic.

Just before my mother died, as she slipped into a coma, she began singing and talking gleefully—to imaginary others—of chicken. "Did you put the chicken in the basket, don't forget the chicken in the basket!" I assume she was referring to a joyful family picnic. Her mother loved picnics and outings. To this day, much to my wife's disbelief, I don't mind actually eating chicken, I just can't stand the *idea* of it. I would rather die than be seen eating chicken!

This revulsion was not shared by a young woman patient who, like my mother, identified with the chicken. From her dreams, she created a two-headed chicken (Picture 6), a sort of monster image, to protect herself. He was called

Picture 6

Guerranero, which to the patient meant "Black War." In Spanish, *guerrero* means warrior, so this animal was a call to war—meant to do battle with the woman's father. You will see from her dream that this animal means to fight:

> I am looking for something in another room—hear a bird outside—peeping—see an animal moving—see a creature—a huge bird, but it has another head instead of a tail—ugly head—I study it through the window. A Hispanic or Filipino boy comes by—I assume this bird is going to eat him— the boy is surprised—almost jumps out of his skin and says, "Wow, a Guerranero!" He has seen them in his own country! It doesn't hurt him. Plus he sees some animals in the room where I am—calls them by name too—I see that they are a family of dinosaurs. A mother and babies. She eats one. I decide this is a great scientific discovery—so I take two, although they might eat each other. I discover I have three. I leave.

This two-headed chicken can scratch, as fighting women do. Its tail head looks like an artificial mask invoking a demon spirit to frighten its enemies. The creature's hair is standing up on end and the eyes are jutting out, dilated. It's fight or flight. This animal means business; its ugly head reminds us of the ugliness of the boar that is associated with strength.

For her, the rear end of this chicken was her father, a man who thought of his children as extensions of himself. He would follow his young daughters about, shouting orders, making demands, invading their space. So, this monster head-tailed chicken could scare him off if he got too close. She pointed out with glee that it had teeth. Yet, from looking at the drawing, I couldn't help but wonder if the whole proposition of teeth and surprise get-up was a bit of a ruse, while the real head looks quite savvy and alive, perhaps angry. Its open beak is giving orders, and it's on the move. There is a feminine quality to the eye and head. This chicken knows where she's going and why, which is also true for this woman. Although she seems coy and unassuming, speaking with a voice younger than her years, she is smart as a whip, clear and determined.

Still, this defensive prop doesn't really work. She is too sensitive to criticism, especially from women in authority. Even when she likes her bosses and has a real relationship with them, the slightest note of disapproval undermines her.

Curiously, in her dream this woman is more worried about the warlike creature eating the Hispanic boy than she is about the dinosaur biting her. Presumably she has grown up in a family of dinosaurs where the mother eats her babies. She seems more intrigued than afraid, rescuing them in a logical manner. Her intellect must have rescued her. After the confrontation with her father, I learned more about the her relationship to her mother from another short dream:

> From a window at home in our backyard, Mom and I saw a little bird, a wren, in a tree. It was a small young bird, light brown with white spots. Mom started petting it. I started petting it too. We were sharing something. Then the bird's color began to fade and it flew away.

She said that she often wanted to share things with her mother, but her mother could not be emotionally present for her. "She can't relate to me. If I try, she can't respond. You can't get in. I can't figure out what she's thinking. If I pet the bird, then I get all confused." When she tries to share this experience with her mother, the bird just disappears. The rational mother does not want her daughter to be emotionally expressive, so she refuses to engage with her in any real way. This mother's cold touch kills all feeling and spirit, represented by the fading of the bird's warm colors.

After graduating from college, this young woman developed a friendship with an older woman who one morning made cinnamon toast for her. Noting her friend's happiness while performing this task, my patient said of herself, "No one else would have noticed her happiness, because it's what people normally share in their relationships all the time." This simple human act was too warm-blooded for her dinosaur family.

Following the dream of her mother, she showed me drawings of horses doodled while talking with me (Picture 7, next page). She said she had been drawing horses ever since third grade.

> I can always draw a horse and know what I'm feeling like inside. Horses have all these things on them, harnesses, traps, lead lines and then you can make them free. The horse to the left is an old wild horse. He is free and if you try to pet him he will run. This represents my feeling free from restraint. But what is now is the horse to the right. He is domesticated. His head is down, his ears are down, so he is more in touch. He is a listening horse, the smaller the better. This reality has hope. If I had not begun this new life, this horse wouldn't have been drawn.

She begins trusting. Yet the horse looks somewhat depressed as the dreamer herself continues to be depressed from time to time.

She continued to draw in the office, this time faces, either sad or happy, to express feelings, rather than using animals for this purpose. She was becoming more open, not just in therapy, but with other people too. She told me a surprising thing: that for the first time she didn't need to know where other people were in the house; she could allow them to enter her space without being prepared ahead of time. Before she had been on guard, "Guerranero," but now she could be herself with others present.

Picture 7

The bird, an animal of the spirit, protects this woman's spirit from being contaminated by her father. These protector birds are sent down from heaven to rescue us. In Christian tradition birds are often disguised in human form as angels because the birds know people are not as willing to accept animals as spiritual guides. But they still appear undisguised in dreams.

Another bird, in a different woman's dream, protects her from the danger of misusing her own creative energy:

> An older man was going to smoke a really nasty cigar. He got out his special bird. This bird cleaned the air of the smoke. It also cleaned up other messes. The bird was floating in the air and I could reach up and pet it. It was very beautiful with fluffy pink downy feathers like cat fur and long trailing floppy feathers on its head, wings and tail. The long feathers were a soft grey color. The man said that this was a very important bird.

The morning after her dream she seemed more cheerful. Although she thought the dream was amusing and interesting, she didn't connect it to her situation. But to me it seemed clear that she had become contaminated through overwork, in projects far removed from her interest, causing her to lose touch with her own inspiration. Her irritable, nasty mood was infecting the environment. The older man smoking, representing her now soured enthusiasm for study, stinks up the room. But diabolically he contains within his nature the miraculous ability to clean up his messes. He produces this magic bird which can restore clean air, allowing the dreamer to reconnect with her creative spirit, seen in the long feathery covering with bright feminine colors.

The bird serves as a caretaker whose function in our dreams is to keep the house, a metaphor for psyche, in order. An example of the quintessential caretaker in the form of a person rather than an animal is P.G. Wodehouse's butler Jeeves, who is forever rescuing his master Bertie from situations in which he has lost his wings.[143]

These are very important images because they keep the spirit from falling into darkness. In my experience women especially hate to use their creative energy for things which hold no interest for them. It is poison to them and they resent it more than anything in the world, as was the case for this woman. She was assigned projects that were not central enough to her muse. She said that although she didn't always understand her dreams, they were nevertheless important: "I have to dip down into my irrational in order to feel better."

The irrational, that inner voice that tells us how things really stand, is also what stimulated another patient to trust himself. He consulted me when he risked rational judgment by changing careers. As a child he had felt cared for by Big Bird of *Sesame Street* at a time when his father was drinking himself to death. Big Bird affirmed the little boy's emotions when his father couldn't be there for him. Being the youngest of three boys, he must have enchanted his mother in a way that protected him from the fate of his two brothers, who succumbed to schizophrenia and drug addiction. All his life he tried to be true to his feeling, but the genuine spirit and real success that he generated did not satisfy him. In midlife he decided he needed to give more to people than he had been able to in the past, and became a psychotherapist.

As part of this training he undertook to work with children in a special project. Because of the enormous undertaking in switching careers and the resultant financial hardship, he had doubts all along the way. He would pray from his heart: "Can the world take what I have to offer? Is it time for this project to be realized?" Months later he was to tell me, "It's happening, people are getting it." During this tumultuous period he had a dream containing images reminiscent of creation motifs in mythology:

> My friend and I are following a big bird around the yard. There are palm trees and palisades nearby. The bird is pregnant and has a long pole which it sticks in the

---

143 See Wodehouse, *The World of Jeeves.*

> ground to make holes for new palm trees to be planted. It circles around and passes us. We are intrigued and follow it. The ground is hard and the pole is ten feet long. But the bird sticks the pole in hard and is able to put six feet of it in the ground so four feet are showing. The pole is long and thin at the bottom but with a bigger bell-shaped top on which is carved and painted, in color, a cornucopia, out of which miraculously spring images of ideas, flowers, children, stars and rainbows.

The man was struck with how forcefully "Big Bird" was able to wield his pole. To be able to make those deep holes in hard dirt with two or three thrusts was quite impressive, he thought. "That's the kind of confidence I need to have about my work; then I wouldn't have any doubts."

Big Bird had come through; he was able to dig the holes for planting that his father was unable to. He said it was a sad thing to see a powerful man like his father shrivel up into nothing, his powerful muscles just withering away. I asked him to tell me about his friend. He said that his friend was a thinking-type person who was always inventing things, many of which became successful. With Big Bird laying the groundwork, the friend supplied the missing link to champion his own creative gifts.

Osprey

Inspired by my patient's big bird, I began to think of my own special bird, one who flies silently in the stillness of the night. His enormous eyes, that could only have been created in an artist's imagination, see into the unknown. His little ears, capable of triangulating sound, enable him to hear thoughts in whispered form. Even though owl is of this world, he has always been a magical bird for me. His *who, who, whooing,* so soothing to the soul, would lull me to sleep as I lay on my back deck and usher in my dreams. Owl was the animal I listened to while I studied the stars. The bird of the night became my guide through the day, helping me to stay true to the deeper, more important things rather than being caught in surface turbulence. This is why I have included owl with those birds who exist purely in the imagination. When owl is called up out of my being, I encounter a mystery even though the bird is standing in front of me.

When I finished working on owl, I was satisfied but still doubtful as to whether he truly belonged with the other strange birds. That night I had a dream of yet another bird that exactly fit the category of owl. Like owl, he was a bird you could find in the bird book, but in the dream he was mysterious, even more so than owl. I was amazed and grateful that my psyche would supply me with a dream image right to the point of my inner dialogue, and I couldn't stop thinking about it. Perhaps that's why, in broad daylight, I became airborne like a bird.

For the first time in my life a car hit me while I was on my habitual bicycle ride near my house in the old army Presidio, now a national park. I flew over the hood of the car and landed on my "good" shoulder, shattering my scapula and fracturing ribs which punctured my lung. Another word for scapula is "wing." Instantly deflated, I was brought back to earth, or rather pavement, with a bang. My orthopedist exclaimed, "Lucky you weren't killed."

Here is the dream that had so captured my imagination:

> I was facing a blackboard in the middle of a long rectangular classroom that was open on either end. A young female student brought in a sculpture from the Neolithic period. Was it terra cotta, I wondered, as she placed it on a waist-high pedestal in front of the blackboard and then walked away. It wasn't clear what this object was; that is, I couldn't make out any of its definition or distinguishing characteristics, so I asked a visiting teacher walking out of the lecture how we should name this object. She left the room to get her book to find out. As I looked at it, it seemed to take form. It was most definitely a bird, at first I thought hawk or eagle, but realized it was an osprey. It had a broad white chest and the head of a raptor. The color of its plumage was darker, however, than that of osprey or hawk.
>
> But the sculpture was presented to us as a mysterious object, part of a larger picture, and representative of that time. The student who brought it seemed quiet, as if to suggest that she knew or understood something special about it, and that is why she brought it in to show us.
>
> She argued that even though it looked like an osprey, it seemed to be more than a bird. It looked like a bird that was something else. What could it be, I wondered? Was it a symbol, and if so, of what? Something perhaps representing that period. How strange that something I could clearly identify as an osprey or raptor would at the same time be something else. What could that mean? Being able to identify the object as a bird freed me from my usual achievement anxiety, often expressed in dreams as my not knowing the material and so failing a test, but that was not the problem here. The problem was more of an intellectual puzzle, leaving me feeling exhilarated, as if I were on to something new and interesting
>
> As I was pondering this, caught up in the wonder and excitement of it, the officious teacher—either as a response to my question or voluntarily and somewhat mechanically on her own—began to talk about how all this was to be advertised on the Internet in commercial or communication language, none of which I could understand. Yet, we were to be examined on this. (There was only one other woman in the classroom besides the owner of the sculpture, the teacher and myself.)

The dream dropped me again into the inner life. I had been struggling with what to do over the Christmas holidays: to work on my book or go away like my colleagues, crammed into houses in the snowy mountains, with not a moment of privacy. The mysterious bird affirmed my decision to stay home. Much better to have a bird to puzzle over, I thought.

The osprey sitting on the pedestal also made me think of the osprey nesting on poles out in the water of Tomales Bay. Years ago, I had spent a day in the spring with the naturalist Jules Evens, inspecting all the osprey nests along the bay. Because of the low rainfall that year, he was concerned that there might be fewer chicks. The less rain, the less food, the less chicks, he explained.

But now that I knew these associations, how was I to understand this dream image, an identifiable fish hawk of this world, and yet a symbol of something else that dates back so far? How can something we know so much about still remain a mystery?

When I ask this question, what comes to mind are the exquisitely detailed sculptures of the early Egyptians, especially the hawk of Horus, the sun god. Standing before this carefully rendered bird in a museum, you actually feel it is living, yet it symbolizes something bigger, something that reaches into the beyond, a god perhaps. It is a symbol of power and empire, like the Roman eagle or our American eagle. The naturalist Henry Beston shares a similar perception from his little house on the shore of Cape Cod:

> Watching the hawk thus a-squat on the sand in the summer intensity of light, with the grey sea bird [tern] angrily assailing her, there came into my mind a thought of the ancient Egyptian representations of animals and birds. For this hawk in the pit was the Horus Hawk of the Egyptians, the same poise, the same dark blood-fierceness, the same authority. The longer I live here and the more I see of birds and animals, the greater my admiration becomes for those artists who worked in Egypt so many thousand years ago, drawing, painting, carving in the stifling quiet of the royal tombs, putting here ducks frightened out of the Nile marshes, here cattle being herded down a village street, here the great sun vulture, the jackal, and the snake. To my mind, no representations of animals equal these Egyptian renderings. I do not write in praise of faithful delineation or pictorial usage–though the Egyptian drew from his model with care–but of the unique power to reach, understand, and portray the very psyche of animals. The power is particularly notable in Egyptian representations of birds. A hawk of stone carved in hardest granite on a temple wall will have the soul of all hawks in his eyes. Moreover, there is nothing human about these Egyptian creatures. They are self-contained and aloof as becomes folk of a first and intenser world.[144]

The swiftness and agility of the powerful hawk make it an animal of the gods.

---

[144] *The Outermost House,* p. 160.

My sculptured osprey commanding the front of the classroom harkens back to the very beginning of civilization—back to when the wild was domesticated, when people settled down and began firing clay pots and sculpture. My first real journey into this period, known as the Neolithic, came as a young psychiatrist through my study of the spiral image.[145] There, the terra cotta figures of the Babylonian Ninhursag and the Egyptian Hathor, goddesses clothed and coifed in spiral imagery and alive with earthy sensuality and fecundity, supplied me with the feminine inspiration absent from my patriarchal Jewish tradition. I felt like young Joseph in the Bible, who after being sold to the Ishmaelites is taken down into the heathen land of Egypt.

I was led again into this agricultural era of the Great Mother, this time by the waterbird. The sculptures of bird-headed goddesses, documented by the archaeologist Marja Gimbutas,[146] revealed the psychic feminine realm of sky and water, informing my fascination with these same long-legged shore birds on my walks on the beaches of Pt. Reyes. Behind the natural world lay the deeper world of symbol and psyche.

All the animals I have presented so far have had a personal symbolic meaning for the people who dreamed them, and therefore they sparked the imagination. The dream always began with a known animal whose symbolic meaning was left for the dreamer to decipher. In this dream of the osprey, however, the initial image portrayed was that of a mystery bird from an ancient period. Only as it came into focus could the bird be identified, and then the dream stated that its meaning was somehow more than a bird. The dream begins in mystery, bridging the unknown to the known worlds, rather than the other way around. In this way, it reminds me that these two worlds are more interchangeable than I thought.

Is that how animals came into being, as in Genesis in the Bible, created as images in God's eye, then to find their place on earth? The osprey in this dream was real. Its photograph appears in the *National Geographic Field Guide to the Birds of North America,* with this description:

> **Osprey** *Pandion haliaetus.* "L. 22-25" W 58-72". Dark brown above, white below, with white head, prominent dark eye stripe. Males are usually all-white below; females have a necklace of dark streaking. Immature plumage is edged with pale buff above. In flight, the Osprey's long, narrow wings are bent back at the wrist, like a gull's dark wrist patches are conspicuous. Wings are slightly arched in soaring. Ospreys nest near fresh or salt water; eat fish almost exclusively. Hover-

---

145 See above, chap. 4.

146 See *The Civilization of the Goddess.*

> ing over water, they dive toward prey, then plunge feet first to snatch it. Bulky nests are built in trees, on sheds, poles, docks; also on platforms specially constructed for Ospreys. Conservation programs and elimination of DDT in recent years have halted decline of species. Now fairly common in coastal range. Uncommon and local inland; seen chiefly during migration. Common call is a loud, whistled *kyew kyew kyew kyew kyew.*[147]

For me, of course, the osprey isn't just another bird in the birdbook. It is classed with the raptors; its hawklike head and great claws make it a bird of prey. Because its diet consists solely of fish, it is often called fish-hawk. They are magnificent birds and beautiful to watch, often hovering over their prey before diving. Because the osprey builds nests on poles in Tomales Bay, it carries for me the spirit of the life of Tomales Bay. It symbolizes the life that awakened in me when I went to live there. But now, the osprey, a fisher by nature, has come to symbolize more: the spiritual nourishment I would take from understanding my dreams. Instead of watching the bird, I have become the bird. The psyche is now the place from which I begin.

In this way the dream breathed new life into a bird I knew, while presenting it as a symbol. This supported, in a reverse way, my impulse to include the owl, a known bird, with those birds which live solely in the imagination. The dream affirmed my connection to the psyche and left me feeling deeply satisfied.

Synchronistically, I began to think about submitting a proposal for a paper at a psychological conference. Encouraged by the fact that the program committee offered a more innovative and flexible format than usual, I began to think what form would best introduce my animals. How could they relate to people? I shared this puzzle with a colleague and he suggested a topic, "Animals in Art; Animals in Life," in which I would present a side-by-side comparison of animals as we know them in reality and the same animal as seen in reflected image. I would begin by showing slides of animals as they are depicted in selected paintings from Western and Eastern art. Then I might talk about the nature of the actual animal that the art refers to allegorically or symbolically yet also conceals. Around these images, I could say something I have learned about the nature of each of the animals in reality and in dreams.

The important point is that the psychic reflection of the animal and the living vitality of the animal are two different things. Jungian analyst James Hillman talks about two different souls, the psyche-soul and the life-soul.[148] The life-soul

---

[147] Jon L. Dunn, *National Geographic Field Guide,* p. 102.

[148] *The Dream and the Underworld,* pp. 104f.

or body-soul with its emotions is related to our waking, conscious state; the psyche-soul appears in dreams or art representing reflected instinct. Animals speak both to psyche and to life; that is, they have their own emotional vitality apart from the reflected image, and yet each enriches our understanding of the other. The animals, by bringing their body to the union of spirit and soul that their image conveys, complete their healing value for us. The reality of the psyche becomes embodied.

The animal in the dream can go either way, pointing to its own relevant life traits or to a psychic image which has symbolic meaning. It's curious that so many of the animals in my imaginary world are birds. Waterbirds started me off on this venture, leading me backward in time. Now birds that are solely of the imagination bring me in a strange way to the present. The birds have gone full circle, from the present to the Neolithic period and back again, allowing me to experience this great range of time in one moment, and reminding me that the world of the psyche is not bound by time.

Owl

So, as I listen to the soft hooting of owl outdoors, under cover, I am in touch with the Neolithic goddess of death and the night. In the dead of night, with great outstretched wings and claws and silent flight, she descends upon her prey. This eerie image makes the owl a symbol of death. Under the darkness of night, the owl carries away the soul of her captured prey and then stands guard over its spirit. Marja Gimbutas found prehistoric owl goddess statues, half owl, half woman, marking graves in southern Europe during the late Neolithic period. She notes that "frequently only her eyes and nose (beak) and occasionally breasts are shown."[149]

The owl can fly noiselessly in order to hunt undetected in the stillness of night. Its outer serrated feathers muffle the sound of the air flowing over its wings, and allow this death visitor to drop silently onto an unsuspecting mouse or vole. It has developed other unusual characteristics which it uses for the hunt. Some owls, like the barn owl, hunt solely by audition; its ears are positioned asymmetrically on its head so that each ear picks up a slightly different range of the spectrum. This biangulation of the sound enables the owl to focus on its prey with accuracy. Owls also have stiff feathers around their beaks, rictal bristles that function similarly to cat's whiskers to help keep track of prey.

Other owls, like the great horned owl, use their large saucer eyes to hunt.

---

[149] *Civilization of the Goddess*. p. 239.

Their huge pupils dilate at night, letting in great quantities of light. At the expense of color-defining cones, the owl has developed a large concentration of light-sensitive rods, allowing it to see thirty-five to a hundred times better than humans can in dim light. If we had eyes proportional to those of the great horned owl, our eyes would be the size of grapefruit and weigh five pounds each. Owls have the most frontally positioned eyes of any animal, thus increasing their depth perception. The all-seeing eyes of the owl inspired Neolithic people to decorate vases with "the oculi motif representing the numinous regenerating eyes of the Goddess."[150]

The first owl eyes I saw close up in the wild were those of the spotted owl at Indian Beach in Tomales Bay State Park, just two miles north of where I lived. Bob Stewart, the naturalist connected with Marin Open Space, led a small group of us out to see them in early February one year. He let me bring my Border Collie, Moss, because he said the spotted owl has no known predators and for aeons has been unafraid of anything. They live in old forests, this one Bishop Pine, and so they are protected from the great horned owl and other larger predators who can't penetrate the foliage. Late in the afternoon we arrived at our destination, a small area of forest where the birds lived. Bob led us to the usual two or three trees where they tend to perch, but they were not there, so we scouted around for some time in search of them.

There, on a low branch just above our heads, slept Mr. Owl. It was dusk now and he was just beginning to stir. Opening one eye and then the other, he began to look about before completely rotating his head, clear around, while maintaining a stationary body; an amazing feat. Then he called out in an attempt to locate his mate, and soon she responded from a short distance away. Bob said we were free to talk and move about as this wouldn't bother the unflappable bird and true enough, it continued to sit just over our heads. Each owl, Bob told us, has so much territory dependent on the number of rodents living there. Owl plucks them off the logs as they scurry back and forth. As the dusk deepened he told us many stories. Alerting us to the fact that the spotted owl is an endangered animal, we were encouraged to look for more pairs of owls on our walks in the old forest. Satisfied in some deep way, we walked home in silence to the last light, listening to the gentle lapping of the bay.

Not everyone lives quietly in harmony with their nature, even for a brief period. I am seeing an artist who is agitated and depressed. She was referred by

---

[150] Ibid., p. 204.

another patient, a co-worker of hers, who said that she was unhappy in her job and frustrated in her art. At the time of her first appointment, I happened to look out the window to see a downtrodden woman approach my office with slow, methodical, determined steps. In a hollow voice she told of her alcoholic father and of her depressed mother who roped the little girl into sharing her depression. If ever she expressed joy she would experience guilt, associated with breaking a secret bond with her mother. After the patient's failed marriage, she broke away from her mother and her homeland and moved to San Francisco to attend graduate art school. These were the happiest years of her life, but after school, to support herself, she found a boring, compulsive administrative job, stopped doing art work, and became severely depressed.

When she first came to see me, she brought a photograph of herself as a young girl of eight or nine playing in the water. Her arms were outstretched toward the sky and she had the most precious smile on her face, as if she were imagining being a bird. This was exactly what she was unable to do under the weight of her Germanic mother's leaden depression.

In the beginning of our work, she would often forget an appointment. When she came she would express doubt as to the usefulness of therapy, or deny her problems, saying, "Things are not so bad," or "Neil, I think it's time to stop." Slowly she began to realize what her therapeutic work had to offer. It could open up new possibilities, new ways of seeing things, new hope, perhaps a return to her art work. She hated her controlling woman boss who reminded her of her mother, and within months of beginning therapy she spontaneously applied for a new job. There were over three hundred applicants for this job, both because of the nature of the work and its prime location, but she got it. She was more amazed by this than anyone, amazed that she could actually leave the controlling boss for another woman boss, better educated, who could value her for who she was. It was a beginning. About six months after starting analysis, she dreamed:

> I'm trying to get somewhere and I can't find my way. (This reminds me of the frustrated feeling I have when I have difficulty trying to accomplish something.) I'm walking into a neat little house. It is an old house in the country with a porch. The house is made of dark wood and it is mine. Before entering, I notice that the porch roof has a pitch to it and I see a big white owl perched there. Instinctively I stick out my arm for the bird to land. But then I realize that I have no protection; my flesh is exposed and I'm worried that the owl will puncture my vein. As she comes down, she lands on my arm and doesn't hurt me. Then I release it. I know it had to go back to the roof. It just flew off and I'm back in my house.

She said that when the bird landed on her arm, it was a special moment. She exclaimed:

> This beautiful bird, this wild owl, has come to see me. Its beautiful peaceful owl eyes reassured me that I wasn't going to be hurt. I had a calm feeling about connecting with the bird, that in fact I had attracted it. The owl made me feel special and I realize now that I need to trust my psyche. I must trust my own intuition rather than asking for outside advice. Knowing the owl is there for me helps me to realize that I no longer have to be frantic. Up until now I have discounted my dreams but I see through the compassionate eyes of the owl that she is wise.
>
> In the past I have always sought help and direction from men. This has to do with my father wound. My father was an alcoholic who never realized his own artistic nature. He was a poet who followed his images through his intuition and feeling. He had a wonderful wildness to him, but unfortunately the way he touched it was through drinking. He painted only when he drank. Much to my mother's concern about the neatness of the house, my father would drag out his canvases and paint right in the middle of the living room. But he also became violent when he drank and took this out primarily on my brother.

She brought in some of her recent paintings for me to see. Into a particularly dark painting she had inserted an old photograph of her father surrounded by light. She was trying to resurrect the creative energy inspired by her father. The darkness surrounding the rest of the painting belonged to her mother and the disappointment her mother felt when her father began drinking and the family came to ruin. She then brought in a poignant photograph of her parents when they first married. It showed a beautiful, coquettish young woman sitting alongside her handsome husband on the bumper of their new car which was to take them west to begin their new life The nostalgic picture was filled with the promise America held for its young people. The time was just before the Great Depression. Later photographs showed a depressed heavy-set woman and a man who vacuously stared off into space.

The powerful and independent owl of the night interrupts the vision of her parents to help her find her own way. The owl represents her own fierce yet gentle spirit who keeps watch over her and frees her from the guilt of no longer merging with her mother's sorrow. Compensating for her father's failed attempts to realize his artistic imagination, the owl brings the woman gifts of the night and thus becomes the bird connecting her back to the creative life.

The owl's wisdom comes from its ability to see in the dark. Knowledge gained in this way, through intuition, teaches us the objective truth about the motivation of animals and people. Sitting on top of the woman's roof, the owl keeps her secret hopes and her spirit alive in the dark night. As this woman learns to trust the white night bird, her dark depression will lift. In an alchemical text, there is a picture of a "bespectacled owl holding two torches . . . flanked by a pair of lighted candles, [who] carries the dark saying, 'What good are torches, light, or spectacles, to folk who won't see!' "[151]

Birds of the imagination light our way, enabling us to find the life that we know to be true. They instill our spirit with a sense of wonder and trust without which we remain just clay. There is not one of us who can live without the white bird in the dark night.

---

[151] John Read, *Prelude to Chemistry: An Outline of Alchemy, Its Literature and Relationships,* p. 81.

7
Returning Home

Town, Nature, the Human World

From the beginning this book has been a quest, a way back. Following the animal trail back to my own nature, I find a path that illuminates and restores. Often what leads me along the way are dreams. Indeed, the dream is at the very core of this mode of traveling.

Even people who are perplexed by their dreams feel their emotional charge. They know from a dream whether they are upset or not, whether a recent decision they have made is the right one. A dream image can break through like a large hairy animal arising from the depths. There is no denying it.

I recently watched a new production of Emily Brontë's *Wuthering Heights,* in which the tragic heroine decides to marry, not for love but for social status. She dreams that she is violently brought back to the heath she loves, to Heathcliff, the man linked with this love. Having made a rational decision that defies her nature, she draws a violent response in return. The dream touches something deep in her. It strikes home.

Not everyone is as passionately connected to their emotional life as was this heroine. They don't know what they feel. They don't have a heath or hearth to call home. They don't know what home is. Robert Frost gives us one definition:

> "Home," he mocked gently.
>
> "Yes, what else but home?
> It all depends on what you mean by home.
> Of course he's nothing to us, any more
> Than was the hound that came a stranger to us
> Out of the woods, worn out upon the trail."
>
> "Home is the place where, when you have to go there,
> They have to take you in."
>
> "I should have called it
> Something you somehow haven't to deserve."[152]

Home is the place where we belong, where without pretense or mask we can

[152] "The Death of the Hired Man," in *Poetry of Robert Frost: The Collected Poems, Complete and Unabridged,* p. 33.

truly be ourselves—like the animal instinctively true to its nature. We come home and we know where we are. One woman who has found a home through our work together described it this way. She said,

> I can feel that center place, that solidity, in my belly. I feel it going clear down to my feet. When I'm not in touch, I'm floating, I'm lost. The more I'm in touch with me, the more seen I feel; the more I step out, the closer I get to that place. It's like coming home. Now, I have a map to follow when I go out. I can read the map to find my way. It's reassuring to know I don't need to ask anyone, I don't need to rely on anyone. I can trust myself.

In a relationship too, if it is right we feel at home in the other's presence. One of the first things women say to me about a man they like is, "I feel comfortable with him. I can be myself. He likes me for whom I am."

A woman whose husband had left her, who didn't have a map, who felt homeless, came to see me in a state of anxiety. She no longer felt comfortable in the home they had shared. She was a trained artist, but as she was not working, there was nothing in her outer life to anchor her. She knew deep down that she had been adrift for a long time.

When I first met her, I could see that she was frightened. She didn't quite know where things went wrong for her. She sat lifeless, yet she wasn't so much depressed as confused. She was at a loss as to how to proceed, as if the separation and divorce had caught her by surprise. What had remained intact was an aesthetic function that she had developed over the years. But even if she decided to draw and paint again, where would she go about doing it? When she left the room at the end of the session, it was as if a spirit walked out. She had no body. She didn't really have a life.

She had dreams, however, and as we talked about them we both began to learn more about the person she was. Somewhere in the middle of our work together, she had a dream in which she felt utterly at home. This was where she belonged. Though a stranger, she entered a dream village and was spontaneously accepted. As she told me the dream, a deep calm and feeling of well-being came over her that I wouldn't have believed possible. This is her dream:

> I was in a quaint old cottage that belonged to a humorous, kindly, middle-aged man. He was going on a holiday and asked me to take his place running the post office he had in his house on the sun porch. He also wanted me to deliver the mail. He told me there was nothing to it; I would easily figure it out.
>
> The old cottage was filled with all kinds of things he had collected and kept throughout his life. The sun porch was off to one side of the entrance along the

front of the house. It had a low sloping roof and a series of small windows with smaller squares of glass on the front.

A long table or series of counters were under the windows and on one were the post office boxes. I started to look in the boxes. There were some letters, but a lot of items in the boxes were small pieces of colored or printed paper notes that children had made to send to their playmates. The town was so small that everyone knew each other and the postmaster knew where to deliver these notes.

As he said, it was easy to figure it out so I decided to go out and deliver the mail. The first bundle was for Gates Street. It was a tiny old town, so I found Gates nearby. It had only a few houses, small ones with porches and front yards surrounded by picket fences with front gates. I gave a letter to a little old lady who came to the screen door with her apron on. Then I looked down two short streets off the main street and found Banks Street near the river. I think the main street was called Main Street. There was also a street called River Street near the river.

Then I saw there were some pamphlets for the Park and Recreation Department in their P.O. box to be delivered, so I went down a small dirt road to find their building. It was in an overgrown forest with a few newly painted buildings. When I approached the end of the road, I saw the office and went in. It overlooked the river. I gave the attendant the pamphlets and realized they were actually published by them. The quaint man must have stored a few in their box in his office for references if visitors inquired at the Post Office about Park services.

When I returned to the Post Office I wondered how the mail was delivered there and someone said it is often just slipped under the door!

Somewhere in the dream I helped the man sort out some of the things he had collected. A table with glass cases was filled with all kinds of stones, some cut and polished, some just polished and some left natural.

Then I am in the old section of Main Street and see a new modern building. I have some mail for them. When I enter I realize it is a familiar place I once went to with my sister. It is a combination art gallery, concert hall and ballet school. I feel happy to be among people who know me.

In the dream it's a small town where often everyone knows each other, old fashioned, historic-timeless, with old streets and cottages. Picturesque. One could live in such a town alone and not feel isolated. You see someone you know almost everywhere you go.

What relieved her so in the dream was that she could identify all the streets simply by noticing how they were placed in space; that is, River Street ran along the river, Main Street ran through the center of town. The streets took on self-evident names. Anyone could find their way. She didn't have to learn or memorize the street names in order to deliver the mail. The task to which she was assigned was one she could perform by drawing on an age-old knowledge, so simple she could hardly say where she acquired it. This is the knowledge that comes to us spontaneously with the feeling that "we just know." We could call this the instinctual knowledge of how things are placed in natural surroundings. Often this knowledge comes through pictorial understanding or images. "A picture is worth a thousand words"—the house by the lake, the big rock in a waterfall, the large oak in a field: all are references to placement in nature. We don't have to learn or remember a complicated set of directions or abstract numerical reference in order to find our way.

This middle-aged dreamer had not always been able to find her way. As a young girl she felt she did not belong in her life. She was isolated. An emotional thread had been broken—the thread between mother and daughter—so her mind did not develop naturally. Whenever she had a problem that required an effective response, she would panic and go blank. She would reach out desperately to find something, anything that might work, as if she were grasping for straws.

Her dream compensated for the lack of relationship between mother and daughter. Her mother had never matured. She would say whatever came into her mind, whatever the unconscious cooked up; there was no ego. The mother's expression was not that of conscious intuition, but rather the leaking out of dissociated, random primal material. What my patient needed from her mother was the knowledge and affirmation to trust her intuition. Her situation was similar to the dolphin patient, who couldn't trust her intuition because it resembled her mother's psychotic episodes. This woman also couldn't trust her own natural responses. When the mother-daughter relationship is unbroken, a daughter can safely venture out into the world as an extension of the original sacred center. If nurtured as a child, then she does not find the world alien or abstract. She need not grasp at things to understand her reality or find her way. Through mirroring, seeing how she is valued by the other person, she discovers who she is.

In this woman's dream the job she is asked to perform is to deliver mail in the age-old way, a way that allows her to meet everyone in the village and see where they live as well as learn about the history of the community. She finds new buildings in old forests, the new as it grows out of the old—perhaps as the man-made road along the river evolved from an animal deer path. It is nature's way, with the postmaster as center keeping the new and the old related. Alan Watts says:

> Everything's "own way" is the "own way" of the universe, of the Tao. Because of the mutual interdependence of all beings, they will harmonize if left alone and not forced into conformity with some arbitrary, artificial, and abstract notion of order,

> and this harmony will emerge "tzu-jan", of itself, without external compulsion. . . . Outside the human world, the order of nature goes along without consulting books—but our human fear is that the Tao which cannot be described, the order which cannot be put into books, is chaos.[153]

The natural order of this village in the woman's dream reflects a natural order in herself. She doesn't need a map. She has her own inner map. She is at home.

At the end of the dream the woman remembers that she has been in this village before with her sister. The personal link is a familiar building from her childhood which combines art gallery, concert hall and ballet school, all related to the arts. As a child she had participated in activities in this central art building. In fact she had fashioned a professional career by becoming an artist, but she had not remembered that her identity in the world was intimately bound to her sister and, therefore, also to her mother. Realizing this connection was too psychologically threatening. So like the woman who made her own connection to the mother archetype by dancing with the bear, this woman, as postmistress of a village, could now honor her earlier sister-mother bond. This new awareness allowed her to sell her house and move to a place which expressed more clearly her artistic nature.

It was the simplicity of how things were placed in nature that allowed the dream woman access to her natural mind. In her dream an ordinary American town comes alive. Its homes, inhabitants, streets and river comfort her, allowing her to naturally find her place in the community.

For people who have developed a tight-knit and overly rational mind, who have functioned well in school all their lives and who not only trust their mind to be able to meet any new task, but who identify their mind as themselves, an experience in a different culture can be radically transforming. Another patient of mine lived in Africa for an extended period, and the exposure to animal life and the land changed her Western way of thinking. She was an attractive young woman who consulted me for just one hour. She was small and thin, very exact in her body movements. She came from a very traditional WASP family. She sought me out because she was hoping she could be treated on an out-patient basis instead of being hospitalized. The problem was that she was returning from a two-year stint in Africa with the Peace Corps and, due to what she called "culture shock," she could not reorient herself to life in America. Her mind was not functioning and she was terrified. She was overtly psychotic.

---

[153] *Tao: The Water Course Way,* pp. 43f.

She had a noon appointment, and it had taken her all morning to find my office. She took buses out from the center of the city in all four directions to the perimeter, returning each time to the central bus station. Only in that African way of following the cardinal points of the compass could she get her bearings.

What I saw was a woman wandering lost in a strange world which just happened to be her place of birth. But in fact she had found her true home in Africa. Her two years in the Peace Corps had been in a remote part of Africa where she saw few Caucasians. In describing her experience there, she said that the African women with whom she lived would pick her up on their shoulders and carry her down to the river where they got water. This physical contact was unlike anything she had ever known. After a year of living in close proximity with women, her boyfriend joined her and for the first time they enjoyed a full sexual relationship. She was for the first time in touch with her body.

Her malaise developed when she returned alone to this country. She was unable to integrate her emotional and physical experience which—though something a new-born infant might enjoy with its mother—was foreign to her. She had no cultural container to hold and integrate what had happened. Yet, because she had opened up emotionally to her deep feminine being, there was no going back to her dry, split-off thinking mode. Her journeying out from the center of the city in four directions was the psyche's way of trying to orient her to an archetypal plan consistent with her life in Africa—something deeper and more primal. But she had no corresponding inner image or dream symbol that would help her to integrate or understand what had happened to her there. She needed an internal reference point. She also had no personal link in the present culture to draw on. In this way she was unlike the postal village patient who all along had a vital, though unconscious, relationship with her sister. This woman needed to bridge these two completely disparate worlds. What images and symbols would the psyche create to heal this split?

I saw her for only that one hour. I offered to see her again, but she said she wanted to check out the hospital located down the Peninsula that was recommended to her, and she never came back. Though I only met with her that one hour, in her wandering, ungrounded state she has visited me many times.

Sometimes we have real-life experiences that are dreamlike in their ability to diagnose our missing pieces and to supply the images that make us whole. Quite unexpectedly, I had such an experience toward the end of writing this book. My best friend—actually, my elephant-other, described earlier in the elephant chapter—invited me to join him on a trip to India. His invitation came so suddenly, and at a time when I was so overworked, that I didn't have time to think the decision through rationally. I acted impulsively.

It happened in this way. Just by coincidence, I had seen an old movie about the Oklahoma land rush, a piece of American history in which my friend's great-grandparents played a role. In addition to being a psychiatrist, my friend was also a writer. For a long time he had been working on a book about his Oklahoma past, and had published a chapter in a well-respected literary journal. But he was also very social, and for two years he let himself be pulled out into the world, away from his writing. I knew this was the case, so when I saw the movie in which people and horses line up on the Oklahoma state line at twelve noon for the gunshot that would send them off competing with one another to stake their claims, I called him, imploring him to get back to work. Responding to the emotional timbre in my voice, he begged me to come out and help him start.

For several days we wrote together in an isolated spot along the Pecos river in the high desert of New Mexico. I was happy to see his stories flow. In return, he invited me to join him, and two friends, one of whom was a professor in oriental art, on a trip to Ladakh in Kashmir, the northern tip of India. There we would see the thousand-year-old paintings in the Buddhist monasteries. Ladakh is a Buddhist culture, more like Tibet before the invasion of China. It is high in the mountains. Leh, the city you fly into, sits in the foothills of the Himalayas, at 11,000 feet. I was told that it was beautiful, and that we would go for a month.

I was ambivalent, for several reasons. I wasn't that interested in Buddhism. I had already planned a trip with my wife to explore the small Canadian islands off Vancouver Island in British Columbia. I also realized that the trip with my friend would take me away from my book. But I had always wanted to go to India. The stories told to me and the books I had read—*Passage to India* for one—instilled in my imagination a picture of a timeless land in which people responded from the depths of their soul, manifest in daily devotion to the divine and experienced in relationship to one another, even to their sacred animals. They could truly be themselves and this was not only accepted by everyone, it was demanded. This was different from how I was brought up, which was to do the expected thing and ignore real feeling.

My other contradictory response about India was that I really couldn't imagine it all. I knew I wouldn't be able to stand hearing from my friends that I had missed the trip of a lifetime, and I told myself, "It's all arranged. All you have to do is go." But I had a strong premonition that I would be lonely.

In the end, I scrapped the trip with my wife, abandoned my book and left. I met my friends in Delhi, and from there it was only an hour's spectacular flight threading our way through a Himalayan pass into Leh. We stayed a little way out of town in a guest house surrounded by Buddhist stupas, chortins and mani walls. Stone walkways alongside running streams led up to terraced barley fields and apricot orchards. Women walked with their animals or in small groups, smiling, laughing. They wore dark dresses of black, brown and purple, with colorful kerchiefs around their necks,. and they tied their beautiful long black braids with ribbons. They greeted everyone with a cheerful musical "Julley." It means "Hello," "Welcome," "God bless."[154] High mountains with snow ringed the landscape wherever you looked.

For ten days we visited monasteries, each one unique and a joy to the eye; so natural did they feel that I could imagine the stone organically building itself. But I was no longer able to keep track of where I saw what mandalas and tankas, which Avalokitesvaras and Buddhas, though I could easily have spent a month joyfully studying one particular painting at Alchi, a thousand-year-old monastery. The fact was, I took in more than I could absorb. I was overwhelmed. There was no point in visiting yet more monasteries. If I was really interested in Buddhist culture, I might have holed up near the mandala painting of my heart. But I longed to see the "real India" I had read and heard about, and I knew that I had better see it now because it seemed unlikely that I would ever return.

So, beautiful as the mountains were, I decided to strike out on my own, to have my own experience. I went over the pass at 18,000 feet on a local bus in seat no. 7, which was no more than a demarcation painted on a bench. On this ride I had my first encounter with Indian people. The bus was so filled with people and luggage that the ticket taker's feet, in moving from the back of bus to the front, never once touched the floor. Like a monkey, he moved with agility from seat back to pole to stacked luggage, with passengers giving him a helping hand along the way. I learned about the Indians' boundaries: from a Western point of view, they have none! Without asking, a man appropriated my wool shirt to place underneath his head and slept with his legs crossed over both the person next to him and me. The man sleeping in the aisle placed his head in my traveling companion's lap. It was an adventure.

Near the top of the narrow pass the bus suffered a flat tire, with, you guessed it, no spare or jack, so all traffic stopped both ways for two hours until somewhat larger tires were supplied by a truck driver tired of waiting. The flattened

---

[154] Andrew Harvey, *A Journey in Ladakh,* p. 24.

tire that was removed was placed next to me in the aisle, towering above my head, as if a Westerner would be more likely to keep watch over it. So, in order to occasionally relieve myself when the bus stopped, besides having to crawl over the luggage and people lying on top of it, I had to negotiate the tire as well. The psychiatrist in me took notes. This was real life.

Traveling by bus and train down the great plains of India to the city of Varanasi or Benares, I arrived at the old religious city on the Ganges. Earlier, an Indian had warned me not to go. Because of the recent heavy rains, he cautioned, there were outbreaks of cholera. "Why do you want to go there of all places, when there are so many beautiful places to visit in India?" he admonished. "There are too many people, the city smells, you won't like it."

When the train arrived at 4:30 in the morning I was unprepared for the mass of humanity that filled the station. Bodies covered the floor from one end of the building to the other, so that it was impossible to thread one's way through the terminal without stepping on someone. Once outside in the night I could feel the fervor in the city. It was palpably different from the overcrowding and pollution of New Delhi. When a man on a scooter offered me a free ride to the ghat I wanted, several drivers who wanted the money threatened him with violence. After many exasperating trials at finding my hotel, a little boy, whose bright eyes lit up his face, took me in hand and deposited me there. The rooms were right on the Ganges. Arriving at daybreak, I immediately went out in a waiting boat to see the worshippers make offerings of flowers from the different ghats.

Here in this holy place, people live close to their emotions, to life and death, as symbolized by the river. They ritually bathe in the river, chanting to evoke the gods, and there they deposit the ashes from the cremated bodies. Human bodies that are not burned are returned whole to the river along with bodies of cows. Sometimes you see crows pecking away at the carcass of a cow while it floats down the river. Unlike Ladakh, where you feel your chest expand from being on the roof of the earth, Varanasi has a closed-in feeling, even though I could look out, as well as go out, on the mile-wide Ganges river. The city is crowded; people and animals move in and out of narrow winding streets filled with shops and noise. Water is everywhere, in the wide high river, in the streets from the monsoon, on the floor of my room blown in through the shutters. I step into the shower soaked through from the humid air; I step out of the shower only to slip on the wet floor. I go out in a boat early in the morning to watch fully-clothed people praying to Shiva in the river. My daypack falls off the seat onto the floor of the boat, only to get soaked with water from the Ganges.

There is an underlying emotional turmoil in the culture which makes it impossible to rest or even think. (E.M. Forster alludes to this in *A Passage to India,* when the older woman at the beginning of their journey warns her younger companion about the difficult emotional climate.) In Varanasi, bodies are carried by chanting relatives who run with them through the narrow alleyways to the burning ghats. Emotion is expressed openly to people, animals and gods.

In the midst of such teeming human energy, I felt utterly lonely and depressed. I realized it had been a mistake to make this trip. I had been pulled in the wrong way. I knew instinctively that the trip was not for me when one of the four members of the traveling party told me she was depressed and felt empty inside. She had been looking forward to this trip because of her interest in Buddhism and her belief that travel to the high mountains would fill her with spiritual energy. She had been to Tibet before, staying for months in monasteries, never ready to return. She felt a kindred spirit in me and referred to me as a fellow wanderer. But I didn't feel any emptiness inside that needed to be filled. There were other hints. She loved Andrew Harvey's book, *A Journey to Ladakh,* which I found boring and adolescent. Because many of my colleagues who were travelers had encouraged me to go, I gave up my wife, my book, my trust in myself, my good sense, and I went.

Overstuffed with Buddhism, missing my wife terribly, suffering the heaviness which inevitably follows a descent from the mountains, oppressed by the mugginess of the monsoon, overwhelmed with the continual haranguing of rickshaw men, noise, crowded quarters, litter, too many people, a veritable barrage of stimuli, I was at a low point.

I thought of leaving, but I didn't have the energy to even think of trying to change travel plans. Instinctively, I knew I had to do something. So I decided to validate my inner experience with an outer one. I decided to visit death itself; I would see the Burning Ghat, the steps along the river where bodies are cremated. Because of recent heavy rains, the river had risen so high that it was no longer possible to walk from one ghat to another along the river front; I had to turn inward into the city and go by a circuitous route. Quickly I lost my way in the narrow winding streets. Then, as if by miracle, the shiny happy face of a ten-year-old boy smiled up at me, the same boy who had rescued me days before as I hopelessly sought out my hotel. He became my trustworthy guide. Never did I feel led by a truer spirit. It was as if I had inadvertently rediscovered a forgotten child in myself, who with lantern in hand was leading me back to the meaning in my life.

Joyous at being found, while simultaneously preparing myself to view the cremating of bodies at the Burning Ghat, I didn't really take in that my little friend had slipped off to the side. Bearing directly down on me was a large beautiful bull whose horns caught my chest and threw me. It was the bull of Shiva, the bull he rides, called Nanda, who had come himself to initiate me. Shiva, creator and destroyer of life, the great Hindu god who reigned over this city, had claimed me. In the moment before impact, I saw the bull out of the corner of my eye. The funny thing was that I expected it to behave like a person and give a little ground as people do, especially on the busy streets in India; when almost colliding, they manage at the last possible second, with much shouting and name calling, to avoid a physical confrontation. But the bull, without proper manners, continued its downhill movement and I felt its full power.

I had never felt an animal's energy directed at me like that. I had ridden horses and experienced their power in my legs and thighs, but I had never taken it in before, not a direct hit. Even though the bull was just walking, I could feel the energy running through it, from the bottom of its feet to the tips of its horns. I could feel its total being. There was a strength and beauty to it. It was truly amazing. The animal was just itself. It was alive and I could experience it. My appreciation of the life in the animal moved from the psychological and aesthetic to something real. Up until now it had been a psychic thing, real but removed. The closest thing I had experienced to this before was the energy released by my Tai Chi teacher. I was stunned, and after the moment of the strike and the realization that the horns had not penetrated my chest, I laughed. A tension had left me and I felt strangely reassured at meeting the energy of the animal. The bull was real and I must be real too. It was no longer an intellectual thing, but an experience reminding me of my animal self.

The animals knew what they were doing. They knew that in contacting me, they would awaken the animal in me, that I would be one of them. Then, like them, I could trust something in my own nature. I could count on my own power to find my way. I, too, had an animal strength that would have to be reckoned with if encountered. I had the same strength as other people and could fight to see my way through. I could be fully in my life like the animal and know the force of that. For the first time in my life, I felt really connected.

I can't really communicate in words what the experience was or how it happened, but ever since I have felt as connected to my life as I do to touching a table. Relating to people is direct. There is no separation, no screen separating us. And I no longer have to try so hard. I feel part of the human race (now laughing as I write this) just as much as the animal must experience its own reality. I met myself thousands of miles away from my home, in the form of a bull whose horns penetrated my psyche, whose horns lifted me up and knocked me down. I came down off the mountain and met the animal of the earth, who lives in the here and now, in the great round we call life. This bull will one day wind up in the river Styx, as will I, with a crow nibbling on our hides, and there will be another bull who will awaken yet another searcher.

There in India, in the most difficult of situations, I finished my book, in my mind that is. I finally knew in my bones what it was to be connected. I knew what it was to have a life of my own and value it. The whole plan of life was simple. All you had to do was follow the meaning in your life. You simply had to respond and take up the tasks that were presented to you. Life would do its own thing. I didn't have to worry about it or try to make things happen. Friendships either worked or they didn't. I no longer had to envy other people's lives. I was home for good. It was a relief.

When I arrived in San Francisco and the Immigration official welcomed me home, I almost cried. My wife was there to greet me. Though I returned fifteen pounds lighter and sick, somewhere deep inside I felt quietly ecstatic. I had brought back an intestinal bug, but instead of being dismayed I found I was happy to sit on the toilet, in a waking dream being revisited by the many different healings that had come to me. There was the healing that came through the move to Inverness, the waterbirds, my dog, and now the healing that came via my trip to India and my return. I am reminded of what William Howarth wrote about the meaning of Thoreau's solitude:

> This rite of passage, going out into nature and then coming home, was Thoreau's greatest discovery; for that became the pattern of all his major narratives—the retreat in solitude that leads to reconciliation with society.[155]

Now that I am more deeply at ease in my body, more trusting in the path that opens up beneath my feet, I can take up the human tasks. I need to learn again to live with people—to feel their warmth and compassion, their care and nurturing. I don't have to take life so seriously. Awakening in the morning, I look forward to what the day will bring. I laugh and am playful. I eat licorice and drink lemonade. My sons are grown now, but if a child wandered into the kitchen where I am sitting with my morning coffee, I would hold her in my lap, the child I wasn't able to hold when I was younger and cut off. While she caresses her

---

[155] William Howarth, *The Book of Concord: Thoreau's Life as a Writer*, p. 30.

blanket and sucks her thumb, I tell her a story while I follow the life in her eyes.

Across the street I watch a young girl, alone, at home in her body, play with a volley ball. She bounces it up with her forearms, then, waiting for its return, positions her lithe body underneath. With supple movement, she sinks with the descending ball, resting it tenderly again in her forearms until in perfect harmony, her body and the ball both spring upward. The ball and the girl have become lovers. It is a game.

How each of us finds our way back is our own unique story. Identification with animals can help us return to a sense of our deepest nature—a relaxation and wholeness of the body, a more trusting relation to the process of life's unfolding, a spontaneous and playful attitude, an intuitive feel for choices and decisions. Dreams are the primary medium for this identification because they give an internal reference point, one charged with emotion. In traditional societies, such as the Navajo for instance, the shaman or healer could draw on the inner mythology of the culture in sand paintings and song to remind the suffering individual of the healthy way. Now we have to do the work individually. There are no maps you can buy in a store. You have to find your own way in. For me it was the animal, the waterbird, the dog, the bull—and so many others—that brought me home.

Animals in My Office

A man enters my office, an anxious man who puts on a smile. He doesn't announce that he is lost, he just looks like he doesn't know where he belongs. He is an overweight man in his mid-fifties, whose tension seems to stop even his breathing. Although he has been a successful business consultant at the high end of the industry, he suffers from a feeling of inauthenticity. "This isn't really me that people see out there. I act professionally but inside I feel like a fraud. I'm afraid people will find me out."

He has a host of medical problems, some of which are related to his weight: diabetes, hypertension, high cholesterol. He is somewhat out of control. Not only does he have an eating disorder, he has difficulty sticking to a schedule. He sometimes misses an appointment with me without acknowledging it later, and I am left with the feeling that he is missing even to himself. Does he want to be here? He doesn't know himself; here is as good as anywhere else. There is a kind of panic that stems from a fear of not knowing where he belongs. Clearly, he doesn't belong in his body. It lugs him around from place to place according to some business plan, but where is he? He has never felt that someday he might be satisfied deep down, with a life of his own.

As he talks, I think of certain ancient cultures where all sickness, mental or physical, is ascribed to "loss of soul."[156] A soul in a precarious situation might forsake the body and become an easy prey for demons, sorcerers or even one of the dead. In such a culture, the shaman has to find the fugitive soul and bring it back.[157] The shaman is helped on his journey by animal guides. They lead him on an ecstatic journey to the underworld. Retrieving the soul restores energy, ease, the vividness of presence. Today, we call loss of soul depression. Sitting in my office across from this disoriented man, it occurs to me that it might be more useful to turn the words about and call depression loss of soul. Such an understanding might help us to find the animal guides we need for healing.

Meanwhile he rants and raves about his mother: "She was in my face all the time, always wanting me to do better. No matter how well I did, it was never enough: student body president in college, straight A's, etc." He felt his mother stripped him of his own feelings. He gets in such a rage that I worry he might have a stroke on the spot.

On the work front, he decides to join a new company. But that doesn't go well and he suffers a financial setback. Realizing he has made the wrong decision has unnerved him. Then he has the following dream, which on the surface appears to be about a sexual encounter. More profoundly, it is about animals, about energy and life. The power of the animal is so strong that even its dream-image will bring vitality.

> I'm in New York and I hail a cab. It stops and a male passenger in the back seat invites me in. I don't like the idea that there are people in the cab, the husband in the back seat whom I mentioned and his wife in the front. But I decide to get in anyway. I tell the driver that I want to go to Chelsea. The buildings and narrow streets look like London, though I know I am in New York.
>
> After the cab takes off, the woman in the front seat begins rubbing the driver's neck, and as she gets closer to him, she begins "making out" with him, right in front of her husband. I look at the husband, wondering how he is taking this. He points to the ring his wife is wearing. It is in the shape of a snake coiled around her wedding finger. It is more of a wrap than a ring as the piece of metal begins at the base of the finger and extends to the finger joint.
>
> Now she is naked with her back to the dashboard looking at the driver. But she says to me, "Do you want to have me?" With that she sticks out her butt, says

---

[156] See Eliade, *Shamanism,* p. 8.

[157] Ibid., pp. 182, 289.

> "Fingerfuck me, my asshole too, if you want," and I do. Then I notice that the driver is going past my hotel, so I direct him back. As I get out of the cab, the husband asks me if I want to continue the play in the hotel, this time all three of us together. No, I respond. I just want to go to my hotel.

Here the animal energy appears in the symbol of the snake. Its energy is calling to him. How wild and free it is and how overwhelming. Even though the snake energy is attractive and compelling, the man is ambivalent. When we are not in a good relationship to it, we are out of control as he was.

The man said the dream was as vivid as if it had actually happened:

> I was struck by how real it seemed for a short a period of time. The streets seemed real; gas lights, brick buildings, narrow streets, all made me think I was in London. Everything was dark except the woman's body which had a glow. She had a beautiful smile. She was Catholic, age twenty-five, and had a perfectly toned body.

From time to time over the years, this man would let creative intuitions creep in. Innovative concepts would strike him when he was relaxed, when he was just being himself, not self-conscious about what an important figure he was in his field. However, he would get so caught up in the far-reaching significance of what these new ideas might mean for him and his company that he would lose the inspiration. Or if he remembered, he would often not have the confidence to follow through and his work would come to a standstill. This is his current predicament; his business is faltering and he is frightened. He can't sleep. He is afraid of the loss of income and the fear, he says, of "falling back into the middle class." He is Catholic and came from a lower middle-class family. His father was the first one to go to college, and for this he was castigated by his brothers. This man is very smart business-wise, but he can't get in touch with the positive snake which might renew him. He needs to tap into his emotions and become involved in his life. He needs to become passionate about something that is vital to him. And first he must inhabit his body.

He sits in the chair, thinking, always thinking, but he is restless. He keeps moving around as if trying to get comfortable, but he never can. He sits far forward in his chair to make contact with me and then pulls back to gauge my response. He always brings a big plastic bottle of mineral water which he grabs from the floor like an alcoholic desperate for a drink. This he compulsively drinks when he is anxious, when something comes up that he doesn't understand or that he is not in control of, hoping that this elixir will cure his ills or at least calm him down. He brings a notepad and pen so when the conversation is interesting he can write it down and look it over later in the week.

So he dreams of snake woman, but she isn't helpful. She has a husband and flirts with the taxi driver. She is provocative and potentially dangerous, possibly leading him into big trouble. Because she is so real in the dream, she reminds him of the debauchery he has known, although the actual experiences depressed him. What he needs is to find the good snake in his life, a snake like the python of Delphi that, whispering, foretells his life direction. This dream snake-woman might give him pleasure, but in fact she doesn't arouse him. She turns him off.

The man has the right idea. He needs to feel alive. He needs to touch the rhythmic pulse, that basic life beat, the heat in a woman's vagina. But he doesn't know how to gain access. He doesn't know how to internalize a passion for living. It is still projected onto women in a rather mechanical, unsatisfying way that leaves him without true connection. He is repulsed by the dream and remains at a loss. He leaves the hour unsatisfied and even has doubts about whether I can help him.

A pervasive feeling of disconnection is one of the great casualties of modern culture. A hundred years ago, we walked on dirt roads; we rode animals that sweated, grunted, whose flesh touched our flesh. We looked into the eyes of the animal and into our own soul. We traveled with the soul of the animal and our own soul. Now we take antidepressants to deal with the problem.

The writer D.H. Lawrence felt that the answer to disconnection was the rediscovery of passion, emotion, sexuality. To realize his vision, he turned to the land, the body, the animal. In *St. Mawr*, he tells of a woman faced with a difficulty in relation to the instinctual. She knows what she wants, but she doesn't know how to bring it into her life. St. Mawr, a horse, becomes her obsession.

> Only St. Mawr gave her some hint of the possibility. He was so powerful, and so dangerous. But in his dark eye, that looked, with its cloudy brown pupil, a cloud within a dark fire, like a world beyond our world, there was a dark vitality glowing, and within the fire, another sort of wisdom. She felt sure of it: even when he put his ears back, and bared his teeth, and his great eyes came bolting out of his naked horse's head, and she saw demons upon demons in the chaos of his horrid eyes.
>
> Why did he seem to her like some living background, into which she wanted to retreat? When he reared his head and neighed from his deep chest, like deep wind-bells resounding, she seemed to hear the echoes of another darker, more spacious, more dangerous, more splendid world than ours, that was beyond her. And there she wanted to go.[158]

---

[158] *St. Mawr and the Man Who Died,* pp. 26f.

My patient doesn't have the sense to look for the animal in this way. He doesn't know that our soul can attach to objects. Sitting across from him, as he balances uncomfortably on the edge of his chair, I have an impulse to open my mouth and let Lawrence speak through me: "A pure animal man would be as lovely as a deer or a leopard, burning like a flame fed straight from underneath."[159]

Perhaps he heard these secret whispers, because nine months later he began to see me regularly. No longer resisting the process, he became increasingly able to give up control. He didn't grasp his bottled water as if it were his mother's breast. When his mother was dying, he called his sister, with whom he had fought his entire life, to tell her that their mother was in the hospital, not expected to live. When she asked him if he thought she should travel, from where she lived abroad, to say good-bye to their mother, he simply responded, "It's up to you," instead of telling her what to do. This once desperate and controlling man was now relaxed. He would share a story and laugh. His body, now fluid and coordinated, moved naturally, like a powerful animal. He had taken on Lawrence's leopard with a burning passion.

Having been lonely myself, I am familiar with the feeling of disconnection. Not having many friends, I used to play with acorns that dropped on our driveway. As I rubbed their rough hats on their smooth faces, these little fellows talked to me. Later, walking on the beaches at Pt. Reyes, I would collect seashell hats and feel similarly warmed. That period was the beginning of my time in Inverness when I began to heal my own instinctual wound. The acorns with hats were now sea-shell hats: I had moved from the vegetative to primitive animal mollusks, but not yet to humans.

This was strongly brought home to me when I was inside the Lakota sweat lodge making a prayer to the spirit of my dog who had just died. The insightful but tough Indian healer responded, "You care more about animals than people." The timing of his statement directly addressed the point I had reached. When my dog died, something deep inside me on an animal level had healed and now I was entering the human world, taking on the socialization that was denied me as a child. By revitalizing this instinctual animal realm, I had become a member of the human race as well.

In *Thresholds of Initiation,* Joseph Henderson writes that "what a man can never experience fully on a purely human level, he can experience upon an ani-

---

[159] Ibid., p. 50.

mal level, and the quality which is thus acquired is expressed archetypally, . . . as the power to be."[160]

Gradually, I came to see that I didn't have to work so hard at being connected. Perhaps the core meaning of animals is that they bring love into our life, love that leads us into relationship and allows us to be more foolish in an animal way, not in a profane way. Even a crusty old man or woman can let a dog in. Freed up, we can enjoy the mystery of relationship.

Recently a woman told me about a dream in which she wanted to catch a beautiful butterfly to share with her male lover, but she was worried that in touching the butterfly she would injure it. Then it flew into her hands, which she cupped in such a way that its wings could extend out on either side without being injured.

The butterfly's lightness of spirit and transformation quality is known to our psyche, and we react to it as a child whose eyes follow the butterfly's flutter and color. Where will the delicate creature land? "Will the bride's bouquet fall to me?" "Will there be horses in my life?" my horse patient asks. The butterfly woman is learning how to let the spirit touch her without controlling it. With it, she can light up those around her as Virginia Woolf describes in *To the Lighthouse,* when the mother, with candlelight at the dinner table, draws the faces of all the children into the round of relationship.

There is a mystery at the heart of connection. Although it is mysterious, it is very palpable and real. It becomes the secret that two people have with one another, and astonishingly the secret is seldom mentioned. Carl Kerényi tells of nature's "sacred open secret," referring to the Greek mystery religions in which the secret was known to all "who lived in the vicinity of the cult sites . . . [and known to those who participated in the mystery rites] . . . but it was unutterable. For [he says] in the profoundest sense it was ineffable: a true mystery."[161]

One reason I had problems with relationship was because I had no link between the inner and outer worlds. I had never bonded with my mother, nor she with me, and I grew up in a household in which feelings and emotions were not expressed. Like many first-generation Americans, my parents grew up listening to their parents' native European languages: German, Polish, Yiddish. It was up to my parents' generation to adapt to this new country. Survival was at stake. There was no time for such frills as feelings, hopes or dreams to fulfill some inchoate inner longing. My father had to settle for pharmacy school rather than

[160] *Thresholds of Initiation,* p. 231.

[161] "The Mysteries of the Kabeiroi," in *The Mysteries,* p. 37.

medical school because he could finish in two years instead of four. He had to support his parents.

It fell to my generation, the second generation, to begin to decide what we, as new arrivals, would contribute to it. There was enough money; what did we really want to do? Kenneth Clark, the art historian, said that civilization began when people no longer had to work to survive, when their energy was available for less immediately pragmatic tasks. But for us, the old survival patterns were still in place. "Eat, eat," my aunts would say. It didn't matter what you thought. "What do the *goyim* (gentiles) know about life. They don't even know how to eat. Who knows when the pogroms will begin again; we will have to move; remember, keep everything liquid." My family really didn't settle anywhere. They were here only to make money and then retire somewhere else. It was a provisional existence. We went to college to land a profession, not to be educated. "What can you buy with a liberal arts degree?" my father would ask. But my friends and I no longer lived separately from gentiles. We dated. We intermarried. We had dreams. The rabbis fretted; we were in danger of being assimilated.

Before undertaking these adult tasks, however, I withdrew. The energy that might have gone into playing baseball as a boy stayed in the family drugstore. I was locked up inside the store and myself. The emotion never became connected to life. Nevertheless, I managed to make an adaptation, a sort of cover-up, like my snake-man. I developed a disdain for anything rational as a compensation for the emotional ghetto where I grew up. Whatever did not speak to me emotionally, I wrote off. How I got through school became an interesting challenge, a bit harrowing at times. I began to put thinking and feeling into opposing camps: the rational and irrational, reality and fantasy, left brain and right brain.

My polarization of these attitudes was simplistic and dangerous. I would think, "Do we look at our life from the inside or from outside? If we are like the woman with her butterfly, or the woman in *St. Mawr,* we can experience this magic; then, we are inside our life experiencing its miracle. Otherwise, we live only as rational beings, biological facts, statistics." This dichotomy is humorously illustrated in a newspaper article in which an artist and a scientist collide:

> A dazzling fireball lit the night sky over West Marin Sunday, and some astronomers believe it could have been caused by a wad of dust trailing Halley's Comet and exploding as it hit the earth atmosphere.
>
> "I thought I was blessed by the gods," said Inverness illustrator Cyndie Wooley, who saw the celestial display. . . . "It was a fireball," she said Monday. "There was no doubt about it. This was no shooting star. It was really grandiose."

> Andrew Fraknoi, chairman of the Astronomy Department of Foothill College in Los Altos, cautioned, that nobody can be certain Sunday night's fireball came from the *Eta Aquarids* (fragments of Halley's Comet). . . . He said it might have been a random piece of "cosmic garbage" that collided with the earth's atmosphere, the kind of event that happens regularly. . . . Although people often see fireballs and think they've witnessed something extraordinary, Franknoi said, "the significance of this is absolutely nil."
>
> For her part, said Wooley, "even if it was [cosmic] garbage, it was spectacular." She added the meteor put a perfect ending on an extraordinary day: "I had seen a bobcat and a great-horned owl, and I had eggs Benedict with portabello mushrooms. I'm a changed woman."[162]

The people I met in Inverness were more like Wooley than the astronomer. They were friendly; they responded to feeling. All I had to do was be myself and things happened naturally. Often in the morning I might want to connect with someone, and then, as if by magic, I would run into that person in town or birdwatching on the road. Inside something was healing. I became quiet. I could feel the well of my inner life sustain me. I became one with the animal in myself or with my dog, whose image changed as he leapt ahead actively encouraging me on. My life was my own. Then, mysteriously, the outer life corresponded. Once I came upon a passage from Rilke that beautifully expresses this correspondence. In a letter to Lou Andreas Salome, he expanded on a line from his Seventh Elegy, "You would cry out as purely as a bird." He wrote:

> The bird is a creature that has a very special feeling of trust in the external world, as if she knew that she is one with its deepest mystery. That is why she sings in it as if she were singing within her own depths; that is why we so easily receive a birdcall into our own depths; we seem to be translating it without residue into our emotion; indeed, it can for a moment turn the whole world into inner space, because we feel that the bird does not distinguish between her heart and the world's.[163]

Once while meditating in my little place in the woods on how inner and outer meet, a hummingbird flew inside. Before letting it out, I felt its hum accompany the hum in my writing. We both were hummers and this made me happy. From time to time I recite this Yeats' poem, "The Lake Isle of Innesfree":

> I will arise and go now, and go to Innisfree,
> And a small cabin build there, of clay and wattles made:

---

[162] David Rolland, *Pt. Reyes Light,* May 9, 1996.
[163] Stephen Mitchell, ed. and trans., *Rainer Maria Rilke,* p. 327.

> Nine bean-rows will I have there, a hive for the honeybee,
> And live alone in the bee-loud glade.[164]

I still feel that people's experience of animals cannot be fully communicated. The animal remains a living mystery.

From time immemorial, humans have made paintings and sculptures of animals in order to carry their spirits and to remind us of their power and necessity. Some of the oldest drawings of elk and mammoth are cave drawings from the pre-ice age. Today I keep paintings and sculptures of animals near me all the time. They bring primordial consciousness into my office and into my soul and the souls of those who see me. Their presence quickens, enlivens and heals.

Behind the patient's chair there hangs a six-foot Chinese scroll two centuries old. A black hawk is perched on a tree branch. Seen from behind with his head in profile, his eye misses nothing. His great claws and legs painted in beige highlight the sleek black body. Not a line is wasted in the powerful graceful shoulders and elegant tapered body. His alert head with hawk beak and penetrating eye is all quickness. This stirring presence fills the room.

One other animal, a clay bull made by children from the mud flats in Africa, small enough to enclose in my hand, sits on a bookcase in full view. With a large humpback and horns on its head, its rather primitive animal face with small holes for eyes and nose reminds me of a drawing on a cave wall. It has both tail and penis. Did it inspire the dream of one of my patients in which large animals came out of the earth to inhabit her room? This bull has taken on new significance since my encounter with the bull of India.

The very first picture I acquired when I began practice was an etching of a little duck (Figure 20). It was given to me by the artist when she became depressed following the death of her husband. Only four inches by five, textured with many lines and yet simple, its feminine body stands on one leg, awakening in the viewer a quiet living presence. However, looking more closely, you can see the duck's watchful eye. Does the calm appearance of its body belie a certain anxiety, as if—rather than resting on the water—it were hesitating, unsure of its direction? Will it be safe? The little duck looks so lovable and perfect in form that it is hard to imagine it may be afraid.

This duck on the side wall of my waiting room has become my most treasured possession. No one has ever mentioned it, though it is the first object one sees upon entering. Yet it underlies my life and practice. Am I the duck who

[164] *The Yeats Reader: A Portable Compendium,* p. 30.

carries patients to psychic realms until they can do that for themselves, even sometimes getting angry with them when they are not self-protective? If and when I retire from my consulting room it will be with this duck tucked under my arm.

"Where are you going with the duck?" someone may ask.

"Wherever it takes me," I will respond.

Figure 20

Acknowledgments

I am indebted to many people who helped this book become itself. John Tarrant initially helped me to shape my vision and to give me the courage to articulate it. Noelle Oxenhandler, my editor and writing coach, was my rudder. Carolyn Grassi helped the material to coalesce.

My life-long friend John Talley let me write alongside him in a little adobe high in the New Mexico desert along the Pecos River, Tom Singer arranged for trial public offerings through the C.G. Jung Institute of San Francisco, John Beebe offered his invaluable editorial knowledge; Linda Leonard encouraged me to find my personal relation to the material. Many other writer and colleagues gave freely of themselves; Eleanor Criswell, JoAnn Culbert-Koehn, Jules Evens, Thomas Kirsch, Naomi Lowinsky, Sachiko Taki Reece, Ami Ronnberg, Craig san Roque, Karen Signell, Susan Thackrey, David Tresan.

I am profoundly grateful to Joe Henderson. Michael Flanagin helped me find many references in the Archive for Research in Archetypal Symbolism. The Scholarship Committee of the C.G. Jung Institute of San Francisco also gave me a grant.

These members of my Tai Chi group connected me in a new way to my own animal body: Sifu Gene Chen, Percy Lumpkin, Don Houston and Ken Yasumoto. My doctor Ben Fong, M.D., kept it alive.

Linda Boyd kept track of all the printerly aspects of the book; she even taught me how to use the computer. Pansy Hawk Wing gave me invaluable information.

Most of all, I am indebted to the many patients, colleagues and friends who let me use their dreams and stories, which have taught me much of what I know about animals. I want, finally, to acknowledge the animals themselves who visited me in the wild and in some deep mysterious way in my dreams. One of these, my dog Moss, has stayed with me throughout all times.

Neil Russack

Permissions

"Happiness" from *Sun Under Wood* by Robert Hass, copyright © 1996 by Robert Hass. Used by permission of HarperCollins Publishers, Inc.

"The Chambered Nautilus" from *America in Literature*. Vol. 1. New York: John Wiley and Sons, 1978.

"Whales Weep Not!" by D.H. Lawrence, "The Elephant Is Slow to Mate" by D. H. Lawrence, from *The Complete Poems of D.H. Lawrence* by D.H. Lawrence, edited by V. de Sola Pinto & F.W. Roberts, copyright © 1964, 1971 by Angelo Ravagli and C.M. Weekley, Executors of the Estate of Frieda Lawrence Ravagli. Used by permission of Viking Penguin, a division of Penguin Putnam Inc.

"O to Be a Dragon," copyright © 1957 by Marianne Moore, renewed 1985 by Lawrence E. Brinn and Louise Crane, Executors of the Estate of Marianne Moore, from *The Complete Poems of Marianne Moore* by Marianne Moore. Used by permission of Viking Penguin, a division of Penguin Putnam Inc.

"Wild Geese" by Mary Oliver from *Dream Work* by Mary Oliver. Copyright © 1986 by Mary Oliver. Used by permission of Grove/Atlantic, Inc.

"Spanish Dancer," "The Panther," and "Sonnets to Orpheus," from *The Selected Poetry of Rainer Maria Rilke* by Rainer Maria Rilke, translated by Stephen Mitchell, copyright © 1982 by Stephen Mitchell. Used by permission of Random House, Inc.

"Elephant Rocks" by Kay Ryan from *Elephant Rocks* by Kay Ryan. Copyright © 1996 by Kay Ryan. Used by permission of Grove/Atlantic, Inc.

Excerpts from "Wilderness" in *Cornhuskers* by Carl Sandburg, copyright 1918 by Holt, Rinehart and Winston and renewed 1946 by Carl Sandburg, reprinted by permission of Harcourt, Inc.

"Octopus's Garden" by Richard Starkey, © 1969 (renewed) Startling Music, Ltd. (PRS). All rights administered by Warner-Tamerlane Publishing Corp. (BMI). All rights reserved. Used by permission. Warner Bros. Publications U.S. Inc., Miami, FL, 33014.

"Thirteen Ways of Looking at a Blackbird" by Wallace Stevens from *The Collected Poems of Wallace Stevens* by Wallace Stevens. Copyright © 1954 by Wallace Stevens. Used by permission of Alfred A. Knopf, a division of Random House, Inc.

"Song of Myself" by Walt Whitman, from *Complete Poetry and Selected Prose*, James E. Miller, Jr., ed., copyright © 1959, New York Houghton Mifflin Company.

"A Blessing" and "Beginning" by James Arlington Wright from Collected Poems by James Arlington Wright. Copyright ©1951. Used by permission of Wesleyan University Press.

"The Lake Isle of Innesfree." Adapted with the permission of Scribner, a Division of Simon & Schuster, Inc., from *The Poems of W.B. Yeats: A New Edition*, edited by Richard J. Finneran. Copyright 1906 by Macmillan Publishing Company, copyright renewed 1934 by William Butler Yeats.

Bibliography

Archive for Research in Archetypal Symbolism. C. G. Jung Institute, San Francisco.

Arseniev, V.K. *Dersu the Trapper.* Kingston, NY: McPherson and Company, 1996.

Barrett, Stephen. "Too Many Pagans, Park Service Says." Point Reyes Light (May 14, 1998).

Beilenson, Peter, and Behn, Harry, eds. *Haiku Harvest: Japanese Haiku Series IV.* Mount Vernon, NY: The Peter Pauper Press, Inc., 1962.

Beston, Henry. *The Outermost House.* New York: Ballantine Books, 1928.

Blake, William. *The Portable Blake.* Ed. Alfred Kazin. New York: The Viking Press, 1946.

Brown, Joseph Epes. *Animals of the Soul: Sacred Animals of the Oglala Sioux.* Rockport, MA: Element, 1992.

Campbell, Joseph. *The Masks of God: Primitive Mythology.* New York: Viking Press, 1959.

_______. *The Mythic Image.* Princeton: Princeton University Press, 1977.

_______. *The Way of the Animal Powers,* vol. 1 *(Mythologies of the Primitive Hunters and Gatherers).* New York: Harper and Row, 1988.

Collodi, Carlo. *Pinocchio.* New York: Philomel Books, 1982.

Comandini, Federico De Luca. *The Octopus: Metamorphoses of an Imaginal Animal.* Zürich: Spring Publications. 1988.

Dickinson, Emily. *The Poems of Emily Dickinson.* Ed. Thomas H. Johnson. Cambridge, MA: The Belknap Press of Harvard University, 1979.

Dunn, Jon L. *National Geographic Field Guide to the Birds of North America.* 3rd ed. Washington, DC: National Geographic Society.

Eliade, Mircea, ed. *The Encyclopedia of Religion.* New York: Macmillan Publishing Company, 1987.

_______. *Patterns in Comparative Religion.* Trans. Rosemary Sheed. New York: Sheed and Ward, 1958.

_______. *Rites and Symbols of Initiation: The Mysteries of Birth and Rebirth.* New York: Harper and Row, 1958.

_______. *Shamanism* (Bollingen Series LXXVI). Princeton: Princeton University Press, 1964.

Fierz, H.K. *Jungian Psychiatry.* Einsiedeln, Switzerland: Daimon Verlag, 1991.

Frankfort, H. "A Note on the Lady of Birth." *Journal of Near Eastern Studies III* (1944).

_______. *Ancient Egyptian Religion.* New York: Columbia University Press, 1948.

Gimbutas, Marja. *The Civilization of the Goddess: The World of Old Europe.* San Francisco: Harper, 1991.

Grimm Brothers. *The Complete Grimm's Fairy Tales.* New York: Pantheon Books, 1944.

Hannah, Barbara. "The Symbolism of Animals." C.G. Jung Library of San Francisco. Privately circulated lectures.

_______. *The Cat, Dog and Horse Lectures.* Wilmette, IL: Chiron Publications, 1992.

Harvey, Andrew. *A Journey in Ladakh.* Boston: Houghton Mifflin Company,1983.

Henderson, Joseph L. *Thresholds of Initiation.* Middletown, CT: Wesleyan University Press, 1967.

Henderson, Joseph L., and Oaks, Maud. *The Wisdom of the Serpent.* New York: George Braziller Inc., 1963.

Hillman, James. *The Dream and the Underworld.* New York: Harper & Row,1973.

Holmes, Oliver Wendall. "The Chambered Nautilus." *America in Literature,* vol. 1. New York: John Wiley and Sons, 1978.

Howarth, William.*The Book of Concord: Thoreau's Life As a Writer.* New York: The Viking Press, 1982.

Hung, Wu. *The Wu Liang Shrine: The Ideology of Early Chinese Pictorial Art.* Stanford, CA: Stanford University Press, 1989.

I Ching or Book of Changes (Bollingen Series XIX).Trans. Richard Wilhelm. New York: Pantheon Books, 1950.

Jung, C.G. *The Collected Works* (Bollingen Series XX). 20 vols. Trans. R.F.C. Hull. Ed. H. Read, M. Fordham, G. Adler, Wm. McGuire. Princeton: Princeton University Press, 1953-1979.

_______, ed. *Man and His Symbols.* Garden City, NY: Doubleday and Co., 1964.

_______. *Nietzsche's* Zarathustra: *Notes of the Seminar Given 1934-1939* (Bolligen Series XCIX). 2 vols. Ed. James L. Jarrett. Princeton: Princeton University Press, 1988.

_______. *The Visions Seminars.* 2 vols. Zurich: Spring Publications, 1976.

Jung, Emma, and von Franz, Marie-Louise. *The Grail Legend.* Trans. Andrea Dykes. London: Hodder and Stoughton, 1971.

Kallins, Wendi. "Return from Paradise (again)." In *Point Reyes Light,* Jan. 7, 1993.

Kass, Ray.. *Morris Graves:Vision of the Inner Eye.* New York: George Braziller Inc., 1983.

Kawai, Hayao. *The Japanese Psyche: Major Motifs in the Fairy Tales of Japan.* 2nd ed. Woodstock, CT: Spring Publicaitons, 1996.

Kerényi, C. "The Mysteries of the Kabeiroi." In *The Mysteries: Papers from the Eranos Yearbooks* (Bollingen Series XXX 2). Ed. Joseph Campbell. Trans. Ralph Manheim. Princeton: Princeton University Press, 1955.

_______. *Asklepios: Archetypal Image of the Physician's Existence* (Bollingen Series LXV). New York: Pantheon Books, 1959.

Kipling, Rudyard. *Just So Stories.* New York: Penguin Books, 1989.

Kluger, Rivka Shärf. *Satan and the Old Testament.* Trans. Hildegard Nagel. Evanston, IL: Northwestern University Press, 1967.

Larousse Encyclopedia of Mythology. London: Hamlyn Publishing Group, 1968.

Layard, John. *The Stone Men of Malekula.* London: Chatto and Windus, 1942.

Lawrence, D.H. *The Complete Poems of D.H. Lawrence.* New York: Viking Press, 1971.

_______. *St. Mawr and the Man Who Died.* New York: Random House, 1987.

Leadbelly. "The Gray Goose." On *Leadbelly's Last Sessions.* Smithsonian Folkways Records, 1994.

LeGuin, Ursula. *The Language of the Night: Essays on Fantasy and Science Fiction.* New York: Harper Perennial, 1993.

Leonard, Linda Schierse. *Creation's Heartbeat.* New York: Bantam Books, 1995.

Leppman, Wolfgang. *Rilke: A Life.* Trans. Russell M. Stockman. New York: Fromm International Publishing Corp., 1984.

Link, Margaret Schevill. *Pollen Path: A Collection of Navajo Myths.* Stanford, CA: Stanford University Press, 1956.

Meier, C.A. *Healing Dream and Ritual: Ancient Incubation and Modern Psychotherapy.* Einsiedeln, Switzerland: Daimon. Verlag, 1989.

Moon, B. ed. *An Encyclopedia of Archetypal Symbolism.* Boston: Shambhala, 1991.

Moore, Marianne. *The Complete Poems of Marianne Moore.* New York: Macmillan Publishing Co. Inc., Penguin Books, 1987.

National Audubon Society Field Guide to North American Mammals. New York: Alfred A. Knopf, 1996.

Neihardt, John G. *Black Elk Speaks:Being the Life Story of a Holy Man of the Oglala Sioux.* Lincoln, NE: University of Nebraska Press, 1961.

Neumann, Erich. *The Great Mother* (Bollingen Series **etc.**

_______. *Psyche and Eros* (Bollingen Series LIV). New York: Pantheon Books 1956.

Newcomb, Franc Johnson. *Hosteen Klah: Navaho Medicine Man and Sand Painter.* Norman, OK: University of Oklahoma Press, 1964.

Nowak, Ronald M. *Walker's Mammals of the World,* vol. 2. 4th ed. Baltimore: The Johns Hopkins University Press, 1983.

Oliver, Mary. *New and Selected Poems.* Boston: Beacon Press, 1992.

Perry, John Weir. *Lord of the Four Quarters: Myths of the Royal Father.* New York: George Braziller, Inc., 1966.

Quigley, Lillian, ed. *The Blind Men and the Elephant.* Illus. Janice Holland. New York: Charles Scribner's Sons, 1959.

Read, John. *Prelude to Chemistry: An Outline of Alchemy, Its Literature and Relationships.* Cambridge, MA: Massachusetts Institute of Technology, 1966.

Rilke, Ranier Marie. *The Selected Poetry of Rainer Marie Rilke.* Ed. and trans. Stephen Mitchell. New York: Vintage International, 1989.

Russack, Neil. "Amplification of the Spiral." In *Journal of Analytical Psychology,* vol. 29, no. 2 (1984).

Ryan, Kay. *Elephant Rocks.* New York: Grove/Atlantic Press, 1996.

Sandburg, Carl. *Harvest Poems.* New York: Harcourt, Brace and World, Inc., 1960.

Smith, Elliot. G. *The Evolution of the Dragon* Manchester: Manchester University Press, 1919.

Starkey, Richard (Ringo Starr). "Octopus's Garden." The Beatles' *Abbey Road* album. Parlophone/EMI Records, 1969.

Stevens, Wallace. *The Palm at the End of the Mind: Selected Poems and a Play.* New York: Vintage Books, 1990.

Storer, T. I. *General Zoology.* New York: McGraw-Hill, 1951.

Watts, Alan, and Huang, Al Chung-Liang. *Tao: The Water Course Way.* New York: Pantheon Books, 1975.

Wheelwright, Jane Hollister. *The Ranch Papers.* Santa Monica, CA: The Lapis Press, 1988.

Whitman, Walt. *Complete Poetry and Selected Prose.* Boston: Houghton Mifflin Company, 1959.

Wodehouse, P.G. *The World of Jeeves.* New York: Perennial Library, 1988.

Woloy, Eleanora, M. *The Symbol of the Dog in the Human Psyche: A Study of the Human Dog Bond.* Wilmette, IL: Chiron, 1990.

Wright, James. *Collected Poems.* Middletown, CT: Wesleyan University Press, 1951.

Yeats, W.B. *The Yeats Reader: A Portable Compendium.* Ed. Richard J. Finneran. New York: Scribner, 1997.

Yuan, Chieh Tzu, and Chuan, Hua. *Mustard Seed Garden Manual of Painting* (Bollingen Series). Trans. and ed. Mai-mai Sze. New York: Pantheon Books, 1956.

Zimmer, Heinrich. *The Art of Indian Asia: Its Mythology and Transformations* (Bollingen Series XXXIX). 2 vol. Ed. Joseph Campbell. Princeton: Princeton University Press, 1955.

________. *Myths and Symbols in Indian Art and Civilization* (Bollingen Series VI). Ed. Joseph Campbell. Princeton: Princeton University Press, 1946.

Index

Entries in *italics* refer to illustrations

Studies in Jungian Psychology by Jungian Analysts

Quality Paperbacks

Prices and payment in $US (except in Canada, $Cdn)

The Secret Raven: Conflict and Transformation
Daryl Sharp (Toronto). ISBN 0-919123-00-7. 128 pp. $16

The Psychological Meaning of Redemption Motifs in Fairy Tales
Marie-Louise von Franz (Zürich). ISBN 0-919123-01-5. 128 pp. $16

Alchemy: An Introduction to the Symbolism and the Psychology
Marie-Louise von Franz (Zürich). ISBN 0-919123-04-X. 288 pp. $20

Descent to the Goddess: A Way of Initiation for Women
Sylvia Brinton Perera (New York). ISBN 0-919123-05-8. 112 pp. $16

Addiction to Perfection: The Still Unravished Bride
Marion Woodman (Toronto). ISBN 0-919123-11-2. 208 pp. $18pb/$25hc

Jungian Dream Interpretation: A Handbook of Theory and Practice
James A. Hall, M.D. (Dallas). ISBN 0-919123-12-0. 128 pp. $16

The Creation of Consciousness: Jung's Myth for Modern Man
Edward F. Edinger (Los Angeles). ISBN 0-919123-13-9. 128 pp. $16

The Analytic Encounter: Transference and Human Relationship
Mario Jacoby (Zürich). ISBN 0-919123-14-7. 128 pp. $16

Change of Life: Dreams and the Menopause
Ann Mankowitz (Ireland). ISBN 0-919123-15-5. 128 pp. $16

The Illness That We Are: A Jungian Critique of Christianity
John P. Dourley (Ottawa). ISBN 0-919123-16-3. 128 pp. $16

Cultural Attitudes in Psychological Perspective
Joseph L. Henderson, M.D. (San Francisco). ISBN 0-919123-18-X. 128 pp. $16

The Vertical Labyrinth: Individuation in Jungian Psychology
Aldo Carotenuto (Rome). ISBN 0-919123-19-8. 144 pp. $16

The Pregnant Virgin: A Process of Psychological Transformation
Marion Woodman (Toronto). ISBN 0-919123-20-1. 208 pp. $18pb/$25hc

Encounter with the Self: William Blake's *Illustrations of the Book of Job*
Edward F. Edinger (Los Angeles). ISBN 0-919123-21-X. 80 pp. $15

The Scapegoat Complex: Toward a Mythology of Shadow and Guilt
Sylvia Brinton Perera (New York). ISBN 0-919123-22-8. 128 pp. $16

The Jungian Experience: Analysis and Individuation
James A. Hall, M.D. (Dallas). ISBN 0-919123-25-2. 176 pp. $18

Phallos: Sacred Image of the Masculine
Eugene Monick (Scranton, PA). ISBN 0-919123-26-0. 144 pp. $16

Touching: Body Therapy and Depth Psychology
Deldon Anne McNeely (Lynchburg, VA). ISBN 0-919123-29-5. 128 pp. $16

Personality Types: Jung's Model of Typology
Daryl Sharp (Toronto). ISBN 0-919123-30-9. 128 pp. $16

The Sacred Prostitute: Eternal Aspect of the Feminine
Nancy Qualls-Corbett (Birmingham). ISBN 0-919123-31-7. 176 pp. $18